TAPESTRY

The Journey of Laurel Lee

ALSO BY LAUREL LEE

Walking Through The Fire
Signs of Spring
Mourning Into Dancing
Godspeed: Hitchhiking Home
To Comfort You

AND FOR CHILDREN:

Barnaby Frost
Barnaby Frost Plants A Seed
A Very Special Birth Day
The Beginning
God's Greatest Day
The Christmas Program
Learning To Count

TAPESTRY

The Journey of Laurel Lee

Illustrations by Author

Laurel Lee

Lighthouse Trails Publishing
Silverton, Oregon

TAPESTRY
The Journey of Laurel Lee

©2004 by Laurel Lee
Second printing
First Edition Hardcover

Lighthouse Trails Publishing
P.O. Box 958
Silverton, Oregon
editor@lighthousetrails.com
www.lighthousetrails.com

Scripture quotation on page 267 taken from the New King James Version. Copyright ©1982 by Thomas Nelson, Inc. Used by permission. All rights reserved.
Poems, illustrations and drawings by Laurel Lee ©2004.
Cover design by Laurel Lee and Lighthouse Trails Publishing.
Special thanks to Audrey Kerwood and Andy Jenkins of Tapestry Standard [www.tapestry-standard.com]for the replica tapestry of Duke William's Ship of the Bayeux Tapestry.
Photos on pages 272, 274 and 288 courtesy of Richard C. Owen Publishing from *Imagination* by Mike Thaler ©2002.
A few drawings have been taken from public domain.

Publisher's Cataloging in Publication Data
Lee, Laurel
    Tapestry: the journey of laurel lee
    1. Lee, Laurel   2. Biography—United States 3. Cancer—Biography
4. Christian life

921   2003117064
ISBN 0-9721512-3-0 (cloth)

Printed in The United States of America

Dedication

The very nature of Christ reached
through my husband, Mike Thaler,
to love me.
Here is the heart and soul
of life and marriage ...

You gave all the dedication,
and these words are just the smallest way
to reach out and say how much
I admire and love you, darling.

Laurel

December 26, 2003

ontents

1966-1967

October 29, 1966
Portland, Oregon

The drizzling rain makes me pause on the porch to button up my coat. Richard, already in his one suit, laughs at my bundling. Since he's finding mirth in almost everything, I suspect it's a form of pre-marriage jitters. My parents are in town for the ceremony, but we've declined a ride with them in order to walk to the church.

I have my dress under my arm in a box. My mother bought it one week ago as my twenty-first birthday present. It's a practical, white wool A line. Summer weather better allows for the wearing of ballet slippers and trailing antique lace.

The exterior of the little cabin we are building on the back of our 1940 International truck looms behind us in the driveway. It towers over the cab. Now with the roof shingled, only the interior needs refining. By spring we'll be ready to start north in it to Alaska, and find our land to homestead.

While avoiding a puddle in a sidewalk depression, I take Richard's arm. The transformed words of a Beatle's song are in continual replay: *I'm Laurel in the sky with diamonds, ... I'm the girl with Kaleidoscope eyes ...*

Richard turns in the wind to try and light again a fat caterpillar-like joint of marijuana. "Think Laurel, we're on our way to something we will never forget." I'm now laughing as easily as he is. It does seem experiences are usually registered as memorable during or after the event. But tonight we know beforehand.

It's cold on the Hawthorne Bridge. Only Portland's oldest black-girded structure has a design that lets pedestrians cross the Willamette. The reflected city lights vibrate below us in patterns imposed by both wind and river currents. The undulating reflections of silver-white street lights and office neon seem like schools of animated tropical fish. I forget everything, while watching the red and green traffic signals appear and disappear on the water.

As Richard pulls me, I remember that in just two hours my parents are going to watch us exchange our legal vows. I look over at the man I'm about to marry. He has an angular face with prominent cheek bones. The collar of his navy surplus coat is pulled up against the wind. His dark eyes seem to be a sum from mixing his Norwegian ancestors with tribes of Indian blood. I was hitchhiking last June, and that summertime ride has brought me to this day. He's the only man I've ever met who was willing to stake out free land. Like me, he's excited at the prospect of living with moose in our backyard and scooping salmon out of rivers.

Once through the church doors at 1200 Adler Street, we find we're alone. Richard locates the light panel and experiments with the buttons until he illuminates the small chapel scheduled for our 8:00pm ceremony. He wants me to come down the aisle and sit next to him while he plays free-form jazz on the organ. Shaking my head in refusal, I know I can't. I have to be alone. Part of it is my realization that this pending act of marriage is going to be much more meaningful than I anticipated. It isn't anymore just a dull legal requirement with mandatory participation, but it seems like something bigger.

Going into the woman's bathroom, I shake out my dress and unfold from tissue a blue mosaic brooch. I even have a package of white nylons and pull them up my legs knowing I'll never again wear anything like this. From now on it's going to be denim or corduroy.

Once dressed, I study my face in the mirror. Carefully, I part my hair down the middle and brush the two long sides until I straighten every tangle. I have no makeup, but I still pinch some color into my cheeks and use a finger to smooth my eyebrows.

I know no friends will be here. Most likely my parents, alone, will be our witnesses. Richard has asked a worker from the ice cream cone factory, where he's now employed, to act as best man. He asked to be paid with a half a lid of grass.

When the music stops in the midst of a rising chord, I surmise that Pastor Merton has arrived. I come out to find him in an impeccable dark suit that I guess is his uniform for conducting both weddings and funerals.

"Okay, you two." I'm glad the minister is smiling. "You didn't want a rehearsal, and am I right that you are not having any bridal attendants?"

Seeing my head nodding in agreement, he continues to instruct us to walk together down the aisle at the scheduled 8:00.

"No organ accompaniment, either. Is that right?"

Richard and I exchange one of those looks that I think means we are already hearing music.

Pastor Merton leads us into his office to wait, then later I can hear his voice directing my parents into the chapel. Sitting together, we are wordlessly waiting on the minute hand. My feeling is for prayer, but I don't know how. I wouldn't even mind natives in body paint encircling us with voices that chant about my womb and all the gardens and hunts to come.

"What are you thinking?" I ask Richard. I really want to ask what his meditation has been all evening. But I won't risk a question that has any chance of yielding a less than rosy answer. It's too close to eight.

"Nothing. Oh, I'm wondering what all the other men that are about to become husbands are thinking. You know, Laurel, we might have a problem in the ceremony because Triple was never able to get those rings finished in time."

Even as he is talking, I can see the bowl of paper clips on Merton's desk. My movement to reach for them communicates my intention to Richard. With dexterity he straightens the wire, then patterns it around our fingers creating the emblems for our pledge. Once the rings are completed, and pocketed, we stand and start our march.

My arm interlocks with Richard's as we walk down the chapel aisle. The room is empty except for my family and one guest. Mr. Horns, my first college art professor, must have driven here from Forest Grove on the strength of my one hand-painted announcement. I stare ahead. A cross above the altar is the solitary decoration. To me, it's a symbol that our two lives now intersect.

I was always the girl in the process of becoming a woman, and the future will be me as a woman, with a girl lurking within. Tonight, I feel, is the perfect balancing of the two states.

Pastor Merton studies us. He steps down from his place of officiation, as the audience titters, to invert our positions. We had no idea there is a prescribed side for bride and groom. Richard is now standing by his hired best man. Yet, the mood is cast. I have to push my tongue against my molars to keep from laughing aloud. We are like clowns up front in polka-dot rags and red-bulb noses.

Following instructions, Richard and I now repeat high faithfulness, eye deep into eye. Merton is obviously surprised as Richard lays the paper clip rings in his palm upon request. But the phrase "With this ring, I now you wed" has no less resonance than if we had platinum bands. After turning as "Mr." and "Mrs." the best man goes and collapses on the closest pew. Richard, too, looks rather pale and feeble. While walking back up the aisle, he begins to pull me over to rest with him on a seat just past the halfway point to the door.

"I really could have fainted," he whispers. "But the one fear that kept me upright was the fact we might have to repeat all of this again. We shouldn't have smoked so much dope." He's barely finished the disclosure when my parents and Mr.

Horns come with well wishing words. We rise, belonging to our company, and take the offered ride back to our rental home.

December 1

"Oh, take it," says Richard. "Our landlady doesn't even know it's there!"

It is barely dawn. I am standing on the driveway by our truck. Around me are boxes of possessions to hand up to Richard. In my arms is a small brown rug that we found rolled in the basement.

Late last night in bed, we decided not to spend the forty dollars for December's rent, but to move into our cabin. Richard estimates he has about one more month of finishing carpentry work before we can actually launch north. He's been restless to start our journey.

"Let's get the mattress," says Richard while dropping down beside me. I follow him back through the kitchen door and down to the basement. We are both nervous that old Mrs. Spicklemire is going to catch us. No one ever uses this bed that's propped  against the wall under the stairs. We are leaving the springs and frame and taking only the mattress for our loft. It feels to me like a gray act, balanced between the white zone of an outright gift and the black of stealing what is used and loved. Both of us glance over at our landlady's house while maneuvering the bulk into the truck. The tag is even up that threatens legal action for removing its factory certificate.

Once concealed, my pulse recovers its normal speed. Maybe the American Heart Association should add stealing to its list of things to avoid. Richard helps boost me through the door. Fold-out stairs are on the list of things yet to be done. Even in these far limits of disorder, our cabin shows artistic craftsmanship. The smell is the essence of fresh-cut lumber. A diminutive wood stove is ready to be installed by a wood counter over storage shelves that still need doors. There are no bookcases yet, and the books my parents brought me lie in cartons. Richard is pushing still more boxes through the door. I can remember how I bragged once about carrying all that I need in a sack between my shoulder blades.

Once our goods are installed, I get in the cab with Richard. Our plan is to go to Triple's and live at his curb for however long it takes to perfect our interior. I have a kind of vacation feeling that comes from setting ourselves free from the tyranny of clocks and a calendar. Only in this diary will I try to notch the dates to a page.

We are earlier than traffic. Only a few long-distance trucks pass us, most with their headlights still on. Off the road, most of the homes are still dark except for an occasional bulb that I imagine is in a kitchen or bathroom.

We park at Triple's but know not to go to the door. His schedule is tipped so far into the night that 11:00am is his morning. To us, his profession is largely dope dealing.

"We need to get rid of a lot of this stuff, Laurel! How many boxes of books do you have here? We should dump them all."

"Never!"

I'm adamant that the books are the last to go. I point to the Tupperware Jell-O molds that my mother brought me, as expendable.

"Okay, Laurel. Discard those weighty hard covers and keep the paperbacks."

I'm sorry to see Mother has included my high school yearbooks. I can see an orange-and-black *1963* on top of a stack. It's almost like a record of reincarnation; it was a past life where I purposely back combed my hair to give myself four inches of body over each ear.

"Hey, look at this." I hold up a black Bible that was once given to me in a fourth-grade Sunday school. In the end, I decide to keep it; it's a history record of an ancient age.

After filling four boxes of discards, I stagger under the weight of them to Triple's front porch. It seems late enough now to knock. Surprisingly, the door has been left open about the width of a foot. I knock and call my friend's name through the crack. Triple's approaching footsteps stop as I hear a single-syllable swear word, then the sound of clicking boots resumes down the hall to the door.

"I got two new dogs," says Triple in his

greeting, while coming out on the porch to pick a fistful of pages from a stack of newspapers.

"I'm afraid they choose to urinate everywhere, but on the printed page. They should belong to a journalist."

I follow Triple into his darkened hallway thinking how much I've always liked him. He may deviate in every way from the scrub-faced business man, but I feel with Triple it's more of a joke than a rebellion.

"I finally got your rings done. Come and look."

I first reach down to touch the puppies. They look like collies covered with a golden down. I can see the trails of newspapers and the puddle that produced the strong odor.

"Laurel, go upstairs. The rings are somewhere on my workbench—first room at the top."

I've never been to his upper floor. One could pencil messages in the dust at the end of each tread. Below me the dogs try to follow but are too small and uncoordinated to climb a step.

The workbench is under a platform suspended from the ceiling by chains. There are marks where two of the walls have been scraped.

I look among the tools and supplies, and find our rings. The bands are silver and border a rectangle of polished wood. Three silver dots are set in the mahogany. While admiring them, I slip on the one with the smallest circumference. Once downstairs, I hand Richard his and let him exclaim with me.

"I want to give you something else," says Triple. "You are going to need a dog for Alaska, and I want you to take one of these. Richard is about to refuse, but I'm faster.

"I would love a puppy," I exclaim, reaching down to the dogs who are biting each other at my feet. Now, with one in my arm, I announce he needs a name. All immediate offerings are dull. Richard's suggestions are like the names of stars in a science fiction book. It's Triple who wins. He cries out, slapping his knee, "You guys in that house should have a dog named Noah."

As our host has our attention, he continues on with a completely new topic. Looking up at Richard, he challenges him to stay here until spring. "Choosing the three coldest months to drive to Alaska doesn't make sense."

"No," says Richard in a voice that's almost fierce with determination. "I want to leave as soon as we can." I also think it would be better if we could earn some more money first, but I add my assent. Richard has been adamant that we can both take odd jobs along the way. To him this means for me to be a waitress.

He's thrilled that I can collect coins from table tops. The change doesn't usually exceed what tooth fairies slide under pillows.

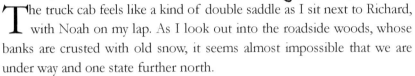

January 5, 1967
Washington

The truck cab feels like a kind of double saddle as I sit next to Richard, with Noah on my lap. As I look out into the roadside woods, whose banks are crusted with old snow, it seems almost impossible that we are under way and one state further north.

"What is that on the dashboard?" Richard's voice has such a sarcastic lift that I look at him. He's dabbing the ends of his new mustache with his tongue where the hairs protrude over his lip.

"It's a rock," I reply with deliberate enunciation of each of the one syllable words.

"No," says Richard.

On one of our trial runs I had suggested collecting things on our dashboard. It would take awhile, but I could assemble a wedge of colored stones, feathers, and evergreen branches that still have pine cones attached. It was never a serious argument, yet it was still a matching of wills.

"Okay, Richard, I was just admiring the rock and left it there. I have the right to put things on my side."

We have the leisure of three thousand miles ahead for dialogues, big and small.

"Sure," replies my husband. "One sudden stop, and it's on our laps."

I have to laugh. I crack open the window and throw out the stone. I notice that the highway signs are a white silhouette of George Washington's head.

"Look, Richard, there's a lot of warmth and light on this dashboard. Custom build a small planter box that we can secure on each side. Then, let's press in marijuana seeds among common garden flowers like pansies that never reach any height."

"There's a policeman following us."

I can see my husband glancing up from the road to look in his side mirror.

"He can't touch us, Richard. We are fifteen miles below the speed limit." Yet, I still feel nervous. I try to concentrate on the intricate network of tree limbs against the sky, but my meditation is punctured by the siren. In my side mirror I can see the red and blue revolving light as Richard releases his foot from the gas and looks for an adequate shoulder for the vehicle.

The cop, who walks to Richard's side, is void of expression as he asks for the driver's license and registration. He's like a robot in a uniform with an authoritative voice and an inability to smile. The dog stands up, and nose to our company, wags his tail.

"He just wants to hassle us," says Richard grimly, as he watches the policeman take the identification back to his vehicle to run a check.

I feel angry that we should be victimized just because we are different. My father, who drives a new Buick station wagon, would never be stopped. It isn't fair that there's pressure exerted on those who choose to live on the edges of the bell-shaped curve of normal.

The policeman is back with a yellow and white layered ticket separated by a carbon. "It's against regulations not to have mud flaps on this size truck. You'll find the fines listed on the back."

"Oh, give us a break," I ask. "We'll just go and correct this today."

I'm trying to address some human particle in him. Maybe once he loved his grandmother, played with a dog or got a present for Christmas."

"Can't do that. Once a ticket is written up, it's in the books."

We just sit there in frustrated rage as he goes back to his squad car and drives away. I can feel hate in me. It comes from being punched by something bigger than we are.

Richard looks for the fine first, then not finding it, passes the forms to me. There's a whole list of snares and costs like stopping at the wrong colored curb. Under "Heavy-Duty Vehicles" is a twenty-five dollar charge for not having mud flaps.

"You know," says Richard, "if this isn't paid, the fine doubles, and it would eventually go to warrant for my arrest. We have no choice but to buy a money order and envelope in the next town."

I immediately translate this new cost into the medium of grocery prices. "This county is stealing two weeks of our food!"

"And almost half the money we have on hand," says Richard. "We've got to get to Alaska!"

The thought of the comparative freedom of the wilderness is our one consolation as Richard turns on the ignition.

There are some construction sites in the trees, which multiply until the forest dissolves into a housing tract as we come into Olympia. The capitol building is a shiny dome in the small city vista. Richard spots a riverbank where we can park with a view. His idea is to fold and attach black roofing paper flaps over the rear tires.

My first duty in making camp will be to insert our stovepipe so it rises above the roof. I'll start a fire, and from our sack of fifty pounds of potatoes put four in for our meal.

Richard has just pulled out the small access ladder to the front door when a green and white city police car pulls alongside us. We freeze, neither speaking nor moving. Only the dog is animated. I call him back knowing he might lift a leg or lower his haunches. I am fearing another ticket; they may fine a dog that fouls the footway.

"Some rig you got there, but there's no camping allowed within the city limits, folks."

Richard asks if there's any place where it would be lawful to stay.

"May as well lead you, myself," says the young patrolman. "We have a state park that is mostly vacant in winter."

Back in the cab, I notice that with a police escort, cars change lanes to give us room. People seem to be staring at us in degrees well above normal curiosity.

I keep a pocket sized book of Zen aphorisms in the glove box. I take it out for an occasional diversion. Opening at random I read, "Only those who appreciate the least palatable of the vegetable roots know the meaning of life."

Again, I wonder if there really is a meaning, or are all the spokesmen of enlightenment like the emperor in his new clothes. The adherents chant how beautiful they are dressed in their philosophies, but they just might be naked and know nothing.

Still self-conscious of public attention, I keep my head down, now patting the dog until we are off the main street and back again in the country.

January 15

Unfurled, the map of Washington has fluttered between us, on the front seat, like some bird with a broad wingspan. I can see by the spot denoting Tacoma that it will be a larger town than Olympia.

"Do you think we stayed too long?"

"Probably," replies Richard.

We camped in the state park for a week. It was like a long, pleasant dream being alone in the woods. The variations in temperature released snow in clumps from the overhanging branches, making plopping sounds on our roof. I experimented with bread recipes, naming most of the loaves after national parks like Old Smokey and Crater Lake. My husband built things. He constructed a hinged ladder that could be unfolded to climb up into the loft.

"Richard, didn't it feel like we were playing house among those firs, rather than really keeping one? We just needed Triple to come and pretend he was the Avon lady."

Richard replies in a half measured laugh.

"What is very real is the gas gauge. We're close to empty. Look, Laurel, after paying the state its fine and buying fuel and groceries, we have depleted almost all our cash."

Immediately I think about us getting in line behind the seven dwarfs who are off to the mine singing, "Hi ho, hi ho, it's off to work we go ..."

We take the freeway exit to city center. Tacoma is built on the shore of the Puget Sound. I can see a pine covered island in the inlet and guess that the Cascade Mountains would be visible if the day was not overcast.

Driving down a street that includes boarded up storefronts, small bars, and an adult movie house, Richard sees a pawn shop.

"Your parents sent us a camera for Christmas. Let's just exchange it for cash to hold us until we're working. It's worth an immediate five dollars."

"No," I cry, feeling alarmed.

"Look Laurel, how could we ever pay for film and developing pictures anyway?"

It's not a matter of logic. I don't want to let go of the camera. It's to record the land we'll claim and the house we'll build. My throat is constricting, holding back my tears as Richard looks for a parking place.

"It's pretty slick how we can use these truck zones!"

I won't even talk. I note he isn't promoting the idea that we can buy it back later. My typewriter is still in Portland. It was far more important to me than the drum he sacrificed for money.

Some Indians are leaning against a wall staring at us. One is holding a brown bag that I guess covers a bottle they are passing among them. I hate poverty. Richard climbs out to seek the camera in the back. I remember how he suggested we leave it intact in the box as soon as we opened it. I wonder if the Noel wrapping paper was still in my hands when he began calculating how to protect it for resale.

The anger in me has prongs. I've already attached one hook into how I'm regarding my husband. Yet, as I watch him walking, with his shoulders rolled forward while he carries the Kodak box, I feel sorry for him. His childhood included living in so many foster homes that he can never feel that anything really belongs to him.

Now, it's self-pity that has me. I'll never again be able to turn over a price tag on a shirt and buy it. Only the rich have admission money for movies, or can order food from restaurant menus. Not wanting those solemn-eyed men to witness my crying, I get out of the truck to walk in the opposite direction from my husband.

The sidewalk is dirty. Amidst all the boarded exteriors, one shop has been renovated. I can see geraniums in pots along the window. *The Salvation Army Rescue Mission* is painted on the glass in precise gold lettering. Opening the door, I see a man in a uniform at a desk. Religious art decorates the walls. Every picture is of the crucified Christ in agony.

"What do you do?" I blurt in response to his welcoming nod. I immediately fear he'll answer with a round of Bible bullets, and I'll be driven out to the street to stand and drink with the Indians.

"We're here to help anyone with a real need."

Since I'm still staggering in the mire of self-pity, I don't have my usual assured footing. I ask if he will hire my husband and me for five dollars worth of labor. I choose Richard's estimate of the camera's value in pawn.

"Sure," he replies. "One of you can wash the car, and I have a stack of envelopes that need stamps."

After assuring him I'll be back, I race for Richard, hoping to spare my Kodak. He's already in the truck, and at my appearance, raises four fingers to communicate it's done and our yield.

I, in turn, tell of our chance for a thirty-minute employment. I lead us back and execute a mock salute.

The Salvation Army man has organized a bucket for my husband and a pile of mail for me. Again, I'm relieved that we can just start to work without having to listen to some tape-recorded speech by Billy Graham.

After collecting five one dollar bills we get in the truck to immediately buy gas. Our financial life is like first-grade math. The Chevron pump, registering five, must be subtracted from the ten in Richard's wallet. We have a five-dollar sum left to put towards everything we need and want in the universe.

We've learned to look for a parking-place base out of the city limits. Choosing a road that traces the water's edge, we pass a pier where I can see crates stamped for Cam Ranh Bay, Vietnam. After passing a manufacturing plant we find an empty expanse of cement. Richard surmises that it was originally intended for factory expansion but never got funding.

Pulling the truck as close to the water as possible, we can see the waves from all four windows. The water looks like shades of gray steel, appropriate for industrial zoning.

In the fading afternoon light, we both look for driftwood to start a fire. The dog runs around us making sounds like a seagull. We are almost silhouette figures picking up our boards from the short rise of pebbled beach. The wood smells like the incense sticks of the sea, pungent with brine.

There's no speech between us. In the quiet of our simple labor, I compare my marriage to a giant sifter; I've been pushed hard against its grate. What I previously considered as necessity was really luxury, and it's gone. Today my camera has fallen through the grid like my typewriter before it. Yet, the pen and cheap notebook diary will always remain. I have no shower, but I still get clean with a cloth and bucket of water warmed on the stove.

I know myself better too, since undergoing the daily scrub of marriage. Illusions are popping like soap bubbles. I'm not as noble as I thought I would be. I can move quicker to resentment than kindness. When the soapy film of my personality dissolves, underneath is dirty water.

First thing in the truck, I mix flour, yeast, salt and water. Richard works the lantern, so I stir in the dark, but knead in the light. While he moves his attention to the fire, I stretch the dough into a long, flat loaf and mark its length with diagonal slashes. Our dishes are bright colored tin; I always take the blue, and he has the red.

After rinsing our utensils from the kettle, I want to read in bed. I leave Richard the lantern so he can have the best light for continuing to carve a coat hook, and I take the flashlight. Since the Zen proverbs are still in the cab, I pull out my old Bible. I feel like slow language.

Usually I undress by the fire, rotating my nude body like a planet in an orbit warmed by the sun. Tonight, I just climb the ladder with one hand and then crawl the few feet to our mattress. My nightgown has been left under my pillow in a wad of flowered flannel. There's no room to rise much above my knees because of the sloping roof. I toss my corduroy pants and turtleneck into a corner. At my feet is the water tank we fill without cost in gas stations. The sheets, a wedding gift, are patterns of monotonous large orange dots. I've taken a pen and filled in some of the spots with whimsical faces on my side of the bed. My elbow is now resting on a winking eye as I open the Bible.

The page has all the words printed in red. It's peculiar because I can see all the previous chapters have the standard black lettering. I can imagine laborers in a 1954 print shop running out of black ink, and momentarily substituting crimson. I want to pick out any paragraph and let some old lines hum in me and then fall asleep. The one time I tried to read it before was nothing but long lists of names.

This time I didn't open to genealogy but what appears to be instructions. I read, *The measure of a man is not what he owns.*

I'm surprised by the truth of it. It sounds almost revolutionary, like something that can be spray-painted in red as graffiti to confront suburbanites. I was expecting some list that commends roast beef for dinner but forbids a pork chop.

But you, take no thought of what you eat, drink or wear, like all the people of the nations.

I lay down the book, chuckling about what I've seen of modern Christianity. If the churches are a boat, they have drifted far from the dock of these words.

Richard emerges onto the platform of the loft. I'd been too engrossed to hear him on the ladder. He carries with him the smell of smoke from the wood stove and a slight essence of kerosene. The one flashlight in my hand moves shadows across his cheek.

"Now listen to this." I reread the two sentences that confront our society.

"Keep on going," says Richard, wadding his pillow up under his chin.

But above all else, you seek first the kingdom of God, and His righteousness, and all the rest will be added unto you.

Neither of us speak. The words feel personal now, no longer for the groups outside, but for us alone together. It seems like more than a phrase on a page but a voice addressing us.

I decide I have to quit reading what is highlighted as "The Sermon on the Mount," and I lay the book face down. I don't want cracks in my perception of reality. Everything is relative, and nothing is absolute. I want to laugh that I was touched, if only for a moment, by a Bible. I refuse to end up like some old woman I once saw leaving scripture pamphlets in public bathroom stalls.

"Oh, come on," says Richard, "read some more." His voice is impatient, and he is even flicking his hand.

I continue to quote paragraphs in a voice a little louder than a whisper. Each passage convinces me further of the logic and purity of Christianity. It seems now to be such a well made gown that I feel too unclean to ever put it on. It all makes me feel that there is a God, and I'm naked before Him.

"This is ridiculous, Richard. There's no way that anyone can wear the robe of being a Christian. It calls for perfection, and all of us are flawed!"

Richard put his hand on my arm. Holding the light directly at the page, I can hardly see him at all.

"But that has to be the point of the cross, Laurel."

I think of the two simple lines that intersect as a decoration on buildings and dangle as jewelry. I grasp there is a flashing reality behind the symbol. It's in the words of ancient hymns. The refrain has always been a holy God and sinful human beings bridged by the atonement of His Son.

"You know we have stolen almost everything."

Richard is not speaking to me. It's as though both of us are facing a mirror that reflects only our excessive greed. I can't stand the sight of myself. I have spent my life rationalizing and forgetting.

Richard takes my hand. It's wet from rubbing my eyes.

"Laurel, I think we must do something like ask to be forgiven."

Too overwhelmed to answer, I let him go first and then take my turn to speak. We use simple words and not the colored language of stained glass windows. We affirm belief, we yield our wills.

In the process of our expression, I feel the garment of Christ being pulled over our shoulders. I am new, and what we are together can be a new configuration of a couple too.

I finally sleep, wrapped in the beauty of the word, *Saviour*.

My blanket seems woven from gold and silver strands. We may have died only to be resting in some heavenly bower with angels in attendance—who are beginning to talk loudly among themselves. Can wings get caught in the slamming of car doors?

I hear the noise of motors and men calling to each other. Opening my eyes, it seems even louder. I slip down from the loft. Out both windows I can see we are completely surrounded by vehicles. Richard slides down beside me and peers out.

"This has to be a company parking lot."

I volunteer that it must be Monday. There's a throng of men dressed in the working clothes of assembly-line employees, and most are carrying dome-topped lunch buckets. It's now so congested, we could never move our rig down the irregular rows to the highway. I can see more vehicles still pouring in to park, filling up the far side.

"It looks like we are here until 5:00," chuckles Richard.

The day is clear. The band of clouds has dissipated, revealing blue skies. Richard moves from the window to start the fire. It's the first act of morning, equivalent to blowing a bugle and raising the flag.

I take the dog, wanting to walk the beach. I marvel at the transformation of my mind. Everything from sand grain to galaxies has meaning. God created the heavens and the earth.

Hearing Richard's voice, I turn back. He is leaning out of the doorway, which is elevated above the mass of colored-metal roofs.

"We have company," he announces. "Laurel, these people are from Tacoma's newspaper."

Looking up, I can see a couple standing behind Richard. The man has an expensive looking camera around his neck, and the woman is holding a briefcase. I feel like making jokes about the Daily Planet, Lois Lane and Jimmy. While waiting for me, Richard must have kept putting wood in the fire. The room is unbearably hot, and with four standing adults, it is as tiny as a closet.

"We got a call from the Northern Line Engineering Company that your camper had been seen in the auxiliary parking lot. We just think there might be a human-interest story here."

I look at the journalist, who, like me, is in her early twenties. I surmise that she has both a checking and savings account. She's wearing a rich suede coat with purple leather trim. The jewelry on her fingers, wrist, neck, and ears salutes the arts. She likes the medium of wide gold. By contrast, I feel unkempt, with my hair hanging down like two spaniel's ears and clad in a boxy plaid raincoat that I wore in high school.

Maybe we were in the same stream while growing up, but all rivers fork with decisions. And this woman, now opening a stenographer's pad, went one direction, and I another. I can feel the gulf as her lead question asks for our credentials. She wants to know where Richard went to college.

"UCLA," I blurt. I'm ashamed that he's really a high-school drop out. Now having chosen a false shiny engine, it's easy to couple behind it a whole train of partial answers.

"So your husband's major area of study is theology," the reporter repeats. Even my body feels off track. The gossamer peace that had let me float from minute to minute is gone. I am full of weight and in some pricking nettles.

"We're both writers," injects Richard, "although I'm just starting."

"So you publish?" she asks.

"Just me," I add. "A children's book."

Now with our past reduced to lines of fiction, the photographer requests us to step outside for some shots. Following Richard, I can see a cloud cover is beginning to wrap the sky again in white gauze.

"Is there anything else you want to add?"

I know it's the last chance to state what sounds foolish and trite; we have found it to be true that Christ is the only way to God. Yet I stand, instead, in mute misery. As they walk away to a late model car, I feel wretched from the paradox of my performance. I kept silent with all the things that should have been shared and fluently expressed all that should have never been said.

In the weak light of late Monday, the cars begin to move. It reminds me of a frozen lake thawing with the turn of motor and ignition. We join the flow to the highway, and Richard turns toward town.

"Let's experiment with coal. I've been thinking how we could bank it through the night, and unlike wood, we'll still have heat in the morning."

Richard spotted a fuel yard on our first drive through Tacoma. He's convinced it will just be a small-change investment for our experiment. I know he carries the burden of navigating our cabin into below-zero temperatures. Often he has expressed concern that the whole water tank could easily freeze in a night.

Even with the window rolled up, I can smell the acrid odor of coal. There are dark piles throughout the yard from trucks dumping it in towering heaps. I choose to sit and wait, with Noah on my lap like a living muff. The street has one gas station and some flashing neon from a lone café. The restaurant looks to me like the kind of place that keeps a large inventory of frozen hamburger patties and pancake mix.

It all adds to my sense of loneliness. I can feel it in the strains of a freight-train whistle and the bark of a dog that's probably been chained far from the house.

"Hey," Richard opens my door and puts Noah on the ground. "We can earn some quick cash tonight. They need some gunnysacks filled with coal, and we'll be paid by the number we can stuff. The manager said we can just camp here behind the gates."

I reserve my enthusiasm until I can see the size of the burlap bags. The mercury lights in the yard provide a surreal illumination. Everything smells like a London street after the Industrial Revolution. Richard shows me a pile of bags that I estimate, from potato packages in markets, to hold close to fifty pounds. Fetching my gloves from the truck, I look at the new gray-cloth palms and sweater-knit fingers. My parents sent them for Christmas— I would rather soil my hands.

The coal is cold. Squatting on my haunches, I feel I deserve both the dirt and the labor. I lied to the newspaper, and it's an ancient tale that children who are bad get lumps of carbon in their stocking.

Abstractly, I wonder if telling the truth would have produced an opposite destiny. We could have been enlisted for a trip south to pick a bumper crop of cherries in a scented orchard.

January 17

We have money. A portion is declared for food once Richard gets the check from the coal yard. Twenty dollars gives me the enthusiasm to even take a cart. Usually, with just change to spend, all the goods can be suspended in one arm. Now, I am in a celebration—real hamburger and not my protein-source pinto beans. I lay three packages of meat across the cart's toddler seat.

Richard has been waiting in the truck cab. He sacked coal long after I washed my arms and went to bed. He has no energy, just the wish to find a truly isolated camping spot along Puget Sound. Back in our vehicle, I put the grocery sacks at my feet. I want to feel crowded by food; I like soup and tuna cans leaning against my calf. I can easily imagine myself at forty hoarding case goods and refusing to waste any leftover crust.

We find a shoreline without factory or fisherman. Behind us, in the distance, is a cliff with a few apartment units that provide living room views of the sea. We pull onto the sand where we are more than a high tide's reach from the water. My husband goes right from turning off the motor to lighting tinder in our stove.

I'm hoping Richard isn't too tired to talk. I wait until we can't see our breath, and our coats can go back to the pegs on the door. I wait until the kettle heats and he has tea.

"Something really happened to us, Richard. I'm changed from that night."

As he nods back in agreement, eyes to mine, I realize we have no words of explanation, nor have we ever heard of anyone else who has experienced what we did.

"It's like my conscience is alive," I state, looking down at the coal dust still embedded in the crevices of my hand.

Lying had never bothered me before, or guilt of such duration that I could still feel it ticking. Fabrications before had always been the art of creating lines for convenience or flourish.

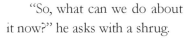

"So, what can we do about it now?" he asks with a shrug.

"Look around us, Richard. Divide in your mind what we took and what was really given to us." I can easily separate gifts from theft, honor from dishonor.

"Even my hammer," says Richard, rising from the chair. "I conveniently picked it up from a construction site," he says while turning it in his hand. Opening the door, he slings the tool out onto the sand.

"What are you doing? We have been forgiven!"

"Look, Laurel, we can't drive back to Portland, Los Angeles, or your Berkeley library and return this stuff. What we can do is put everything out there visible on the rocks. Think of it as a gesture of giving it all back by giving it all away."

Completely animated, he is acting like he is lighter than air.

"I think the whole point, Laurel, is to show what we believe by what we try to do."

It seems to me far out and radical, yet I'm flooded with a sense of respect for my husband. As I begin gathering up the boxes of candles first, my emotions swing to a kind of hilarity.

I carry our matching raw, wool sweaters out to the rocks and fold the arms across the chest. I'm careful with the books too, so they can't slide down and damage any pages. It's not a fast job. We both have a long past of gathering petty merchandise. Richard carries out the bags of flour that he took from the ice cream cone factory.

"Laurel we still have the chairs and the mattress."

I clearly acknowledge that we stole them from Mrs. Spicklemire's basement, yet I'm not enthusiastic at losing their comfort. My body seems to have its own voice on where it wants to sit and sleep.

Following Richard inside, I climb up the loft to quickly strip the bed of its sheets and blankets. While maneuvering the bulk of the mattress through the opening, Richard's eyes look up, and his gaze sweeps past me.

"You know that water tank was hoisted too. I had some guys from the factory help me get it from a lot where they were tearing down houses."

"Does the tank have to go too?" My voice has little volume. All that I can think of is hauling water and storing it in covered buckets. I have taken my gravity-fed faucets for granted.

"Look, Laurel, we want this to be the clean start of a new life. I'll bet we will recover these things that we are now giving up, but in a right way."

As my husband turns on the sink taps to drain the weight from the tank, I ask him to preserve some of that water in containers. There are already cups that need washing and dinner plates and pots ahead.

The late winter sun is feeble as we finish our peculiar cleansing. At times, it has looked as though there will be more outside than left within. I wonder who will be walking along the dunes and rocks to find these things, a strange array of dry and perfect treasures washed up by the sea. I print FREE in large letters on a blank page ripped from my diary.

There's still hot tea on the stove. This time we have nothing to sit on around our windowsill table.

"I doubt if it's even five yet, but let's go up to bed anyway, Laurel."

My husband is leaning against the bookcase, and I see he's exhausted beyond any idea of waiting for a dinner. While taking our tinware to the sink, I'm amazed to see a section of a rainbow. Its prism is on the face of our cast iron stove. I'm sure a scientist could list the angle of the afternoon light rays refracting through the curvature of our kerosene lamp globe, but to us, it is a sign and wonder.

It is warm in the loft and dusty where the tank has been. We cannot afford to use many blankets for padding underneath us, as the upstairs heat is as transitory as embers. The orange dot pattern wrinkles at both ends with no mattress to fill the elasticized fitted corners. Bare earth can yield for bony hips, but boards are resolute. I speculate on the long hard nights ahead unless we can find some thrift shop with a fumigated mattress.

I can hear a car pull up outside our truck and stop. As its motor idles there's a firm, loud rap on our door. I worry that it's the police and we're getting a citation for littering.

Climbing over Richard, I lower myself to the door.

"Hi, my name is Bill Roedecker, and this is my wife, Anne." While gesturing towards the bluff, he says they live there in an apartment. "We saw your picture in tonight's paper and thought why not come down and ask you for dinner."

We follow them to their car. All the colors of our goods on the rocks are muted by night into shadows.

"You are on the front page, kids."

Anne turns in the seat towards me and speaks of her simple soup and bread meal.

The Roedecker's warmth makes their apartment homey. It is full of hand-made things; there are afghans in the bright colors of Woolworth's yarn. The pillows too are hand quilted with shiny polyester scraps. They act like relatives and not strangers, offering us the use of their shower. Richard grabs first that gold ring of unlimited warm water.

Anne brings out the evening paper. It is shocking to see our black and white image below the caption, "City Couple Lugging Home To Quiet Alaska." I had assumed we would be in an auxiliary section. There just hadn't been any hijacked airlines or assassination attempts to move us back to an end page.

When I get the bathroom it's so full of steam it could grow jungle plants. The mirror is a shiny sphere of water. I find there's nothing mechanical in singing the same line of "thanks," over and over. Joy swells in devotion.

Anne lights candles and directs us to chairs. The tapers show every evidence of nightly use; they are almost stubs in their glass containers. Bill reaches for Richard's and his wife's hands, while Anne takes mine. My husband and I fumble with each other's knuckles, a little unsure of this procedure. As our host utters grace, I realize we are not the only ones whose attention has been tapped by God.

Bill tells us he and his wife have moved from a farm to town to start a new business of trying to manufacture rocking horses. Richard says we are back to the business of driving north in the morning.

January 18

New lanes keep adding to the width of the freeway before Seattle. By the time the city skyline is visible there are six of them for each direction. Every vehicle passes our International, which is pushing its maximum at 45. We reject the city exits because the streets will be flanked by parking meters. Our rig pushes past the high buildings of Seattle.

Both of us are tired from sleeping on the loft's wooden floor. We pull off to Everett, the first town north of Seattle. Looking for a parking place, I wonder how many tree limbs birds survey to find a crook for their nests. What do rabbits look for before their forepaws scratch out warren tunnels? We want views of water. Richard pulls our home over three parking stripes at the Everett yacht club. The adjacent wharf is lined with fishing boats bobbing in the current.

I jump from the truck proposing that we first seek a thrift store. Most of our silverware had left an import shop in my pockets, and so it was abandoned in our purge. I know I can buy forks out of bins for pennies.

My husband doesn't answer. Instead he takes my arm and strolls with me along the dock. My eye contrasts the working boats with the sleek pleasure crafts.

"If it's a Salvation Army thrift store maybe we could exchange work again for, say, a mattress. I would love to sort and categorize donation boxes."

Making no reply, Richard pauses to watch a man sitting beside an open tackle box with his fishing rod.

"Think about restaurants, Richard. The tips are always pockets full of change, and courtesy meals for employees, plus an eventual minimum wage pay check."

"I don't know," he replies.

"Oh, come on Richard," I retort, feeling irritated by his inactivity when we have so many pressing needs. "It could give me the opportunity to bring my faith into my work. I've never seen anyone offer a prayer of thanks before they eat the way the Roedeckers did. That could be my special contribution. I'll serve the plates and say a silent grace for each customer. Waitresses can arrange food. I'll always design a cross out of French fries. You might think of it as a visual provoking."

"Oh, crazy," laughs my husband. "What I want to do first is look for a church before we make any plans."

We pivot with his declaration. Seagulls rise and fall along the horizon. The birds are moving in lines like the rapid scribble marks of tiny children.

It's easy to find a church but not as easy to find one with unlocked doors. After two attempts Richard waits in the truck while I run up the wide sidewalks to tug on all manner of unrelenting handles. I know there are different denominations, each with their own subtleties and emphasis, but I know nothing more. I have no experience to help me define the differences between Baptist and Lutheran. I've even stopped reading the signs by the time my pressure pulls open a door and reveals a vestibule.

Motioning first to Richard, I walk inside feeling a hush of respect. It's easier to whisper in here than talk. I want it to be a little like the movies with a couple of widows in corner pews, but we are alone.

There's a padded kneeling bench up by the altar. My attention is commanded by two stained-glass windows; I don't want to shut my eyes. There's an alpha and omega in swirling colors like the eyes of God, who sees from beginning to end.

Richard breaks the silence. "Do you know what we are going to do?" Leaving no pause for me to answer, he announces, "We are going to sell everything we own and just trust in the Lord."

I'm stunned. I say nothing. It's either silence on my part or shouting at him. Neither of us can remain kneeling. Everything had just been peace and order. Now I am outraged—and afraid. He has used his cast iron voice, which leaves no room for debate. I have to walk outside.

"No, we can't give up everything. This is our truck, Richard, and our dream." I am crying. Already I know that every argument I can produce is hopeless. My next question, "Why?" wavers from my mouth.

"A lot of roofing materials were stolen, for one thing, and we also need to tell our families and friends what we experienced. It could happen to them too."

"I can write letters, Richard, and we can work here to send back the money for construction materials."

I glare at him then look over at the truck. It was always going to be a part of my life. It would have its own half acre on our homestead site. I would walk by it with my grandchildren and say, "We came here, in that, all those years ago."

Richard is firm. I hate for him to state, "This is what we are supposed to do." It doesn't seem fair for him to invoke the invisible for credentials.

"What next?" I ask, but I still refuse to turn and look at him.

"We are going to find an auto dealer or a trailer mart and sell this rig." Richard goes and climbs in behind the steering wheel.

"Are we ever going to Alaska?"

"Sure. Let's hitchhike up there in the summer. By then we'll have more money." I can look at him now, wanting my eyes to seal it as a promise.

Richard chooses a used vehicle dealer who has an immense lot to the side of a glass showroom. I watch my husband's process through the door, his conversation with salesmen in suits, and then the employees motioning to a manager.

Dropping my gaze, I pick off a dog hair from the corduroy grooves on my pants. I have this feeling I've known in doctor's offices when a shot is being prepared, and in moments the needle is going to enter my arm. As Richard opens the cab I wonder how much this is going to hurt.

"I have a hundred and fifty dollars in cash! We don't even have to bother with a check. Let's pack what we want to carry with us."

I didn't imagine that the feeling would be amputation, not inoculation. Following Richard, I try not to think this is the last time I'll touch the door handle, feel the distance to the curb, hear the sound of the door of our home opening.

Taking a pillowcase from the loft, I must choose the few things that I can carry with me. Everything practical can be replaced, there are billions of bread pans. What I can't duplicate are my peculiar pieces of art. Opening my antique tin for plug slice smoking tobacco, I put in my rock fossil imprinted with a fern and my blue wedding brooch. I prop my *Moby Dick* drawings along the side of the bag to keep them from being crushed. My Bible comes and notebooks with anything else I can grab. It all weighs too much to go on the end of a stick like my hobo costume of Halloweens past. Instead I hug it all in my arms as I climb outside.

We have to walk. I can't bear to stand and hitchhike so close to our cabin's front door. Yet, thirty feet away from my last and lost home, a pale blue Thunderbird pulls to the roadside.

"Thought you kids could use a ride."

Since neither of us solicited transportation, it feels like Providence. With our acceleration to the highway, I look back. Richard whispers, for consolation, that he can build it all again.

"I'm heading for Portland, kids."

Acknowledging that this is also our destination, the driver and passengers settle into a long-distance silence.

A post on the Columbia River bridge welcomes us back to Oregon. Continual signs enforce a lowering of the legal vehicle speed until we enter the city center at a few miles per hour.

Getting out in the park blocks, I see the benches are all abandoned due to the winter temperatures.

"Tomorrow, let's continue to make our way to the south," says Richard. "I promise we'll be in Alaska by this summer."

January 26
Nevada

I like most of the cheap hotels. Even though the price is rarely over six dollars and the bathrooms are always down the hall, each one is different. Carrying my pack down the stairs for another morning of desert hitchhiking, I admire the boxes of Indian arrowheads mounted on the wall. The artifacts were not arranged in rows but elaborately laid in patterns like formal gardens of old stones. The stairs are unique too. There are dabs of silver metal rounding out each corner that would normally collect dust.

While looking down, I admire my new cowboy boots. Richard and I each got a ten-dollar pair. They feel as comfortable as a baby's bed for the first half of the day. By night, though, my feet cry to come out of them.

My husband has already gone outside with his pack and the dog. I pass the rocking chairs that flank a cage where we paid our money. The desert morning is already shimmering with million-mile vistas in every direction.

We fall into step, our gait as equal as walking bookends. The few houses, gas stations, and cafes are clustered together to make a stand for civilization against the barren landscape. No matter the gallons of water lavished on lawns and flower beds, it all looks precarious. The wind and elements could easily reclaim Little Burg, Nevada.

Using both hands, I pantomime rolling a giant joint of fresh air. After licking the invisible ends, I lift it up and suck in enormous amounts of healthy oxygen before gesturing to give it to my husband.

Only two cars pass, and the drivers keep their eyes averted from our solicitations. While letting Noah off the leash, Richard picks up some rocks and challenges me to target practice with cactus.

"You know, we have less than fifty cents left, Laurel."

Since we are neither hungry, thirsty, nor dirty, this news doesn't threaten my present moment, but I'm well aware how it will challenge a present hour. It's like seeing the train tracks and knowing we are going to be tied to them. The locomotive of some need will come.

"Well, we were dumb then, Richard, to buy these boots. Twenty dollars could easily get us all the way to Los Angeles."

"If these shoes pinch, you're right, but since they are utterly comfortable, you're wrong!"

While I laugh, I begin to compare the shadows of Joshua trees. I'm looking for one wide enough for both of us to stand out of the sun and rest. Above us, a vapor trail in the sky precedes the sound of a jet engine.

A speeding car brakes for us. It even runs partly off the shoulder and into the sand. Now, running with Richard, I think about a whole tin roof covering us, and maybe air conditioning.

It's one of the varieties of Ford sedans. I see a couple in the front, and the fact that all the windows are open communicates there's no system forcing cooled air through jets. There are two doors, and the woman has to lean forward while pulling back the seat.

Our clean shaven driver has on a cowboy hat. His companion has the kind of hair that is short and curled on top, while the rest hangs long with a wave, roller width, at the end.

"We're Mr. and Mrs. Johnson."

Because she giggles with her announcement our driver adds they have recently taken the vows of what, for both of them, is a second marriage. Between them is a Styrofoam cooler. We take the offered sodas and share the last of a box of Broasted chicken. We are now as dependent on God to eat as the wild creatures that have no cupboards.

The proximity of meat propels Noah up from the floor to beg. Tearing off some skin, I drop it into the cavern of our dog's mouth. We still have in Richard's pack over half a bag of puppy kibble.

Since they are eventually going east, Richard suggests a town where we can get out that's still hundreds of miles away. Now speeding, we ride through what I imagine are Western movie sets. Cattle drives and Indians are over every hill.

Once we are dropped off on the roadside again, my shoulders feel sensitive to the weight of my pack as I hoist it on. Dragging myself along behind Richard, I'm flooded with yearnings for a home. There's a need in me to put flowers on a table. I want to cut up old pillowcases into squares of cloth that can be embroidered.

While thinking of stitchery projects, a green-and-white squad car pulls up beside us at the curb. The length of the vehicle equals the exact length of the space that I've lagged behind my husband.

Richard inquires about camping facilities, or any place we can lay our bags out for the night. The patrolman is young. There's some hesitation in his reply, "Nothing like that is available here. There's a city ordinance against hitchhiking wherever there is any housing or business."

I know what's ahead; we'll trek well off the road and make camp. All that I can think of is a Walt Disney movie—*The Living Desert* that featured sidewinder snakes, scorpions, lizards, and fuzzy spiders.

"Well," added the policeman, "there is one other place. No one is in our jail. It's been quiet for a long time, you can stay for a night."

I ask for a lift and climb first into the back seat. Looking straight ahead, I refuse to sneak a glance at Richard. The extensive radio equipment along the dashboard looks as though it could intercept the signals of Air Cuba.

A senior officer lays down a magazine as we are ushered into the facilities. Doing his best to suppress a grin, he's in complete agreement about us using the accommodations for one night.

Finally we are alone in a cell with the door wide open. There are two twin sized beds mounted like shelves into the wall.

"I really don't like this at all," says Richard, opting to go out immediately and walk the dog.

I'm just happy to avoid being ground level with the night's reptiles. Taking my coat from my pack, I fold it into a pillow. I remember the last and only time I was in jail. It was in the early fifties with my mother. She was a Brownie Scout leader and took our troop on a field trip to the police station. I remember asking then if the door could be opened so we could try the bed. My request was refused, and it remained, until now, a forgotten and ancient curiosity.

January 27

Opening my eyes, I'm inches from a drab stucco wall. The morning light reveals smudges and grime. Spots of paint, shades lighter than the rest, have been splashed over what I imagined were once penciled obscenities.

There's still one small slogan even with the ripples of my sleeping bag. The P has been obliterated, leaving the message KILL THE IGS.

Once I sit up and stuff my coat into my pack, I'm hungry. "Richard, the state would feed us breakfast if we were malefactors."

"Ha," he replies. "I would rather starve, and so would you, than to have this door locked!" His voice is unusually heated. Richard Lee has a past that I've asked him about and received only abrupt and partial answers. I know my husband has spent some time in jail.

In a single file we walk out, and I thank the officer on duty. I follow Richard, knowing we have a couple miles to go before we can hitch. I'm fixated on something to eat. Looking into café windows, I glimpse the motion of syrup being poured over pancakes. Men press toast crusts into eggs fried over easy. A customer stands up, forsaking half a plate of hash browns.

The roadway is sand and dirt. One house got the city sidewalk, and the next one didn't. A car behind us honks, and a driver motions for us to come aboard. The vehicle's right front has been smashed in what must have been a major accident. The automobile is also such a dull gray it's not a paint at all, but some chemical coating preliminary to color.

"I'm Jim." He is bearded with electric chin whiskers curling like tiny springs. "What's your sign?"

Berkeley has schooled me for that question, but I credit God who made the constellations.

"So you're a couple more of those Jesus freaks." Unknowingly, he has tapped a need within me.

James Moore

"Where have you met them?" I ask, thinking I have to meet others who had an experience like ours. *Every generation must have its creatures that really make it to the ark.*

"Ah," says Jim. "They're turning up everywhere. One of the biggest grass dealers in L.A. has thrown away his stuff. Now, that's crazy!"

Once we learn our driver is going to an area of Southern California where Richard's parents live, we settle back, and I try to nap for most of the long ride. Late in the day, we climb into the hills. Full-color billboards advertise future housing projects. Richard gives instructions where to drop us on the highway shoulder. I think how the land is endangered. Its sunburned grass is about to be covered with cement patios and wall-to-wall carpeting.

Richard's father and stepmother live in a retirement community. I wish we could call them first—I feel some anxiety. I met Bart and Ruby briefly in the role of their son's girlfriend, and now I've been a wife for three months.

Almost in their door, Richard smooths some wrinkles from the front of his shirt. We pass our one comb between each other.

"Why, Bart," shouts Mrs. Lee, "Richard's here! I thought it was the cleaning lady."

"I'm the lady that needs a cleaning," is my single thought as I follow my husband through the door.

"How about a kiss?" Ruby asks her stepson and then notices our boots and dog.

We are instructed to retreat first and deposit our shoes, packs, and pet back outside. Ruby explains it is the rug: "Don't ever get a white carpet for your home!"

Bart Lee comes out in a bathrobe to shake his son's hand. "We thought you kids were on the way to Alaska."

Ruby adds that there's not much on hand to eat. "Will you be here overnight?" she asks. I follow my mother-in-law and husband through the breakfast room to the small den. She instructs us how to pull out the couch in there to make a bed. She's sorry now that they picked a one-bedroom floor plan. While she's talking, I take a handful of peanuts from an open can on a portable TV tray.

"Now, make yourselves some toast. We'll be done with our bathroom that has the tub in just a few minutes."

First in the kitchen, I see there are several bottles of amber-colored alcohol pushed back against the wall. As we were told, there isn't much in the refrigerator but the loaf of sliced white bread. Richard wipes up the crumbs in between the sets of toast.

Bart Lee, now in a short sleeved shirt, joins us. His hair has been recently shaved into such a radical crew cut that there's no length for texture but just a dark and grizzled shading.

"You know, there are still a lot of relatives back in Minnesota. Anyway, here are some wedding gift checks that came in late that we've been holding until we could get an address for you."

I fill a bowl with water for our dog. My concern about what we are going to do next has lifted. Without even glancing at the amounts, Richard pockets the checks and offers me the first shower. He further suggests we take a walk with Noah around the golf course.

"Okay, how much?" I'm squeezing the ends of my wet braid that's hanging down my back. "Don't make me guess."

"Seventy-five dollars, total," Richard replies. "I have a plan. Isn't the sun wonderful? I'm not in any hurry to get wet and cold right away. The rest of the world is still in winter. Let's take this money into Mexico, and if we camp at a trailer park, cooking our own food, we can last till spring."

I look over at my husband, who is staring at a party of men in pastel shirts playing golf. I counter-suggest that we work and save. I'm sounding much like my own parents, who I now credit for their emphasis on thrift and practicality.

"It's your decision, Laurel. I'm going into Mexico, and you can come with me, or not."

I'm immediately sad. His threat makes this feel like the most serious altercation we have ever had. Only, in part, can I blame our exhaustion.

"What about our dog?" An animal without a veterinarian's certification would not be allowed to cross the border.

Richard replies that he has a good friend right in the valley who has a fenced backyard. "Look, Noah will have a rubber ball and a tree and will live awhile without a leash."

We both know he's won; the tug of war for our direction is over now. As we turn back to the house, he estimates the traveling time to San Diego.

"Then Tijuana, is such a short distance. We'll change dollars to pesos and take the cheapest bus further into the interior. I'll eventually get you to the Alaska Highway in probably three or four months."

I shrug my shoulders. I guess it's not my job to be a conscience that purports hard work and a savings account. My character has its own dirty spots that need some scrubbing before trying to disinfect a husband.

April 17, 1967
Alaska Highway

We are both filthy. The paved road ended in the first town after Dawson Creek. It's already evening, but it looks like late afternoon. Every ride that passed covered us in a great plume of dust. I can see it on my skin. My hair feels coarse, and my clothes have lost some of their color in this fresh film of dirt.

"Where should we camp?" Richard asks.

I laugh in reply. There are hundreds of square miles radiating from every compass point. We could put a tent anywhere. Having seen two wild moose after St. John, I'm only wary of choosing clumps of grass. I don't want to think about being trampled.

Richard points to a natural glen of poplar trees. After knocking a mosquito away from my eye brow, I follow my husband up a slight incline. While waiting for rides, there have always been tiny buzzing insects, which prompted me earlier to break off a branch and wave it over my head.

"Did you hear what that one driver said about Yukon law?"

The question needs no answer; we were together when it was explained that the Royal Mounties consider it a misdemeanor to pass someone on the highway that motions for a lift.

Richard pulls out the tent, which we unfold and secure with stakes. I'm thinking about one woman I met today who was in overalls putting in her own transmission. Our driver had pulled up to her cabin as a neighbor, just to ask about things.

"What a gal," he had said to me once back on the gravel highway. "Homesteading women know how to be completely self-sufficient."

Richard is pulling out his green mummy bag.

"Don't expect to be kissed tonight, as there's too much danger of creating mud."

I crawl in the tent behind him dragging my sleeping roll. A number of mosquitoes have come in with us. Unfortunately, there's no netting on the windows.

"What was that lady's name that we met for a few minutes?" asks Richard.

It's bad enough the mosquitoes want to draw blood, but the fact that they buzz continuously makes them intolerable. Somehow, a few have crawled inside my sleeping bag, but most seem to be swarming by my ears and sizing up my cheeks for a landing. I'm getting hot, and more uncomfortable with my twisting and waving.

"Imagine," says Richard, "she butchers and wraps game besides being a mechanic."

There's definite awe in his voice. I can't even hand him the right tool, and I don't buy meat if I can see blood in the grocery meat packages. The driver said she was a typical homesteader and had lived alone on that claim for a number of years.

Sitting up to kill bugs, I can see them actually sifting through the window like a fine vapor. There are itching welts along my forehead and arms. I hate insects that whine and pierce my skin.

Richard tells me to settle down. I'm turning into a windmill beside him.

"You know, Laurel, you're going to learn how to do all that too. Once we get a truck, I can show you about maintenance. I bet, in no time, you'll be hunting and trapping too."

"Aren't these bugs bothering you?" I know my voice is shrill.

"Not particularly," says Richard. "I don't bother them, so they leave me alone."

It's such an untrue thing to say that I instantly feel hostile towards Richard, and that woman too, who can quarter dead moose. I start to cry. My face is dirty and sweaty. My bug bites itch, and I'm rubbing my eyes with such vigor, I'm sure I'll lose all my eye lashes.

"Good grief," says Richard. "What's your problem?"

His tone reminds me of a statistic that the divorce rate is higher in Alaska than any other state. I think of a way that I can keep the bugs from crossing my face, like Sherman's march to the sea. There's an extra bra in my pack with a lacy cup. I insert it in my sleeping bag as a breathing hole. I finally fall asleep after watching the insects probe not more than one inch from my eyes.

April 18

Walking along the serpentine highway, we are hoping to come upon a mileage marker. We want to know the distance we have traveled from Dawson Creek. Some of the lakes look blind with ice. There's a lot of snow on the mountains, and if we should dig, there's a permanent stratum of frost.

We can see the dust first. It is billowing up, dissipating into the air behind a Volkswagen van. If it passes us, we'll instinctively turn from the road, blind in its wake and hold our breath. It's in range now, showing a Yukon Territory license plate; besides numbers, the tin is stamped with a miner bent over a gold pan. It brakes, and we thrust back the sliding glass doors.

"I'm Ogertschnick." Our driver has an accent reminiscent of European cafes. Wearing a blue Hawaiian shirt, he says he's a bush welder going to Whitehorse, the capital of the territory.

"There's going to be a bingo game tonight, but unless the stakes are high, I won't play. Gambling is about the biggest entertainment we've got in our camp."

I lie back against my pack, still tired from the emotions and conditions of the night. I'm slouched enough to see a band of sky above the trees. Eagles and the smaller hawks glide without effort.

The sidewalk in Whitehorse is simple plank boards. Among some rustic cabins and shops are a number of bars.

"You'll find the Indians starting to line up even before the doors open," says Ogertschnick. "They get treaty money each month from the government."

Three log cabins are built on top of each other, which our host explains was the first hotel back in the gold rush. The one movie theater is playing Hitchcock's *North by Northwest*. I exclaim over a couple men walking with guns strapped to their hips.

Once out on the street, I feel compelled to get clean even if I have to lie naked in my sleeping bag, in the corner of a laundromat, while everything is washed and dried.

"Richard, let's get a cheap hotel room."

"Why? We don't need that! We can camp anywhere."

His speech makes me feel like crying again. I can't bear the idea of another night like the last one. I walk briskly ahead of my husband to try and gain some self-control—dirty, tired, mad dogs foam easily at the mouth.

"Laurel," Richard takes my arm. "You'll only get covered in dust again tomorrow. We still have over eight hundred miles of dirt road before we get to the state border."

Out of the corner of my eye I see a couple of Haight-Ashbury hippies stroll by. It's the beadwork on their sleeves that I first notice. The two men have their hair pulled back into long braids. They look like rich drug dealers on vacation.

Maybe they are staying in a facility where we could put our bags on the floor tonight and at least sleep away from the mosquitoes. I run ahead, crying out, "Hey you guys, please stop a minute."

They swivel and stare. They are not city boys on an adventure, but full-blooded Indians wearing ceremonial clothing. Their eyes are piercing as I back away apologizing.

Richard has caught up with me. "What is wrong with you?"

Men with guns pass on either side of us. Everything feels violent and primitive.

"Now there you two are." Ogertschnick pulls up in his Volkswagen. "I went to get myself a motel, and the only unit left has two bedrooms. Why don't you share it with me?"

April 22

I watch the trailer attached to the hitch of the pickup truck. We have been riding in the truck bed for two days with our legs stretched out under tarps. This vibrating brown-and-white tin box distracts from my vision of raw river beds, forest, and craggy mountains.

We reach the Canadian border station and find an officer in uniform. I can hear Mr. Potter's voice complain of the dirt deposited in their trailer from the past 1300 miles of gravel. His wife echoes him.

Obviously the border guard has heard it before. He has his fast, polite reply. "We are just free with our real estate."

Richard nudges me and points at the Alaska state flag. The sound of gravel that has been such an integral part of this journey is gone. We are on quiet black asphalt.

The outskirts of Fairbanks don't look like much. Almost every business is constructed along this main road, and behind it is a wave of simple houses with tiny yards. It's like going back in time to see the building of America along the highway and railroad lines.

We're eager to get out. Already we have rolled back the tarp and moved our packs. The Potters pull to the roadside. We know their plans are to find a local trailer park that they showed us in the guidebook.

We walk towards the center of Fairbanks, which is an area about four blocks long by three blocks wide. I want to buy mosquito netting, and Richard recommends we purchase a cheap canteen. Often we were thirsty in the pickup but could do nothing but stare at lakes and wish the rig would stop.

One side of Fairbanks is bordered by a river. After buying a staple loaf of bread, we walk to its banks. I read aloud the signs that we are eight thousand miles from Bombay, and the furthest city from this northern spot is Capetown, thirteen thousand miles away. I decide that I want to see them both before I turn fifty.

An older man is seated near us on a bench rolling a cigarette. Stripping off my pack I put it at the far end from where he is sitting.

"Breakup is earlier this year."

I have no idea what he means and turn from balancing my sack to look at him.

"Breakup?" I ask. This isn't the type of person who offers comment on how the deprivations of Alaska affect relationships.

"That's when the ice on the Chena River here melts enough so it can begin to flow. Everyone makes a bet on the day, and it becomes a rich little kitty for the best guesser."

"We're here to make a land claim," says Richard.

"I wouldn't bother with these Yukon flats. Go over towards Anchorage. You can buy maps there at the Bureau of Land Management, then go stake the piece you want."

He stops to suck on his cigarette.

"After you register it, then you've got to build something you can live in."

His words have the effect on us that a bow has on an arrow. Walking back along the main street, I think how the old man referred to winter. There's an exterior thermometer on almost every building, registering now fifty-two degrees. To us, the phrase, "forty degrees below" is an experience awaiting us.

"Laurel, I really haven't counted the change in my pocket, but our money is low enough that we'll have to find some work in Anchorage. That city is about four times bigger, so we should have some opportunities."

We've both been meditating on realities. Side by side we are considering cash and the cold. Again, I wish for a watch. The sunlight is like a makeup that covers the real age of the day.

After a stream of cars passes us, we get a short lift along the turnoff to Anchorage.

Mount McKinley, captive in ice since before history, broods in the distance. A sign states that we've entered the refuge area for bighorn sheep. There's no sign of house or human. Nature here seems at full stature and evokes in me a passion for the land. More than the beauty, it's the sense of freedom. There's plenty of acreage with inspiring views back in the lower states, but with it comes building inspectors, and permits and fees. I have come home, and I'll think of the mosquitoes as my little watchdogs that scare away strangers.

A station wagon stops, and a middle-aged woman says, "There's still some room for you I'm sure." The back seat of her car has been collapsed to accommodate cases of canned food and paper products. I let Richard fit our packs between a Hormel chili box and an eighteen-can carton of Campbell's soup. Sliding to the middle, I glance at our driver, whose polyester sweater and pants are stretched over hills of fat. "Run me a little restaurant up by some mining claims; it's on the other side of this parcel of state owned land."

"Short winter this year," she comments. "We didn't get our first real snow until the very end of September."

"What do people do?" I'm becoming increasingly curious about the occupations of people held in small rooms for six months when it's dark outside.

"It's different with everyone," she murmurs. "Some couples sure fight a lot."

Something about her chuckle implies she has been in a few arguments herself. "A lot of us can't wait for spring, but we love winter best. A friend of mine, a taxidermist, just stuffs some of the animals from his trap line. I like to cook, eat, and read. Some folks keep dogs and do a lot of sledding with their teams."

Hilma suggests we stay in one of the state-maintained emergency winter shelters for the night.

"Look at that!" she cries. "Damn nuisance—should shoot 'em all!"

"What?" We ask in unison. We can see nothing through the trees but a lake and an occasional grayling breaking the surface where it has thawed.

"Beaver dam," she explains with her lips twisting out the words. "They mow the trees down until the bank erodes, and that can flood this road with the spring runoff."

Hilma points out the last curve before the shelter. Pulling to the side, she offers us a couple of cans of food. "You'll find that the door will be open. There should be a pan and wood for the stove."

It's a mystery how the bugs are waiting for us. I'm not even out of the car, and I can hear one whine by my ear.

Once inside, I see the beds are the same government issue that illegal aliens use in detention centers. I look around and wonder what Richard and I would do in here for six months. What we'll be able to construct this summer will be less than a third of the size of this room.

Rolling out the sleeping bag on the lower bunk, I think how much I would like to sew a quilt, and then maybe the following winter I could use it to cover a baby. Once in bed, I begin to consider names for infants. Sorting through the proper nouns of old classmates and characters in books, I settle on Matthew and Hannah.

Above me Richard is pretending to be a fat frog
that unrolls his tongue and lives on bugs.

April 23
Anchorage

We are standing under the awning of a sporting
goods store to escape the deluge of rain. Looking over
Richard's shoulder I can see a display of tents where the placards advertise
they can withstand Arctic cold. I can't help but wistfully compare our little
triangle of canvas with these aerodynamic designs.

"What do you want to do?" I ask. While speaking I'm also checking to
see if it's cold enough to make a subtle vapor cloud at my lips, but there's no
ghost of winter past.

"Let's go find some café, Laurel, where we can figure a plan."

Before moving from the one protected spot of pavement, we pull out our
rain ponchos. Richard points to a bakery down on the other side of the street.
As we open the door, the smell of the fresh bread reduces me to want.

Choosing the table furthest from the door, we balance our two hot rolls
on napkins.

"We have seven dollars left, Laurel, now that we have just spent this change."

"Look, as soon as this storm clears, I can start asking for work in restaurants." We both know that the baker just told us it could stay this way for days.

While savoring the last bites of bread, I wonder where we can stay. An
emergency winter shelter is too isolated for daily work. I dread thumbing to
the city outskirts and putting up a tent in pouring rain. I suggest we find a
church and see if we can sleep on a classroom floor.

One congregational building within the block has an open door. Seeing the
sign that indicates the direction to the church office, I feel like part of a divine
ethics test. Will they give to those who ask of them?

A woman rises from her desk to greet us. She looks from our faces to
our feet, checking whether we've tracked mud down the hall. Fumbling somewhat in her speech, she says they are neither licensed nor insured to provide
casual accommodations.

My dignity feels fragile, and now I must turn from her and not have less of it.

"Wait," she cries. "Just a few blocks away the Salvation Army runs a relief
center." Thanking her, we leave the same we came and head up the street.

Miss Esther Thornton, in her full salvation military uniform is leading us
upstairs. Her knot of hair looks like a compact snowball at the nape of her

neck. Her instructions include separate living quarters for men and women, separate tables for dinner, compulsory meeting attendance at 7:30, and no alcohol. We are allowed a maximum of seven days of residency.

The dorm isn't the expected corridor of beds, but a series of rooms with four metal cots. The women that I glimpse through the doorways appear to be mostly Indians or Eskimos. Seeing the facility's commander they drop their voices and regard me with curious eyes. Wearing the poncho over my pack, I must look like I weigh three hundred pounds in dripping plastic. With a gesture that points to a door, and a reminder that chapel will be soon, I'm sent into a room.

Two women, sitting across from each other, stare at me. One has shocking yellow hair. Because of the exposed one inch black roots, she looks like a university experiment testing the rate of hair growth. The other roommate is also an Indian, but her hair hangs in traditional braids except for bangs that are set in pin curls.

Giving first my name, I struggle out of my poncho, then turn to learn of my companions. They are each from different government land grants north of Fairbanks. Their answers to my rudimentary questions are brief and terse. In addition they ask nothing of me, so I'm to return the same courtesy.

After stowing my pack next to a dresser, I unfold a stack of linen and make my bed. The wind outside sounds like it's being forced through the neck of a bottle. Yet, hearing it from inside a warm room muzzles the weather. It now feels domesticated, on a leash, where outside it was wild and threatening.

We descend for the chapel service. I look for Richard as the men come down a long staircase across from us. There's a shuffling for the seats closest to the assembling body of the opposite sex. A few bearded, long-haired boys are present on treks north, but mostly the residents are native Alaskans.

Miss Esther has attired herself in a Salvation Army regulation bonnet. Like the headpiece on a nun's habit, it reflects an age before the automobile. One incongruous thing is the music on the piano. She has taped what must have been disintegrating sheets onto sturdy cereal box wrappers. So, the colors of Kellogg's Corn Flakes and Post Raisin Bran enliven the rack above the keys.

The commander opens in music. Her choice is a series of hymns written in the nineteenth century. Even her message conveys a feeling that her attire is being held out by ancient hoop skirts and has a silk bustle. Nothing fits this audience, born in the wild. I wish for a chance to speak—

A trapper kept sled dogs, and one of the pups he loved was lost ...

They need a local parable.

April 28

I'm tired of looking for a job again today. It's been an exercise in hearing all the variations of "NO." Richard is helping unload a truck for three hours. No one seems to be hiring in the city at all, but there have been some calls to the mission for casual labor, always at minimum wage.

Crossing over to Cordoba Street, we are planning to meet at the Bureau of Land Management. We need to study available areas and exactly how to mark our claim. I look up at the etching of a buffalo above the double doors. To me it's peculiar that the creature chosen for their logo is almost extinct. How long before the game here will be gone and the rivers polluted?

There are cases of green maps of the wilderness inside, like a library, only with volumes of land. It's overwhelming to consider that every point of the compass radiates into property we can claim. I've asked the Indians at the mission what to look for, and their advice was to pick a stand with tall birch and native grass because a garden will do better there. We are to avoid blueberry bushes because they grow where there's no depth of soil over the permafrost.

Richard strides through the door and joins me, announcing we have another nine dollars, but there are no work opportunities for tomorrow.

I've been staring into an enlarged map of the state that is divided into numbered sections. Less than one percent of the available land has been surveyed. Now, we are to choose the area for our plot and then go over to the geological survey office to purchase our specific maps.

I feel paralyzed by the range of choices.

"We'll need highway access," says Richard, which narrows our concentration to the property that borders the few red lines of road.

We need advice. Looking over at the employees in a separate area of desks, I see seven people. Their casual suggestions could affect our whole lives.

I choose the desk that has rocks and pine cones as paper weights. A woman stooping over an open drawer has her back to me. She turns as I make my request for direction.

"Try the country off the highway before old Valdez. That area is called the little Switzerland of Alaska."

After joining Richard, I want to wave back another thanks at her, but she's gone to a filing cabinet. It was never her desk at all.

Taking a typed form of instructions on how to walk off and mark boundaries, I fold it into my pocket.

"Let's go over to E Street," says Richard. "I would really like to leave tomorrow for Valdez. There's no work now, and maybe something will open

44

by the time we get back.

I follow him outside, adding that our total grubstake is fifteen dollars, and the map will be our first subtraction.

April 29

"Let's just lie down in the middle of the highway. Look, Richard, maybe it will take this extreme act to produce a ride." We are on the Valdez turnoff, and there has been no traffic for over two hours. We can't stop walking, though, because of the mosquitoes. They darken the air by their numbers. Both of us have a piece of mosquito netting over our heads. I look into the deep forests on either side of us through wrinkles of mesh. We should have hats with brims to suspend the material a little distance from our eyes. Instead, I only have a scarf, and Richard is in a knitted cap.

We are each carrying the top of a branch too. These we swish above us to discourage the bugs from landing on the net and buzzing by our ears. It is exhausting. Regularly I have to change hands for the labor. It has been a revelation on the wonders of the horse's tail that is flicked in barnyards with an impressive range.

We can hear the motor of the car before seeing it. Realizing we look more menacing than desperate, we cast our branches to the side and tear off the shroud of net.

The passengers are an Indian family, who simply brake in the middle of the highway. Four small children crowd over in the back seat to accommodate us and our packs. When asked where they are going, the driver only replies, "Ahead a piece." The silence of these people duplicates the dark silence of the woods.

Slowing the car, the father turns up a rough embankment made by a tractor and chain saw. His wife gathers a package from near her feet. I can now see a log cabin up the rise with a couple walking toward us, waving a greeting.

We are observers of neighbors presenting silver-scaled fish to neighbors. I follow the women. Jean tells how she and her husband came three winters ago from Idaho to take the maximum homestead of 120 acres. I notice her calculation of time isn't expressed in "years," but by the sum of their winters.

"It has been a lot more difficult than we expected."

My eyes blink in adjusting to the darkness of the cabin's interior. It is one square room with a very few small windows. There are kerosene lights on wall brackets. The walls are studded with nails holding miscellaneous tools, guns, and even parts of chains.

Returning to the car, we are invited to continue with them and unroll our bedrolls in a broken station wagon that they own. Once left by the vehicle, we see that it has no wheels and is propped up on cement blocks. With the windows up, we can sleep completely free of insects. All of its seats are down allowing ample room to completely stretch out.

Waking frequently, I looked out on a long dusk, then sunrise. This view of an unending evening is the one thread that stitches together all my squares of colored dreams.

April 30

Once back to the highway, I can look down to where the empty road becomes as narrow as a pin point among the trees.

At the appearance of a jeep, we are immediately at attention and raise our thumbs with the flourish of a full salute. The driver wavers. We can see the brake lights flicker with indecision. We stare at the disappearing car when unexpectedly he changes his mind and stops.

"My name is Smith." He laughs. "I'm the only Smith in Valdez." Richard pulls out his packet of maps.

"I know exactly where there are tracts of available land waiting for claims." The driver takes one hand off the steering wheel and taps the folded green maps on my husband's lap.

The dense woods thin with the altitude of mountains. We see glaciers and spots of clouds caught below us.

"Maybe, you would rather go into Valdez first."

Richard decides for us to go into town, buy food, and check for jobs.

"There's no work there," says Smith, "but you should see the place."

There are swallows that soar out of cliffs, riding updrafts of wind. Slow huge moose feed in some of the gullies by the highway. They lift their ponderous heads to regard us as we whiz by in seconds.

We descend through Thompson Pass, and there are views from some streets in Valdez of Prince William Sound. The town has far more saloons than grocery stores.

We spend everything but a dollar and a half for food. Richard puts most of the tins in his pack. Our provisions, if we are careful, can last almost a week. While walking to the end of town, I notice it's colder here than in the woods, but there are fewer bugs.

An old man in a checkered shirt stops for us. He's chewing tobacco and keeps opening the window of his pickup truck to spit outside.

"Weather is changing again," he crackles.

I look, and there is a new band of clouds obscuring some of the peaks.

"Lots of land available here because people want the flatter parcels to do all that cultivating that a claim requires."

"We are interested in the minimum of five acres," says Richard. "That way the size of our garden never has to be inspected."

The old man laughs, approving the sentiment that the less regulations over a citizen the better.

Richard and I are both staring out at the roadside. It seems to be galloping away as we look for possible features that appeal to us. After passing a creek, my husband cries for us to be let out. We want water on our property.

It's almost completely overcast, so fast has been the bundling of the sky into clouds.

After our driver leaves us, I ask Richard where we are. Instead of a sure finger pointing to an area of the map, he shrugs his shoulders. "No idea." We will have to walk a mile at the most to find a location marker.

A single drop of rain hits the page extended between our hands. With haste, Richard folds it. I want to pull out my poncho immediately after experiencing the Anchorage storm.

All the mountains have now disappeared into a thick fog bank. We walk quickly, feeling vulnerable. I'm thinking how the bears must be out of their winter dens by now and starving for meat. I can almost see them raking the air with extended claws, saliva dripping out of their open mouths.

Richard points out the markings of a side road and suggests we explore its first bend. There's no evidence that any recent vehicle has been here. Fortunately, it isn't wet enough yet for there to be mud. The forest, now around us, does make noises. Trees crack, and birds cry.

Our trail ends in a clearing with a log cabin. An acceleration of rain makes us run to the front door. It's futile to knock; no one has been here for a long

time. Richard tries the knob and the heavy door swings open revealing a small, dark room. The stream of outside light creates a division between the kitchen side, with its wood stove, over to the hand made shelf constructed to hold a double mattress. The dirt makes it all feel like a past tense life.

A mouse darts across from the far corner over to the wood box.

"I bet this is an old claim, Laurel, that the people are holding onto for an investment."

I haven't moved my eyes from the wood box. Mice are creatures in plural.

"This is much better than our tent," declares Richard.

Only because of the weather, I think. There are mists of webs that hang like gauze across the small windows. Beyond the spiders is a view of the streaming rain.

Richard wants to bring the cheer of a fire. There's a sink with a hand pump instead of faucets. Wanting to wash the table, I crank it vigorously, but nothing comes out.

Once in our sleeping bags, I can hear the mice and some sheltering crickets whose hind legs saw night songs.

May 1

Once awake, I check the windows. It's not raining, but neither is it bright with sun.

Back on the road, I'm sorry we can't see the towering mountains. Their frozen majesty is still shrouded by clouds. Richard has the map protruding from his hip pocket. I've pulled out from my diary the official guidelines for describing a claim.

"It says we must tie our description to natural features and mark each corner with a substantial monument like a mound of stones. If possible, the land must be taken in rectangular form and the lines follow the north, south, east, and west of a compass, unless one of the boundaries is irregular, like a river or a cliff."

"What else?" asks Richard. He can see I'm holding three full pages of rules.

"The rest concerns warnings of what is unacceptable. It says all mileposts, road junctions, bridges, and towns often change and should only be utilized to supplement natural features.

Don't you love that sentence, Richard? Alaska acknowledges that the handiwork of man is feeble and temporary compared to creation."

I can see by his face that I'm flying away from him with my own colored wings. We both sigh. Marriage calls for such tolerance. Sometimes, I don't make any sense to my husband, and he hates me always writing in a diary. I could let myself be lonely because he doesn't follow some of my ideas, and I have to translate for him many of my similes.

Richard kicks a rock, and a simple game is born. My shots veer the most, nor can they go as far.

We haven't been looking for a ride, but I still raise my thumb because we still can't pin point our position. The map has perceptibly aged since its purchase five days ago.

A middle-aged couple stops and explains that they are establishing their own acres on Fish Lake.

"Why don't you get in, and we'll drive slowly to find some marker that matches your survey papers."

It would have been much more than a mile's walk, but finally we come upon a white post that provides our exact location. Everything our eye now sees is available.

Cities are full of those who have been caught in monthly payments for avocado green or harvest gold furniture sets. They work at jobs they don't like and stare out windows at neighbors who have the latest automobiles for no money down and easy terms. Somehow, through a million hooks that could have caught our lives, we have made it to the country.

We ask to get out by a meadow where there's a stand of poplar trees whose new leaves seem to be clapping in the wind. Great moments have music. I'm hearing "BORN FREE," and Woody Guthrie's "THIS LAND IS MADE FOR YOU AND ME." Others may hear symphony, or even a choir, but my inner ear is rejoicing with pop and folk.

There is a creek. It may come from a spring. We have dropped our packs and begin to run as much as the rocks and foliage allow. There's no sense now of the required metes and bounds of surveying. First is discovery, and then the work.

Richard, ahead of me, shouts back that I'm to hurry. He is now out of sight. We are both in a strip of woods, whose tree roots are nourished by the creek.

I understand Richard's exclamation. There is a real waterfall with a little more than ten feet of sheer cascade. The sound of it is full of life. Imposing the seasons upon it, I try to imagine it in winter when it's turned to fairy castle spires of ice. I lay the future across it too. Our children will learn to walk in range of its shower.

"Richard, this is perfect. It can be a natural corner for our claim's description."

We now have to determine if it should be in the back or front of the land we want. We must walk through the property on either side too. For us, who only knew suburban yards, five acres is a sizable lot.

While piling the corner rocks, I've determined where I want the house and garden. We have staked our parcel that is part meadow, woods and water.

"You know what I learned, Richard. One of the Indians told me that the best cabins are built out of drift logs. They start petrifying as they float. He explained that some kind of chemical process replaces the wood fiber with silica. It comes from the dissolved sand in the water."

I think of construction as Richard's scholarship. It's his artist's canvas, but he doesn't even give me eye contact. I thought I had big-time information.

"Should we stay here tonight?" I ask.

My husband wipes his forehead with the back of his hand.

"We could," he murmurs. "But then again we have so much work to do, let's start back to Anchorage."

As best as I can determine, we have a full legal description that we can submit. Our corners are distinct. Four diary pages declare that this area has been claimed, and they are secured with rocks at each corner.

"If only we had the money," I complain, "to just come back and use both spring and summer to build."

On the highway we mark the entrance to our property with stones. Richard takes my arm and leads me away until the entrance gate to our claim is out of sight.

Because of the steep grade, we can hear a vehicle laboring in its ascent. We pivot to see a new, blue Volkswagen van. I hope we can escape the pesky whine of insects.

There are three men, who move over some personal suitcases to make room. They are all pastors riding back to Anchorage after attending a minister's conference. The driver, Reverend Weeks, extends a passage back to the city. He wants to know our names and ages.

"Twenty-one and a half," I declare, and then am instantly embarrassed. Only children add on the fraction to give their age more stature.

The day held so much exertion that I fall instantly asleep. It is late when Reverend Weeks opens our door and gives instruction that we can sleep in the church multipurpose room. A preschool uses the facilities by day, and we have to be up and out by eight.

Finding a stage, we pull the curtains across to create a smaller enclosed space for our night.

May 2
Anchorage

The imposed darkness of sleeping where there are no windows worked against us. Children's voices wake us. School has started a few feet away from where we have been sleeping. The teachers must be in a play yard where they wait outside for their pupils to arrive. One voice would have alerted us in time. Instead, the entire student body is marching toward us with high-pitched chattering.

Richard dashes for his pack to pull out his Levi's. I have to stifle a laugh; I can imagine the curtains being opened and everyone shrieking at the sight of this man in his waffle-knit long underwear.

A teacher's voice commands quiet and asks everyone to get a carpet square. I'm racing too, up now and buttoning my pants.

"Does everyone, boys and girls, want to hear Mrs. Music this morning?"

As voices chorus a sustained "YES," I can see the piano behind us. We have seconds to become orderly. There's no time to fold sleeping bags. We pile them into a box at the corner.

One girl screams an accusation that David is poking her. I'm glad for the diversion. Our plan is to inquire everywhere for employment. In the past I only checked with restaurants. Today, we must get work. I grab toiletries while young David gets his lecture on what hands are for.

Richard moves our packs to the wall and picks up his shoes. It's so dark it's hard to see anything but shapes. I'm holding both toothbrushes and a comb. Richard pulls me to a fire door. We slip outside just as the curtain opens for the magic fingers of Mrs. Music.

Once in Anchorage, Richard wants us to meet at 5:00pm in front of the land office so we can hitch back together. He has me copy down the church address, just in case one of us is delayed because of employment. I could end up in the pink dress of a Dunkin Donuts girl working a swing shift.

My exuberance begins to wane as I'm told in department stores that they are not taking applications right now. I'm losing the heights of my morning's expectations as people shake their heads, "no," with false smiles of regret.

I walk to the very edge of the city where I catch views of Cook Inlet, an immense body of water that is supposed to be comparable in size to the state of Rhode Island.

I turn back thinking of a job I would really like; I know the Dewey decimal system by heart. It would be wonderful to work in a library instead of some of the souvenir and fir shops where I inquired. Books are like a kind of embalmed mind. The dead may be scattered, but their voices live in the library.

Sent to the head librarian, I walk the length of the room endorsing myself for confidence. I can recommend and quote the best in fiction; I know many of the cabbages and kings of literature.

"We just have a full staff, Miss. Check back with us about every seven months."

There's no air left in me now. I'm defeated and hungry but won't spend the fifty cents Richard passed to me when we parted. I vow never to give ear to that slick pronouncement made about vagrants—they could get a job if they really wanted one.

I find my husband leaning against the wall. People are streaming out of the double-office doors beside him. His immobility makes him look like the seller of a hot watch, just waiting for the right customer.

"Nothing," he says, speaking out the word even before I reach his side. We talk no further and move to take advantage of traffic that will be moving to the northern suburb.

I go first to Richard's pack to get a large tin of pork and beans. We have bakery bread, too. Richard bought a whole loaf for his lunch. There's a church kitchen, and I reach for the can opener in a drawer.

"I want us to go back to Portland," says Richard, coming over and leaning next to me against a cupboard.

"Don't be crazy," I cry. "You're just discouraged because we've had a bad day. Tomorrow ..."

He cuts me off feeling too weary to be exhorted.

"No," he says. "Remember, I tried for days before we left for Valdez, too."

I fill two plates with food, and carry them out into the large room. We choose the stage and sit a little distance from each other.

"Laurel, we are completely broke!"

"I still have the fifty cents!"

Richard sneers. "At least I can get a job in Portland."

"We can't quit, Richard. Everyone has stories of how they just held on a little bit longer, and it worked out."

"Sure," he says, "in storybooks. If we ration the food we bought, we can make it back down into the States as long as we get good rides. Come on, Laurel. Get mad at God, not me; He could have opened anything today, but He didn't!"

Putting down my plate, I stand up, too disturbed to keep eating. Our argument is like an Indian arm wrestle with two points of view. Yet, questioning why God hasn't given us what we need pins my hand to the mat.

All through this whole argument, never have I believed we might go back, until now.

Walking away from my husband, I survey the back wall of the nursery. There are clusters of children's drawings that were once duplicated from a coloring book on a copying machine. It fits how I feel. Nothing is the right shade. Wild colors cross each other, and every stroke extends way beyond the lines.

Without a word, I walk outside, not knowing where I'm going or when I'll be back.

The mountains are quartz pink in the evening light. I keep walking to find the right place to be alone. It doesn't take long to find a swatch of raw country. I climb over some fallen tree trunks, a tractor pushed together in a heap at the end of a development. I sit, and behind me the city sprays insecticide, while before me is a dense and tangled woods.

I cry until I'm exhausted. There are so many graves in a life where countless hopes must be buried. I wanted to tack moose horns above our door and put a giant thermometer on a window ledge. I'll never see the waterfall again, or know the contour of what those mountains looked like.

I feel I've lost Richard too; at least I've lost the way I used to perceive him. He has taken a much smaller, human form.

Gingerly I touch my eyelids. They are sore and swollen. My back aches from hunching over, and I slide off the log, onto the dirt, where my shoulders can lean against the wood.

Spreading out my hand, I look down at my wedding ring below the wrinkles of my knuckle. There's a tracing of dirt, too, in my nails from establishing the corners of our claim. Everything feels gone, but God.

There is nowhere else to go. I want a life that reaches further than my perception. I have to surrender to the fact that God can be trusted, and He has a plan for me.

May 6

The pitted windshield outside the arc of wipers is full of bugs. Richard and I are both up front on the bench seat next to Reverend Weeks. The weather is warmer today than what we have known. Motioning for Richard to crack the window, I appreciate that the pastor is giving us a lift to the junction toward the Yukon. Our packs, in the back, are full of washed and folded clothes.

"This is the only highway east. I'm sure you'll get a ride straight through to Canada."

"Oh, one last thing," says Reverend Weeks. "My wife packed some food that you can use today."

Taking the lunch from his hands, I can feel the weight of fruit at the bottom. Once he's out of sight, I open it, hoping for candy bars. No one could miss the envelope that stretches across the entire bag. It is cash. There are four twenty-dollar bills, a ten, and a five.

Richard whistles in surprise, and takes the fan of bills and smooths them into one roll. He taps my arm with it as if he were an English gentleman touching me playfully with a glove.

"Tell me what you would do, Laurel, if I said, let's go instead to Valdez and try to work there. This could stake us while we look for jobs. It's only early spring."

Richard severs two branches to make fly-swatter tails. There are lots of bugs hatching in the small pools I can see across these flats. This water, created with the thaw, will evaporate through the summer. I survey the landscape, feeling that Alaska was one of the last toys of my childhood. I did want it with the passion of a face pressed against a window glass.

Our conversation stops when a battered car pulls to the roadside. A man with shoulder-length hair gestures to us. He has removed his back seat from his vehicle to enlarge his space for hauling supplies. There are garden tools and a scruffy dog that springs up from a scrap of throw rug.

"That's Jake. He's part timber wolf."

The dog does have yellow eyes, but I still doubt the lineage.

"I can only take you about eight miles; that's where I turn toward my claim. I've taken five mind-blowing acres. Hey, you guys look cool. Open the glove box."

Richard reaches for the knob. Inside is a large plastic bag of marijuana.

"You must use a lot of oregano," I say, feigning ignorance. "Are you Italian?"

"I grow it," he boasts. "Not on my land, but in a secluded place that still doesn't belong to anyone. When I can get it, I fertilize it with bear dung. There are some papers there if you want to roll a few joints. Hey, take a pinch for the road."

I let Richard speak for us and decline.

"Have you ever been to the Haight?" I confirm that I once lived in Haight-Ashbury.

"Are they into crystals there?" Our driver pulls out of his pocket a small piece of rose quartz. "I never go anywhere without it. You know, it's thousands of years old and full of the energy of the earth. It releases vibrations that give me direction."

"Have you ever considered the Bible to be the source of instruction?"

He laughs at us for the last mile before turning off onto two tire ruts that cross a meadow. I'm glad to be going. Maybe we do climb to Heaven over the ruins of some cherished schemes.

I like the feeling of a fresh wind blowing now against our backs. *I can bury lots of little hopes, but never Hope itself.*

The Disciple
Is Not A Volunteer

He Is Called

1970 to 1975

Matthew and Anna Arrive in the World

Laurel and Matthew 1970

Laurel and Anna 1972   Matthew and Anna 1972

Matthew 4 1/2 years old

Anna 3 years old

JULY 1975

Portland

I stand looking at our home, choosing a part of the sidewalk where two cracks intersect making a giant X. It is an old wooden frame that could use another coat of paint, and more front-yard flowers. Once again, I think how it is the smallest house on 73rd Avenue, and probably in all of Portland. It could have less square feet than any other single-family dwelling in Oregon.

Crossing the lawn, I know I have to tell Richard that I'm pregnant again. Also, I'll have to find some kind of prenatal program for low-income families.

Five-year-old Matthew spots me from the front window. He pretends the sill is his own piano. He sings louder as I reach the door, "Thank God for garbage trucks." It is just one of his original's. Anna, age three, squeals and rushes to embrace my knees.

"You were gone for over an hour," says Richard as he comes to get the grocery bag. He wants me to start frying potatoes for dinner and tells me how Anna spilled the last of our milk.

I must try to turn up the valve on my own tank of oxygen. I better take some deep breaths; everything is going to work out; I've just got to trust in that, hope in that, and not in how I'm feeling.

This is pure air, as my own thoughts are already polluted.

September

The family practice clinic is located in a separate building within the multi-service cluster of the University Health Science Center. One physician cares for the medical problems of the entire family unit. I was assigned to Dr. Michael Mainer, who was in his third year of residency.

Once a day, I swallow an enormous pink vitamin pill that tastes like stale candy. Once a month, I ride the bus to Emma Jones Hall at the top of the hill where Dr. Mainer records the early prenatal questions and answers.

My weight is always the first data of his inquiry. He chided me the month I splurged on homemade peanut butter cookies.

"Oh, I was wearing these hiking boots on the scale," I said, while clicking my heels together.

"Well, maybe," he answered.

Every night I experience a phenomenon that I regard as a mystery of my pregnancy. As soon as I sleep, I perspire until the discomfort of my wet night-clothes wakes me. I blame the number of quilts I have used to make the bed.

My body produces such an abundance of water in the night sweat that I pretend I am trying to turn into a mermaid, but I cannot complete the chemistry.

The sweats seem to have courted and married a cold. Together they have produced a healthy cough that turns every night into a long passage to light.

The cough always wants to be heard—

"I will not cough," I say, and count as long as I can. The Cough wins.

"I will hold my breath," I say.

But the COUGH wins.

"I will suck green cough-killer drops," I say.

But the **COUGH** wins again.

It never goes away, but has come to stay.

the night was a long passage to light.

October 3, 1975
Friday

When the cough coughed all night, I went up on the hill again.

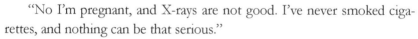

Dr. Mainer pulls up on his bicycle just as I arrive at the door.

I declare that I'm sick, and he tells me to get a chest X-ray.

"No I'm pregnant, and X-rays are not good. I've never smoked cigarettes, and nothing can be that serious."

He listens, but does not waver. He declares, "I'm going that way," and walks me towards the X-ray department. He instructs me to bring my X-rays back to the clinic. Stepping into the elevator, Dr. Mainer introduces me to Dr. Stu Levy, who operates the elevator buttons as if we were all in a department store, calling out the merchandise on each floor—

PHOTOGRAPHIC EQUIPMENT
PHOTOGRAPHY
NUMBER 3

I walk out with Matthew and Anna following me like curious puppies.

The technician shields me with a lead apron over a white gown. After I am dressed, they summon me to take an additional set, and refuse to say why. Neither will they let me take the X-rays back to the family practice office. This fact makes me feel heavy, as if I'm still wearing their shield. Even the air feels dense in the waiting room, and no magazine can engage my attention.

The kingdom of my two children tap dances through the day. Wonder lies at their every corner: Imagine seeing a machine that takes pictures of the inside of bodies. Imagine seeing real pictures of real bones on real lighted screens. They also lay on the carpeted floor to watch the Otis elevator, with all its cables, go up and down.

After we are ushered into the examining room, I sit under one of the bright posters that contemporary doctor offices always seem to have.

"What does the sign say, Mother?"

"Oh, that is so true!" agrees Matthew.

Three physicians come into the room, with a grim set to their faces. The oldest one is introduced as being from the surgery department. He snaps up my own bone poster on a neon screen, and indicates an extra white sac hanging next to the lung. Another has in his hand my first enrollment papers that include my family's medical history and asks about the notation of cancer on my mother's side.

He wants to know how many children I have, while indicating a real concern about my pregnancy, now starting its sixth month. As they examine me, the doctors exchange, with their eyes, their verification of swollen lymph nodes in my neck. They go outside to talk their serious talk in the hall, and I can hear them, even through my children's chattering. The word *tumor* is distinct.

My first thoughts are for my plans for the future. They are like little buds, but I have always believed that their summer unfolding will come. I want to go to remote villages and teach at some of the outposts of our planet. I even have a brochure and application for an international agency that both trains and sends people. Page one, side one, asks about any medical conditions.

Dr. Mainer comes back alone with the request that I check in the hospital by Monday afternoon.

To me the most surprising thing is my own unusual calm. Grace and shock might have something in common.

> *When it rains all winter and our house shrinks*
> *to where my outstretched arms can touch walls;*
> *I go outside and shout at the hedge—*
> *"HOW MANY PEOPLE CAN*
> *WE FIT IN A PHONE BOOTH?"*
> *When the children both cry at once, demand at once,*
> *fight at once, and break at once, then the violin strings*
> *in my mind snap, and I have no melody.*
> *When Richard walks through the house,*
> *his head turning into a growling bear,*
> *I completely faint away inside.*

I call my husband from the hall phone, outlining the events of the day and the pending hospitalization. Once outside I keep thinking how this is the experience of seniors. Being only 29, I'm getting a glimpse of the concerns of the elderly. I better think again how wisdom is the principle thing.

After six hours, we are finally done, and Matthew demands to build a fort. "The woods are dry today," he argues, "and we've done it before."

Anna wants to go look for red leaves. She is sure she can find one shaped like a horse.

Instead, we go right for the bus, where my body executes all the correct mechanical procedures to transport us, but my mind keeps sorting images.

October 4
Saturday

I call the church to activate the telephone line prayer chain. The doctors were too serious for me not to be serious. I make an appointment within myself to really consider dying. I want to look in the face of death, sit on its lap and smell its breath.

I have seen life as an ongoing stream that I was just immersed in. I've always felt that its path would take me to the outermost parts of the earth. Portland was supposed to be a temporary camping spot for the nurture of young children. In one stroke, I cut with some mental shears that fifty-more-years river, leaving me a short stretch.

Finally, I cry; I weep in abandon. I want the privilege of guiding the arrows of my children and giving them the exhortations that can shoot them into the high place.

I am so melancholy. My memory pulls out special days and old ways that had had their fragrance.

Even the meditation of death progresses. It is like a dark glass I have to pass through. Death is the last enemy.

I am sitting in the middle of our overstuffed couch with a wad of toilet paper on my lap. We never have tissues. I have tried to muffle my grief as the children are sleeping. I feel completely out of focus with emotions. I am looking at things either too close or too far. I needed something to grind my lens.

Music comes. Chorus and voices, in tones and scales, in patterns and textures, repeating a joyous sound: **"He who liveth and believeth in me shall not die but have everlasting life."**—Jesus

I feel free. I know it will all have to be faced again; some more black and white runs, and once in living color.

October 6
Hospital

I have never really been in a hospital before, except to walk in and out with a new baby.

After being admitted and issued a paper bag of necessities (including toilet paper), I am delivered to a bed. There is a voice coming from the hall ceiling that spends its days and nights calling doctor's names. I have landed on another planet and am suffering some manifestations of culture shock.

My first morning brings a group of family practice doctors to cluster around my bed. Dr. Mainer makes his introductory remark: "This patient weighs one hundred and sixty pounds." I feel instantly reduced to a country fair 4-H Club exhibit. I cannot be silent as a sheep before my shearers, but with a touch of sarcasm repeat:

"Yes, this patient weighs one hundred and sixty pounds." Then I am so embarrassed, I want them to just go away. One by one they feel my swollen lymph nodes. Then they leave to complete their rounds.

When I was first introduced to my chest X-ray, the doctor had said, "This presents certain ethical considerations in regard to the pregnancy." From that time on, I knew the baby was threatened. It is ironic that my first roommate has come for an abortion and is as equally advanced in her pregnancy.

At an appointed hour, the yellow curtains are drawn around her bed, and she is given an abdominal saline solution. I feel anguish.

I have my own recreations. Two physicians, aided by a nurse, come to get a sample of bone marrow. I studiously avoid their tray of tools. I lie on my stomach and bite my pillow. There is a lot of pain, and it seems to go on for a long time. So, I pretend that the practice of Christian faith is against the law. I am being tortured to disclose the list of the underground believers, but I refuse to betray anyone for deliverance. Later their excavation site doesn't hurt anymore, but my jaw still aches from biting the pillow.

That night at eleven o'clock, I meet another surgeon, Dr. Hood. He has been elected to biopsy a lymph node, and thus we will know my malady. I ask him to share with me the possible ramifications of the tumor. It is like he pulls out of his lab coat a terrible stack of cards. The deck is *Great Infirmities*, and he spreads them before me: Cancer of the lung, Hodgkin's disease, Cancer of the lymphoid tissue, Tuberculosis.

He leaves me with an assignment—scrub the left side of my neck with betadine, an antiseptic solution. This process is to be repeated in the morning. A nurse attacks my left neck with vigor. A stretcher comes for me. Because of my pregnancy, I have no narcotics to make it a twilight journey. Overcome by the strangeness of the surgery corridor, I try to hum some brave, little tune. Once the orderly steps on a button, the doors open into an odd country inhabited by people in green hats and baggy green shoes.

After all the betadine preparations on the left side of my neck, Dr. Hood, without any obvious examination, has the nurse scrub the right side and cover me with sterile cloths. They cover my head and I cannot see. As they begin their incision, they put their tools on my face. I don't think I am going to be able to handle it, until words come to me like a standard in my mind—

That which is seen will pass away,
That which is not seen is eternal.

The conversation in the surgery room seems so ludicrous; the nurses are talking about the cost of their new shoes. I am returned to my room feeling as if they have left some small tools inside my neck.

My next hurdle is waiting the days until the pathology report is complete. I have found that the day shift lives *by proper procedure*, and there are established guardians of rules and regulations. But the night shift is free, indeed. To some degree, I invert my schedule—sleeping as permitted by day—and up at night.

The head night nurse gave me my chart to study, and I poured over all the comments and suggestions of what my illness might be. "Hodgkin's disease" was the most frequent notation, so I began to gather and learn all I could, although my resources are limited to the floor library. I found a medical journal that outlined the indications of the disease's spread—the stages, the cell-type categories, and an outline of treatment. The article has two quotations, which I memorize:

1. Pregnancy does not seem to affect the course of the disease.

2. The disease doesn't have any known effect on fertility, pregnancy, or on the children conceived by a parent with Hodgkin's disease.

I frequently do my reading in a doctor's anteroom, and there I have a confrontation with a young resident. He rebukes me for my study. He tells me to stick to articles I can understand, like those in Reader's Digest. I'm not tolerant; I silently name him, *The Creep of the Week.*

One morning during the family practice rounds, I tell the doctors all I have learned about Hodgkin's, feeling like I am giving a talk to a college science class.

That afternoon, Dr. Hood comes to see me. He has just received the laboratory report. He holds my hand while telling me I have nodular sclerosing Hodgkin's disease. He suggests that I begin radiation therapy as soon as possible. But before the therapy begins, it would be best, he states, to have an abortion. I will not consider an abortion, despite of all his persuasive logic.

Later, Dr. Mainer comes in with the same news. I tell him that really I had been the very first to know.

The stitches are removed from my neck, and I am issued some medication because of a hazy urine culture. A nurse explains how this medicine can cross the placental barrier. So I bury the pills in my hospital plants, and after I'm discharged, let them rest, unused, in my home medicine chest.

October 12
Hospital

We learn obedience by the things that we suffer. On Sunday afternoon, I am readmitted through emergency with severe abdominal pain.

Sunday is not a day for doctors; Dr. Mainer has to come, just because of my call. Upon examination he states, "You have a rip roaring urinary tract infection." He then asks if I had taken my prescription.

Oh, humble moment.

He could have yelled, pushed me off the table, and told me what he had planned for Sunday. But he exhibited true mercy. From that time, I always took my medication.

My outline for Monday is to go to the radiation department. I am terrified. I feel I am being pushed in a little cattle car to Auschwitz, or one of the other extermination camps.

My fears multiply as I look into the treatment rooms from the corridor. I have never had an aptitude for machines—single cell or complex.

Patients are treated behind lead-lined doors that read:

Red lights are turned on while the technicians rotate knobs, watching the cancer victims on TV screens.

Once ushered into an examination room, I can feel my terror. I hate hearing that I will get permanent tattoos to mark the field of treatment. They talk about the risks for the fetus, and that my hair will fall out.

A real prayer can just be one word long, "HELP." Even a well-directed sigh can count.

I remember the story of Naman, who had leprosy. He sought a prophet of God who told him to dip seven times in the Jordan River, and he would be whole.

Naman balked at the word; but once he obeyed, he became well.

Maybe, in being immersed in radiation, I can also be restored.

I can face the staff with calmness. Their plan is to start the treatments, delivering two thousand rads over a period of two-and-a-half weeks. I ask again if it could all wait until after the baby is born.

They position me under an enormous cobalt machine. My imagination conjures a modern episode in *The Perils of Pauline*. There is a fast approaching science-fiction torment.

To my relief the technicians return with Dr. Mainer, halting the procedure until the ultrasound diagnosis is complete.

I jump off the table, hop on one foot, clap my hands, refuse the wheelchair transportation service, and go my way rejoicing.

I am interrupted at dinner, when a transportation-service orderly comes to take me to ultrasound. There I lay on a cot as they cover my abdomen with oil and, with a gliding tool, etch the infant within me on a screen. Their measurement estimates the gestational age at thirty-two weeks, in contrast to my own twenty-seven week calculation.

Because of the acceleration of the due-date, the therapeutic decision is now to postpone radiation until the baby is born. I am discharged with a pending follow-up appointment in the high-risk pregnancy clinic.

I am sick at home, but my family surrounds me. Our house is so small, I can be in bed and look into every room but one. So, even in bed, I am in the bosom of my family.

Our agreement in marriage has always held to a strict division of labor. Richard did the man things, and I did the woman things, without crossing our streams. By necessity, Richard has begun to clean our house and cook our food. With great amazement, I rest on the couch and watch him make dinner. Anything in life now seems possible. It's like turning the course of mighty rivers with a bare hand.

He has always been good with the children, but he has increased in that capacity too. I strain my ears to hear his bedtime serial stories of sailing ships, walking sticks and trains. Bedtime was more than what had been my hasty guidance through toothbrush hygiene and the sleep time prayer.

My symptoms are getting progressively worse. My weekly chest X-rays show that the tumor is enlarging, and the lymph nodes are increasing in size. Night sweats drench me. I am so short of breath that I cannot read aloud, and I can hardly sing. Still, I cough, although *Red Bomb*, my cough syrup, reduces the rack of it to lower-case letters. Going to the doctor is my chorus; it repeats itself after every verse in my life.

During one visit to the clinic, I am asked if I would make a videotape in the basement of Emma Jones Hall.

I have been feeling like a soap-opera star through all the suspended decisions. I can hum violin music, look at the wall, and invite anyone to tune in again tomorrow.

I ask the nurse about the tape. She replies, "It will probably be used in the death-and-dying series in the nursing and medical school studies."

"Oh," I answer, sobered.

The day of the taping Dr. Mainer takes me down the stairs into an illuminated room. I sit in a newsroom chair across from a pleasant-seeming man whose gray hair is a crew cut. When the interview starts, he changes before me into a machine that ejects hard balls for me to bat answers back to. It is alive with high fastballs and curves. My inquirer is without mercy. He keeps my mind swinging.

Finally, he says, "Is there anything you would like to know?"

"Yes. Who are you?" I ask.

He is the kind who answers questions with questions. "Who have you heard that I am?"

"Dr. Tollhouse," I reply.

"That is close," says Dr. Taubman.

Later Dr. Mainer explains he is the staff psychiatrist.

I have a perfect understanding of why the world calls them *shrinks*. My brain seemed to collapse the rest of the day from his probing.

There are some that are ever-learning and never-understanding.

I follow my appointment in the OB clinic with Dr. Montoya, the chief resident. He looks like a pizza baron. He wears a tomato-sauce tie. He throws his words up and out, baking everything with the intensity of his expression. He goes through every progressing abdominal measurement and date, concluding the ultrasound is right.

I have a little calendar where I've marked my last period, which would still put me in the six-month chute. I speak what I feel is true, but I'm more concerned for the baby than myself. Thus, I am relieved when Dr. Montoya confirms they will use a drug to induce labor as soon as the infant has sufficiently matured. This induction will supersede radiation therapy.

I am also seeing Dr. Mainer, who agrees with my calculations, but we flow with the more expert opinion.

As much as I thrill to Richard's help, there is one drawback. He doesn't cook with a great repertoire. For breakfast, we always have very hard eggs; the yolk could support a fork in a vertical position. This is accompanied by a helping of pork and beans. Dinner is mostly hamburgers with very boiled vegetables and a lettuce wedge.

I begin to lose my appetite and think it is a symptom of a progressing disease. Then one day I just don't feel like swallowing anymore.

I share this with Dr. Mainer by telephone. He says, "This is worrisome."

October 31
Hospital

Following Dr. Mainer's orders, I am admitted into the hospital that same Friday night. Dr. Steve Fredrickson is on call. I have never met him, but was advised he would be my weekend attending physician.

When he comes into the room, I declare, "You must be Dr. Fredrickson."

He replies, "Just call me Steve."

It usually takes so long for a doctor to drop his occupational manner with a patient and share anything personal. But Steve is first a person, and he uses a doctor's vocabulary only when relevant. I notice another thing too—he is the first physician whose classic black bag is not embossed with his title in gold letters. Personalness removes strangeness, and it's a comfort.

A patient is continually exposed to groups of medical students and department specialists. I find I can classify doctors into three styles of patient management:

1. The doctor who shares only the very immediate—that present moment.

2. The doctor who shares the next step, and explains in some detail its construction.

3. The doctor who points to the vast landscape ahead, showing not only bridges and cities but every possible avenue.

There are always exceptions. I had one fourth-year student from hematology who told me glibly I had five years to live. I could laugh at him because I knew my disease, and knew I knew more about it than he did. I have continued to study Hodgkin's disease, reading from books and current journals to protect myself from every wind of doctrine by physicians. I also want more understanding to refute my imaginings when I feel so sick and fading.

This is my third time in the hospital. In addition to the other symptoms, my admittance sheet states: "Onset of dysphagia." The progress report is more graphic: "Today intake has been minimal, but patient noticed difficulty in swallowing, with sensation of food becoming 'hung-up' in throat."

I was scheduled Wednesday for a barium swallow to see if the tumor was affecting my esophagus. Simultaneously, the nurses made summaries on their page ... "Complained of being hungry." Another noted ... "ate well at breakfast and lunch, requested double orders."

I realize it was Richard's cooking that has precipitated this hospitalization. I feel trapped, forced to walk through yet another bullring. The humor of the circumstance is apparent to me too. I wad the ludicrousness of it up and stuff it in my hospital gown pocket.

I continue to make primitive observations. The surgeon wants to abort, the radiologist wants radiation, and the OB specialist is concerned for the infant. Can this be the essence of the multidisciplinarian approach? It must be too simple a generalization.

November 1

I am taken to the site where barium swallows are administered. I have to stand between machines, and I'm given a cup of thick, white fluid. Nothing could have prepared me for such a horrible taste, and I gag and spew it from my mouth. The technician is very serious when he asks if this is how I swallow. I brace myself for the cup, and manage to get the barium down. There is little evidence of obstruction.

I am transferred to the OB floor, where there are a number of women with high-risk pregnancies. But the majority is young mothers who come and go. There is such evidence of joy among the delivered citizens. I am always sighing within myself that everything will go well for me.

This is a terrible way to spend a Sunday morning.

I am transported to diagnostic ultrasound, where their etching device locates a pocket of amniotic fluid. By extracting a sample of this water, the lab can determine the maturity of the fetal lungs.

The package of tools for the tap looks medieval. I feel like an early picture in the sequence of the history of medicine.

The lab report is returned, marked "immature." Examination determines the fetal size to be a mere four pounds.

Somehow, Dr. Mainer has begun to concur with Dr. Montoya that the gestational age is now thirty-five weeks. I know it is thirty weeks, and I even argued with Dr. Montoya in a dream.

Ambassadors from all the specialized countries of medicine come to see me and examine my culture with their varied proposals of aid. They have a United Nations meeting to decide my governing-treatment policies. Delegates come from hematology, neonatal pediatrics, family practice, and the OB service. They are moving now down to the conference room. I feel it is my right to go.

From an access closet by the delivery corridor, I remove a full doctor's outfit and dress myself, disguising my bulk into what I hope looks like another doctor who could deliver a baby. Only my eyes show through the headgear. I plan to grab a metal chart board and hang around, back to the door.

Alas, Dr. Montoya finds me touching up the last of my costume. He sends me soundly to bed, saying, "You can't go because we yell at these meetings."

And I bet they take off their shoes and pound them too.

The hematology staff chief has given me a bedside discourse. At the conclusion of his talk he asks his colleague, Dr. Bagby, to share his perceptions with the group: "Immediate radiation therapy is required as further encroachment on the superior vena cava will endanger the life of the mother and the fetus ..."

When we were children, we played a little game called *telephone*. We would sit in a circle. One would whisper some news to the one next to him. And around and around this little word would be passed until the last to receive it would speak what he heard. We would laugh at how it had been jumbled.

The progression of the hematologist's words from my bedside to the group, through Dr. Montoya, and back to me doesn't vary by one jot or phrase. I am not ignorant of the danger of radiation to the fetus. Dr. Montoya has been emphatic that there is even a chance of skeletal damage.

Tears well up in my eyes, and this is just another heavy little corner, in the afternoon, here at the medical school.

November 4

I gird my mind and go to radiation therapy. They were unable to obtain my progressive X-rays, and no one from radiation therapy had been able to attend the conference. A staff member examines me and states he is not convinced I am really in need of radiation. In consideration of the pending due-date, he feels that the decision to initiate therapy is completely mine, and I should consider it well.

Transportation is called, and I am returned to my room.

I am feeling real stress. All men are liars. If I had any strength, I would run away for the afternoon just to look at one solid thing, like a tree.

They call for me again. They had located my X-rays. Those pictures have cancelled out all the radiologist's morning words. The radiation must begin at once. The betatron machine is chosen because it emits the least scatter.

I am rolled under its girth. Earphones are applied because the machine roars as it works. They put small rice bags on my neck and a lead apron over my abdomen. I can feel the baby moving within me, and my mind doesn't wander from God.

The day of the second treatment, peace of mind rolls slowly back and fills me. I spend the hours of that returning tide with my watercolors, painting a little picture. I recall the lines from Isaiah—

"When thou walkest through the fire, thou shall not be burned; neither shall the flame be kindled upon thee."

My days lay in bed, except for the radiation call.

I crank the hospital cot up as high as it will go, to give my eye the best of the panorama from my window. I watch the movement of the city and the progression of the sky. Sometimes boats pull logs, bound in chains, up the Willamette River. It is a provision for my spirit.

The nurse's note reads: "Patient prefers to have bed all the way up. Refuses to let me roll it down. Climbs in and out of bed with help of chair. Was told how dangerous this is. R.N. notified."

On the second floor, the nurse's notes hung at the end of the bed. But the OB floor policy is to enclose them in an inaccessible chart. I found if a nurse was conscious that the notes were available to the patient, it produced one kind of recording of physical movements. The notations tucked within a chart held at the desk were another style, often dealing with their perception of the patient's emotional realm.

I found what seemed like tender concern from a nurse would elicit my tender confidence, only to find it distorted and recorded for the hospital world. I felt betrayed and limited their probes to the external.

Some notes make me sound a little insane: "At 0500 still awake and ravenously eating an orange—short of breath—no complaints." Another: "Poor breakfast. States, 'Not hungry,' had milk and juice. Saves food from the trays and places on window ledge and in drawer. States, 'Hate to waste food.'"

The OB floor could swarm with a great influx, until they would even put patients in the supply room. One Friday the rooms were crowded with extra beds.

I prevailed upon Dr. Mainer for a weekend pass. I am sorely missing my little children. In my transportation to radiation, I ride through the outpatient pediatric clinic and ache through that track seeing the small faces.

I get to go home, and we are all precious together. Everything has so much color. Richard keeps our old wood stove so stocked with lumber that the corner of the house has a tropical warmth.

Matthew found in a plastic bag of fruit one more mottled than the rest. "Look Mom, it has Hodgkin's disease."

Anna climbs up on my lap, dragging my old yellow bathrobe, rubbing its nylon lining and sucking her fingers.

In its sweetness is a sadness too. I feel I am carrying an hourglass of our fleeting time together. I drag my feet all the way back to the hospital.

My roommate of the previous week had a cold, and I have breathed in her sneezes. At home, what was tropical by night was arctic by morning. By Tuesday, November 11, I have bronchitis. I have severe chest pain which wars against my cough center—"I must cough" versus "No, that's real pain." As *they lock in combat, I can't even breathe.*

The tumor was swelling from radiation in its own death process, and I'm experiencing an acute shortness of breath. They hang an oxygen water-fountain box above my bed. They fasten this pure air into me with nose prongs. I keep thinking, if urban air pollution continues, we'll all be wearing some kind of portable unit like this in a few years.

A university hospital is a learning institution, where the young students are reared to become old and wise doctors. Dr. Bagby brought a class of students into my room. He had me sit in a chair. He moved a stethoscope across my back and had me continuously pronounce the letter *E*. As I understood him, he explained how the letter *E* would sound exactly like an *A* as it crossed the chest mass.

Then it was the student's turn. One by one, I continually made the letter *E* for them. I blow *E*s out in the air. I become hysterical in my imagination. I feel we are making a tape for a preschool show on the alphabet. I think that I've turned into a Cheshire cat, and this is my only vocabulary word. Unable to bear the absurdity any longer, I begin to say *A* in the exact same tone. No one even notices. We have all gone insane.

Doctors and patients are at two elevations. I know everyone by their belt buckles. They are subtle, midline bumper stickers. I read them in profusion.

There is the grass roots category with metal marijuana leaves. Mike Mainer wears a stylized eagle. One doctor friend has a Mickey Mouse head. It seems the minority have a simple functional rectangle.

I am always meeting new doctors. Dr. Leslie Dillow comes into my room reading my chart. After some study she asks, "Didn't it hurt to turn thirty?" I am so used to objective questions that I really have to think if I had had any symptomatic problems on my birthday.

Directly after radiation on November 13, I am taken to ultrasound, where Dr. Dillow performs another amniocentesis. I am disturbed because the baby is moving within me. A good-sized needle is inserted in the amniotic sac, to extract the fluid. Dr. Dillow exclaims that she can feel the baby kicking the needle, and I'm very upset seeing that the sample is not clear, but bloody. I'm sure the baby has been pierced.

I refuse to wait for the wheelchair service and walk back to my room. I know the evidence obtained is important, but the means seems as primitive as when they used leeches in medicine shows. Then my ward nurse tells me that last year a fetus went into intrauterine shock when the cord was inadvertently pierced. I rage.

An order comes for me to go into a labor room and be fastened into an abdominal belt to measure fetal heart tones. As the ticker paper rolls out onto the floor, it is within normal limits, except at random there are utterly irregular, abnormal-looking scratches. It seems like the baby was having cardiac arrests. I take the strip back to my room. The floor doctor reassures me. The bloody tap is the result of merely nicking a blood vessel in the placenta. The scratchings that look like heart failures are ordinary fetal movement.

Machines give me screams when I don't understand.

Give me the answers in this doctor-man's land.

The view from my window, which has been sustaining, turns into an enemy. Its message is the distance from my family. It speaks louder to me each day.

The chart doesn't record homesickness, but I begin to suffer this malady of separation. I have never had this disorder before. I find myself thinking of our little house with the vines growing over the front porch. There is a stained-glass window hanging over an antique couch, given to me once while I was walking to the grocery store. I spend my mind on such details.

When Dr. Mainer makes his rounds in the morning I tell him in a solemn tone, "I've lost my will to live," pause, "in the hospital."

On November 14, I completed 1700 rads of radiation. On November 17, the X-ray shows that the tumor is shrinking. That afternoon a man, whom I have never seen before, comes into my room to state that I can be discharged this day.

Good-bye for now, and another plastic identification wristband is cut away for my bedside trash bag.

I am put on a schedule for once-a-week visits to Dr. Mainer, who now concurs with my original due-date for the baby. It is decided to let me go full term as a result of a hematology and radiation consultation.

I have a fur coat, which was once my mothers; it became my winter pleasure. One December doctor's visit Matthew hatched a plot as we waited in the examination room. He turns off the light, and it is a windowless black. He waits on his hands and knees behind the examination table. He wraps his animal stature in my fur.

"Well," says Dr. Mainer. "What's this?" upon finding such a dark room. With a ferocious growl, Matthew crawls out to attack the physician.

Dr. Mainer reaches the light switch, and the rest of our time is routine.

I respect Mike Mainer immensely. I was always a person-patient with him first, not just another case. This is based on a feeling, not words.

It is rare for our conversation to go beyond what is strictly medically relevant. He keeps disclosures of his inner being on a strict budget.

I was told once that the residents make twelve thousand dollars a year. That sounds like a pirate's cave of treasure to me.

When Mike Mainer told me he frequently moonlights in the emergency room, I am surprised. I know he works an abundance of hours as a third-year resident. I apologize for being bold and rude but suggest that free time for walking in the mountains is sweeter than gold.

"Buy clothes in a thrift store for a change," I exhort.

He laughs, then replies that school loans are due.

I increase in bulk in December. I am so pregnant that even when empty seats are available on the bus, people spring up and offer me theirs too. I know I will probably never have another child, and even these enlarged, uncomfortable days are put on special tapes in my mind. I only hear one line from the *Christmas Story*: "And she was great with child."

December 31

My official due-date is the last day of 1975, and it has been arranged for me to be induced at this time. As I leave for the hospital, I give the baby basket a last look. It has been a strange forest that I have carried this child through.

Richard and the children drive me to the hospital, with the children singing all the way, "This is the day, this is the day." They drop me off at the hospital's north door with final instructions—Matthew wants a boy, and Anna wants a girl. Neither care what color the baby is.

It is standing room only in the labor room. Others must have tax exemptions to worry about. I have to be rescheduled. Unable to reach my husband, I ride the bus home, glad for two more days.

Richard says, "What are you doing here?"

I reply that it isn't the day after all.

On New Year's Day, I take the children roller-skating along the sidewalk. I pull them and hold them up all at the same time. How we feel can be just like a wind of weather; I am happy. I am full of life, in me, around me, on each arm.

January 2, 1976
Hospital

I went to the hospital admissions department and my assigned labor bed is under a window. An amniotic hook is used to break the membranes, as this might also stimulate natural labor. Then I am surrounded and attached, plugged into and connected to machines.

The first baby born in outer space.

A fetal heart-monitor belt is buckled. An abdominal contraction belt is buckled. I have an IV, and a special box that seems to have a green flashing light. At 10:45 they begin the drip of pitocin, or *induce-juice*. My body believes it and begins to make contractions.

The abdominal contraction belt transmits the tremors to a graph that I can watch. It is like a child's drawing of hills on a strip that rolls out and makes piles on the floor. The baby has its own paper recording its own heart.

Having once lived on the OB floor for two weeks, I have friends among the staff. They come and sit with me through labor. The machines are at my front, and my sisters gather around my back. The floor doctor asks if I had ever been induced before. For some reason I thought he asked if I had ever been seduced before. We all laugh, and the humanness overcomes the machines. It feels like a home delivery.

At one o'clock, I have dilated six centimeters. A scalp electrode is applied to the baby's head, and there are more wires. At 1:20, I am given oxygen through nasal prongs.

When the contractions reflected on the graph look the same as Mount Hood, visible from my window, I close my eyes. Richard comes and holds my hand. The contractions intensify. My sisters apply pressure to my lower back.

At 2:15, I am rolled into the delivery room and everyone comes with me. Mike Mainer dashes in, just in time.

I am permeated with a sense that all is in order, and my mind seems to expand to the universal of women having children, not in any time-space sequence, but from the beginning to the end. The baby has nearly crowned; I keep forgetting to watch the mirror.

At 2:35, Mary Elisabeth is born, instantly cries, and the room full of adults seems to move back a generation.

My sisters move with me down the hall. They knock at the nursery door, and the baby is held up. She weighs almost nine pounds. They all exclaim in the talk of women. I feel I can run the length and breadth of the world.

I am moved into a postpartum room where one nurse delights in pushing my abdomen. I understand the *uterus-shrink* principle, but she maneuvers as if she were in a great contest to press all the air out of an air mattress.

It is the original birthday party, and my eyes can see balloons pinned to the ceiling, and it seems there should be cake on the dinner tray. I am given the same window berth in Hospitalization No. 4 as in my previous captivity.

Some infant formula company has given the hospital a sign, which is put in the hallway to prohibit visitors. They wheel down the babies in long trays of portable beds.

They bring me my baby for the first time with instructions not to nurse her until she has been given sterile water. Newborns are like birds puckering their faces; something is about to come; I nurse her. A mother with her infant has had to be painted by every generation.

Saturday and Sunday Mary Elisabeth is mine for a brief season, with a circle just around us, and all the cares to come have to recede.

Mike Mainer has gone on a vacation, and Steve Fredrickson is my overseeing physician. I have more than a new mother's schedule.

So short the rest, so often the test.

January 3

On the way to nuclear medicine, the wheelchair driver snatched my chart away and carried it himself, not to lead me into temptation. I only wanted to distract my journey with nurses' notes, which can sometimes provide four-line comic relief.

I am injected with radioactive isotopes so that a liver-spleen scan can be performed. One of the doctors stretches my limbs out on a table. I can watch my liver and spleen glisten on a wall screen as if they are loaded with Mexican jumping-bean, gold-dust.

On the other side of the room, another patient is placed on a table and a technician takes a shuttle and passes it back and forth over her body. She keeps pleading for water in a way that makes the word sound like six syllables. I think, "So this is what it's like to make a James Bond movie."

They will give me no sign of what the test revealed.

I am instructed to wear a lead apron when I hold my baby. I'll have to use a formula for a given period of time and discard all breast milk.

1. The baby is wheeled in.

2. I have to wash with an antiseptic cloth, turning the first smell of mother into a deodorizer.

3. I'm girded with a lead apron adding forty pounds to my postpartum weight.

4. I'm given a bottle with a whole list of ingredients ...

5. My breasts say, "Now what's the matter?"

I use a breast pump that looks like a bicycle horn.

Who cares? She is a healthy baby. But I want the doctors to confirm that with me.

Upper-mantle radiation treatments have now been scheduled to resume, and I want to know if I can be simmered by rads and still nurse Mary Elisabeth. A note has been written requesting a conference with a neonatal pediatrician and Mary Elisabeth's mother.

The resident physician comes to see me. He is the original Dr. Elevator-Driver who pushed the button for the *photography* floor on that first real day. Stu Levy has a face one cannot fully forget and one cannot fully know because it is full of hair like the burning bush, but the flame is in the eyes.

Our second encounter is framed and hung on a wall back in my mind. In speaking of Mary Elisabeth, he said the words from the book of Daniel, without knowing it: "After examining her ... she appears more vigorous than the rest ..."

I feel I could levitate on the bed, and Stu asks, "Just what are you into anyway?"

One can choke with the joy of a joke that is never said. I want to declare, "The American Girl Scouting Movement," but I swallow the line.

"Jesus," I reply.

He then asks me if I have ever heard of Richard Alpert.

"Yes I heard him lecture in Haight-Ashbury ten years ago. All I remember is that he admonished the audience to get some psilocybin because of the realms of love to which it elevated the inner man."

Stu goes on to say that Alpert went to India and found a ragged *holy man* who was being worshipped. Alpert wondered at this until the man revealed the secrets of Alpert's heart, and Alpert embraced him too.

Oh beggarly elements. Alpert took the wrong trail. There is one way. I am adamant. I had to hush myself for in saying too much, nothing is heard.

I have some of the usual postpartum problems. I am constipated. During Steve Fredrickson's rounds, I share my complaint. It takes courage for me to broach such private business with Steve. Sometimes invoking the word doctor can pull a mask over the clinician's face—like when the imitation glasses are attached to the plastic nose. I don't have that prop with Steve.

He prescribes a common, bad-tasting remedy and rouses me from sleep the next morning with excessive jokes about the medicine's effect. Often the way up is down, but I have no mental set for what I consider a delicate topic. Let self-reproach and remorse come later; I kick his leg twice. But, friends can take such abuse, where a doctor and a patient can't.

Once I'm ready to go home, I find he has put a whole pint bottle in my medicine discharge sack.

I dress the baby myself for the first time. The nurse carries her to the car. It's a state law. I have to be seated in the front seat before she will put her in my arms. Richard stows the whole load of samples that infant supply manufacturers want associated with the newborn's nurture.

A song of the family is the new one being introduced to her brother and sister. Anna has triumphed in the fact we have a daughter. Richard told me that she stuffed dolls up her shirt during my five-day stay. Then she would whip them out exclaiming, "It's a girl!" to Matthew's continual chagrin. My son comes and peers through all the January blankets. "Well, she looks just like a boy." So the unity of the spirit is now maintained in a bond of peace.

I am not an untried mother. I fully know that an infant takes more maintaining than just being arranged in Carter's new layette. The baby's up at night; the little children are up by day.

Sleep is an illusion, a mirage. As one attempts to act upon it, as if it were a reality, it only vanishes while trying to seize it.

I am like a robot performing every function from rote memory. It's a perfect self-denial, a baptism that can change girls to women in that exhausting underwater swim.

There were night watches when the baby would not stop crying. I often thought that the world needs a gifted chemist to put another concoction in an aerosol can. *Baby Hush* could be sprayed at bedside to produce instant slumber.

There were nights that I imagined, deep in my pillow, that I was nailing boards between myself and the sound. I would hammer planks over the wail, trying to build a quiet box to sleep in.

On January 13, I return for the lymphangiogram. It's strange to watch dye and oil going through your toes, being absorbed into your system. I ask how long these chemicals will be in my body. "Oh, for years," declares the technician.

There is a screen that separates me from a man undergoing the same procedure. Our names are on a blackboard where the times and amounts of fluid are recorded. At random, X-rays are taken to check the absorption rate. It is like we are in a contest to see who can be set free first. My feet and body ache to move, but under great penalty of loosening their devices and thus repeating the ordeal. I fall in and out of low blankets of sleep, rigid.

I win over the other contestant, and he groans. Then I stand, and bend, and inhale, and exhale for the first series of X-rays. It is a very strange way to spend the day; even my urine turns blue.

Early the next morning the telephone rings, and I run to the ring to keep it from sounding. I want to keep the children asleep, and I juggle noises with schedules to keep it all moving. But, I start to bleed—filling the floor, a mess by the door.

I sit down. Matthew gets up and takes in the scene. "Well, thank God, Mother, that you didn't do that on the Oriental rug." That five-year-old perception starts me laughing.

L ater that morning I have to take the children and divide them all into different homes. It's sad that the Lee family pie is again cut into pieces and distributed. I feel locked into hospitals.

A medical chart is just data, plus data, plus data. The information from the previous tests is available. The liver-spleen report states, "Spleen appears mildly enlarged, with a mottled liver." I don't bend and fold upon hearing this, as most medical authorities don't consider the liver-spleen scan significant in regard to Hodgkin's disease. And the lymphangiogram, which is regarded as relevant, is normal.

It is determined that a placenta fragmentation had been retained and was discharged in the initial bleeding.

I am discharged too. I feel like a bird that has escaped from the snare of the fowler.

I have to have the stitches from the lymphangiogram taken out of my feet. Once at the family practice clinic, Steve Fredrickson takes off my shoes and socks. As he bends over my foot, he pretends to be a shoe salesman.

"What size shoe do you wear? What kind are you interested in today?" He waves to indicate a stockroom that before our imagination began was just a row of hospital gowns.

"Oh, I want the kind with stiletto heels, and pointed toes."

He acts dismayed. "Those are really out of style now."

"I know," I reply, "but they are the best for kicking doctors."

After that sentence, he transforms back into a regular physician; a visiting medical student just stares at us.

I resume the wife-and-mother hike, but I am wearing a backpack that has cast iron pans in its sack. As an outpatient, I have to go for treatment every day. Radiation has been initiated on the upper mantle with the intent of delivering 4,000 rads in eight weeks. It is an uphill climb.

At 1:00pm, the infant, the children, and I enter the radiation hall. The department head, Dr. Moss, once remarked, "We only see a nursing mother once every five years." Sometimes I emerge from the treatment room to find my children darting on stools with wheelbases in between the stretchers and wheelchairs.

The path has such steep rocks. Within myself, I am so exhausted that life loses all its colors, its past, and its future. I am pressed down by each day.

The radiation field was etched on my chest with red ink. Within the target area were outlines of my lungs. Lead blocks were built to protect those organs.

At home, Anna takes a red flow pen to make lines on her own chest to be like her mother. The children are exposed to more than I can bear myself. They play doctor an inordinate amount, creating a doctor's office behind the couch. There they take their stuffed animals to an invisible Dr. Mainer, who seems to live back there for a while. The diagnosis is simple; everything either has Hodgkin's disease or a cold. Sometimes Matthew is the physician himself. He uses a chain and a lot of wet Kleenex in his treatments. They help my perception—*Bum thoughts come, Looking for a handout.*

On the top of the hill is a veteran's hospital. It has American flags at the front entrance, unlike hospital North and hospital South. Every afternoon a van brings the veterans over to the radiation department for treatment. They come at the same time in the afternoon that I do, and I know their faces.

Greyhound bus drivers honk at each other while passing on the highway. Women with tiny children the same age, smile at each other in supermarkets. The veterans and I have cancer; it puts us in one fraternity.

Once I followed them through the lobby of the hospital—old men wearing brown and white striped bathrobes. There was a murmuring behind them after they passed.

"Did you see those red marks on them? It's for the radiation machine." It's like they are passing lepers, and everyone whispers, "Unclean, unclean."

I will then hurry to get in the elevator with them so we can all ride up to the fourth floor together.

I grow accustomed to the look of the radiation department. The fact there are snowballs in stretchers who have almost finished their roll down their hill doesn't make me wince. I can finally look into a melting face. It is just real.

The mothers with the sick little children are the hardest for me. They are always perfectly tender with their injured ones, who need no tether; they don't move.

I feel a cosmic apology that mine have to emphasize the contrast of health. Anna loves to climb the coat rack to the top. The other mothers are at the other end of my tunnel. Their children are leaving them, I am leaving my children.

Where are words
That say good-bye?
I'm just going,
I will not die.
I think its best
To shout it out—
See you later, alligator,
After a while, crocodile.

Sometimes due to an influx of patients or a mechanical failure, we have hours to wait on the turquoise-blue plastic couches. Matthew and Anna challenge each other to do a standing broad jump and measure their flight by squares of linoleum. The office personnel stiffen their faces into they-could-get-hurt looks.

Magazines become more than a turning page. They found all the trains and animals the first time. They line them up on the floor, etching a boat in glossy color. The rest of us in the waiting room have wet feet. Purses become fish.

The employees of the radiation therapy department are in three categories: the doctors, the technicians who operate the machines, and the office workers. With such a grim casualty rate, they take release in celebrations. They mark staff birthdays with a wild tribute to the sugar industry. They would transform their back room employee table into a grandiose potluck confectionery. Having been here so long, I have been invited into their inner sweet circle. Under the influence of so many diet admonitions, it seems to me a shocking display of sugar castles. One doctor confided that they gave him two birthdays in one year. I have never seen one raw vegetable on a toothpick.

My strength is breaking down into half-lives. My body is in rebellion. My lot has become the baby and the couch, while Richard has to care for the rest of the ranch. When he has to work late, I am helpless as the treatments accumulate. With my authority weak, it is like the sheriff has left town, and it is Wild West days for the children.

One evening I told Matthew to get some granola cereal. As I moved in and out of consciousness, they decided to play cows and poured the cereal all over the table. Cows don't use spoons or bowls. Then, it occurred to Matthew that cows don't eat off tables. So they poured their nutritious flakes all over the floor and ate them, mooing on their hands and knees.

What a sight to bless a mother's weary heart.

It is time to bring more authority into town. One call to my mother, and she is coming on the afternoon plane.

We will all be in subject now to the fastest gun, and her reign of order. To further ease the exhaustion, my mother plans to take Mary Elisabeth home with her.

I was warned that the upper-field lung blocks were originally calculated on the simulator for my girth as a nursing mother. Thus, I cannot wean the baby without threat to my lungs. I need my mother to stay as long as she can to keep from having to use manual expression to maintain a nursing mother's dimension. And more than that, it is very hard to see my baby girl fly off to California for an unknown period of time.

But, Mother has her airplane reservations and is eager to go back to a comfortable twentieth-century house with her bundle.

We make an appointment for a complete pediatric checkup before the flight. The family practice clinic gets three generations. Steve Fredrickson is temporarily replacing Mike Mainer in looking after us.

Before being ushered into the examination room, I find Steve peering through his glasses into a microscope who shares, in brief, my situation.

Dr. Fredrickson does such a thorough examination of the newborn. A rash and stuffy nose elicit great concern. He asks if my mother can remain until this is stable, while simultaneously giving my leg a tap.

A few days later, I finish the upper mantle radiation. I nurse the baby for the last time, and Richard drives Mother to the airport. Matthew and I sit and cry, and hug each other. He has decided that Mary Elisabeth is his very favorite sister.

My friends have a baby shower for me on the very night that Mary Elisabeth has left. I open a pile of miniature clothes, which we pass around the circle of ladies. We make limericks for the game:

There was once a baby named Mary
Whose days in the womb were quite scary
She had a rough time
But she came out fine
And now all the saints are so merry!

We eat cake, cutting a glazed, healthy stork into squares.

My friends are well-lit houses where I can go and rest along my way.

Four inches of hair falls out as a result of the radiation treatments. It fills my brush; I pile it on the counter. My neck looks like someone has put a bowl on my head and shaved around its circumference. I have an inverted receding hairline. When I try to braid it, my nakedness makes me look like I am wearing a cheap wig several sizes smaller than my head.

There has been some question among the radiation therapy doctors about removing my spleen. This is a routine procedure for determining the stage of Hodgkin's disease.

The fulcrum of the consideration is in the preservation of the ovarian function, as the ovaries could be moved to midline and shielded during the lower mantle radiation. Thus, I would lessen my chances of being thrust into menopause. On the other hand, it could be an unnecessary major surgery, and the doctors report certain possible problems once a spleen is removed.

I try to manage my own decision, wading through a series of medical school generalizations. Everyone I ask has a concise laparotomy lecture. I take my question from the realm of theory to experience and ask the faculty what they themselves would do. Again, some say "yes" and some say, "no."

I entered carrying a black and white question and leave holding every shade of gray.

I call Mike Mainer and pack together this great gray ball of considerations and roll it to him. He decides on the laparotomy, and I have peace. It is nice to just be able to think in four-line poems again.

There is a very short span between the completion of upper-mantle radiation and my scheduled surgery. I say, "Stomach, you'll never look this good again ..."

February 29
Hospital

I am admitted under surgery's banner. The greeting orderly puts me in a ward with four beds in a tight row. As he writes his "white female admitted, ambulatory" introduction, he asks me how to spell, "disease." The lady in the next bed is testing the smoke alarm's sensitivity by keeping her hot cigarettes rolling.

"Please move me," I ask. I am taken across the hall and put in a two-bed room under the window.

One of the surgery team members comes in, identifies himself, and begins an examination. He leaves the room, and another man comes in and asks the same kind of questions and gives me the same kind of examination. As he leaves the room I think it is odd, but when a third comes with the same procedure, it seems to be very funny—and it might be very disorganized. I do not want the surgery department to be disorganized. But they all come back together; it is the admission plan.

I have two days before my operation. I am offered every color of Jell-O, and every flavor of bullion cube. I fast, and embroider a bird on an old coat.

A hospital patient can have a multitude of roommates. A certain quality of the hospital experience is in that particular interaction. There are a lot of different kinds of animals in the hospital ark.

I've had roommates so young on the OB floor that they come from the part of the world that sighs over rock 'n' roll stars.

I had a roommate so old the nurses and I called her, "Gramma," and she ached in every direction.

I once thought they brought a man in to share my room, complete with tattoos and after-shave lotion. He was a she with cancer of the uterus; she was tough by day, but cried at night.

I had one roommate who would flip her front teeth out and then draw them back with her tongue. She talked all the time in streams without reason.

There were sweet little sisters, and ladies whose years had bent them into ways that were their own.

There are groups within groups. No one knows from where the wind blows or where it goes.

Somehow, I hear of a Bible study held every Tuesday morning at seven in the hospital South cafeteria. It is led by Dr. Ritzman, chief of staff of the cardiac division, with his wife, a doctor also. They pray for me; they already know of my pending operation the following morning.

The head of the radiation department, Dr. William T. Moss, is a most eminent man. Not only is he a frequent speaker at medical conventions, but he has written three textbooks, which have been widely distributed in schools for the study of radiation oncology. He exudes professionalism.

Once, in the hall, he quietly remarked about my coming laparotomy: "Put a tape across your abdomen and write 'ouch' on it." In that minute, we were both ten years old, and I almost fell off the chair laughing.

March 3

I am scheduled for an 8:00am incision. I'm up very early and watch the sun rise over the hills and city. I feel at rest. My mind tries to elbow my peace to get its attention: "Can't you be a little nervous?" But somehow, I feel unshakable.

I am given a preoperative sedative. It makes me feel like a little child trying to stay awake, not wanting to miss anything. Somehow, the ceilings receive great attention, as I am wheeled into the surgery room. The anesthesiologist, who ordered the ingredients of this haze, is present. I tell him, "I am remembering everything." These are my last words.

I wake up in a body that is not sick, but tortured. I am in a room, which seems to be full of people stretched out in my state. It is as if we are on a battlefield of beds, and some nurse in the distance is bending over to tend the injured and wounded soldiers. The face of Dr. Ed Temple, one of my surgeons, blurs in front of me. I just moan for him, as any dying soldier would do, and go back to sleep.

What a great capacity we have for pain.

My first night's consciousness is nothing but torment. There is a tube down my nose, reaching into my stomach, attached to a suction machine that is not working properly, and has to be replaced.

The call light in our room is broken. My roommate and I share one hotel desk bell between us to ring for aid.

I cannot talk or move my body. I can only grab a nurse's arm and pull her close to me and whisper, "I need more medication."

She replies, "You just have to expect it to hurt."

I feel utterly dependent on others for survival. In the morning, Mike Mainer comes, and I tell him I need a stronger dosage to counteract the pain. He understands. He says, "It's like going to hell and coming back."

Morphine is my consciousness-decreasing drug. For a while, I have no awareness of the sequence of day and night. It is either dark or light when I open my eyes. I have chest congestion and want to cough up a thick mucus, but it hurts too much. My body rages with a fever in its own global warfare. I am taken on a stretcher for chest X-rays.

After one injection of morphine, I have a hallucination. A girl is weaving by my bed. She holds out strands of colored yarn for me to see. She is gentle, and I can see right through her.

I tell the night nurse, and she must have told a doctor on the floor. A very hip, young medical man puts his head around my yellow curtain to inquire if I was having a good trip.

Somehow, I begin to mend in such small little ways. They help me get up and walk. I feel as if I'm a tiny bug walking up the wall and across the ceiling. My world begins to open to time and shifts and people.

When the doctors on family practice rounds come to see me, I have the overwhelming impression that they are visiting a kitchen sink. Not only do I still have the hose in my nose, but inserted in my wrist is a tube leading to a gravity fed water bottle, and my urine is collected in a plastic bag. Oh, humble kitchen sink, my porcelain is indeed chipped.

Friendships grow, and as they change, show their depth. Some are slow in the knowing and the growing, but last. With Dr. Cris Maranze, it is fast. It feels to me like we were always friends.

Cris is the family practice doctor who rotated into my surgery team after the operation.

She has very long hair. Mostly she has to twist it into rope and tie nautical knots to have a sanitary-code head.

She wears a white coat. One pocket bulges with mini prescription books of pills and dosages. The other holds a tool that illuminates her hearing of inward processes.

When she comes at night, we build ladders, attach extensions to them, and climb up into ideas. In the morning, she comes with the surgery glee team and asks if my bowels have moved yet.

One night she makes a confession. She introduces it by first swearing me to secrecy. I assure her I will never tell anyone. She declares it is only in a best friend category that she can allow such a disclosure. I wait. "My real name is Harriet, and no one knows it." I'll never tell anyone.

I tell Cris how I've learned to live on fifteen dollars a week for groceries. For driving a school bus, my husband earns 64 dollars a week. It is a lifestyle that makes my mind as sharp as a stockbroker over the price of in-season produce. I am a merchant ship of store sales.

Laurel with doctors Stu Levy and Cris Maranze

She wants to know the stories of a lady at home, and I want to know the stories of a lady as a doctor.

I recover into an air of comforting optimism about the findings from surgery. Everyone agrees, as a group, that it had looked and gone well. One of the team is a medical missionary candidate, and I nail him alone to tell me the truth. He, too, agrees it looked good.

The staff member who dictated the operation record for my chart said under *Findings*: "The spleen was grossly normal," and the postoperative diagnosis was the same as the preoperative diagnosis: Stage II out of the four possible stages of Hodgkin's.

I rest in the confidence of my doctors. On the morning of my pathology report, I remark that the paper will be final that afternoon. The attending physician says, "That's right, but I don't expect them to find any abnormality."

Nothing prepared me to see such a grim Dr. Mainer come in and stand by the window, and such a serious Dr. Temple enter and lean against the wall.

"I have some good news and bad news," says Mike Mainer, avoiding all eye contact. "The spleen was enlarged, weighing 220 grams, involved with Hodgkin's disease, consistent with nodular sclerosing. The good news is I've talked with hematology, and you won't need any chemotherapy."

Mike is talking as if he is reading a paper he typed before coming in. He leaves the room. Dr. Temple stays with me.

I am stunned. I know I must be in Stage III. I can count my thoughts and emotions, as if my head has broken into a lot of little pieces and they are falling slow enough for me to number. I am mad at every encouraging word, and that I had believed them.

We all stand two inches tall; I was set up for a fall.

It is winter, and they have taken my only coat.

This very moment I can see birds flying north again. They seem free, and I feel bound.

I have studied Hodgkin's disease. Like an examination where the answers are on a page in your textbook, I can see the survival rate graph for the third stage. The print is too small to read, but it is a reduced residue of years.

"I HAVE THREE LITTLE CHILDREN NOT EVEN OLD ENOUGH TO GO TO SCHOOL."

This is such a searing thought, like an AT WAR headline, that I say it out loud.

Dr. Temple takes some Kleenex out of the drawer and wipes my eyes. I hate to pull people into my drama—let them be free. So I pull out my defense mechanism, gird myself in its armor, snap the visor over my eyes and ask, "How will this affect the managing treatment policy?"

Dr. Temple replies, "You will be scheduled for regular X-rays and liver-spleen scans."

"But, I don't even have a spleen anymore."

"Oh, that's right," he says softly, and leaves the room.

I am alone. What can I do with my mind? It is like I am in an elevator and my will can push the up or down button. My feelings are overwhelming; self-pity can be my express ride to the basement. I decide to fight it, and so I sing through tears. I pick ancient words of all that can go wrong:

Although the fig tree shall not blossom,
Neither shall fruit be on the vines;
The labor of the olive shall fail,
And the fields shall yield no meat
The flock shall he cut off from the fold,
And there shall be no herd in the stalls.
Yet, will I rejoice in the Lord,
I will joy in the God of my salvation.
The Lord, my God is my strength.
(Habakkuk 3:17,18)

The volume of the song can be turned up, where I sing out loud, but eventually I cannot even turn it off. It is the Holy Ghost radio station.

My agony actually turns into joy, which is beyond understanding. And joy is one with peace. I am in a very high place, and I want to look around. For a very brief time, I am on top of an embroidery instead of on the bottom side where the knots are and the threads cross. It is a perfect work.

I fall asleep making plans to go to Dr. Ritzman's Bible study.

March 9

I can walk, but only with considerable discomfort. This is a little offset by bracing a pillow against my abdomen.

I get an extra large pair of men's drawstring pajamas and insert a feather pillow, firmly drawing the strings as tightly as possible. I put a long maternity dress over this configuration, plumping and smoothing, looking full term. It is my only chance of being able to cross from hospital North to hospital South. I take a wheelchair, but abandon it as it requires too much effort.

I move slowly through the early-morning hall. The corridors are vacant until I see a doctor whom I hardly know.

The physician looks at me, and his face turns into vaguely funny shapes.

Curiosity swings far beyond politeness, and he reaches out to touch my stomach. I draw back quickly and say, "Almost due."

"Yes," he says, "almost due."

Later, I am told that he came into the clinic and asked, "Am I going crazy, or is Laurel Lee crazy? Didn't she just have her baby?"

I make it to the Bible study. When I return to my room, I feel like a great athlete.

With an abdominal incision, joy can be a real problem. It hurts very much to laugh. Sometimes I have to try and think of the most terrible things to sober a good humor, but my comic sense triumphs.

I have conflicts with some of the nursing staff. I wait until I really need pain medication before requesting it. Occasionally, I ask a little earlier than the prescribed interval, but always within a thirty-minute reef of the allowed time. They always refuse, once stating I have a mere ten minutes before it can be administered.

The rules are made for the patients; some nurses believe the patients are made for the rules.

I see another thing too. The registered nurses are often so busy maintaining IV bottles and pills, that jobs are given to the aides that are beyond their capability or their sensitivity.

Perhaps my discomfort is producing intolerant observations. Our whole situation is exaggerated by having a single hotel bell with which to summon the staff.

At home, Richard is involved in a pediatric thirty-two-hour rotation. Matthew and Anna both have the influenza. Thus, I cannot be discharged home, but a house from our congregation opens up where I have never been before. I leave the hospital for this unknown hospitality.

The family has several children, and their pictures take up two of the dining room walls. Most are grown now, and only two are left at home. I know the mother died of cancer last year, and I am sensitive to this grief.

They take me into a back bedroom, offering me books to read. The stack includes a magazine, "Cancer Victims and Friends." On the cover is a picture of shiny crystals of laetrile. Inside are reports about a Tijuana clinic and an underground railroad that transports those in need.

The books contrast the nontoxic approach to cancer, through diet and natural supplements, with the toxic approach of radiation and surgery.

My body doesn't feel well, and I have a stream of people coming in to aid me in my transfer to the natural way. It is done out of true concern, yet it is overwhelming.

There are many voices urging me to consider my diet:

(Hippocrates, 424 B.C.)

BOOK A: Take nothing into your body that has been cooked or processed; if necessary sell the stove and buy a good juicer.

a. Give up meat immediately.

b. Give up milk in every form forever.

BOOK B: Only a pittance of the millions spent on cancer research has been used for nutritional investigation.

a. Experimental cancers develop most rapidly on low protein diets.

b. I have yet to know a single adult to develop cancer who habitually drank a quart of milk a day.

My host takes twenty-six pills with his dinner and confides that this is a lot less than at the beginning of his treatment. He opens his chest of drawers to share with me, and it is stuffed with bottles and bottles of natural supplements. "You are a junkie," I cry. Then my eye notices a white satin banner with the word, MOTHER in gold lettering. It is from a funeral wreath.

I decide to chance the flu for the night and call Richard to come and bring me home.

On one of my last nights in the hospital, I had spoken to Richard on the phone. He told me he had been cleaning our home's one closet.

When I get into the house, I find he has taken all of my clothing and deposited it in a grocery store lot Goodwill box.

I shout, "What did you think you were doing, getting rid of your dead wife's estate?"

"I thought about that," he answers.

I lost my very best, hand-knit, white sweater with red hearts on the shoulders. I'll find another cardigan, I argue back in my mind. It doesn't matter.

March 14

The clouds in the Portland sky are folded together. The children and I ride the airplane up through the mattresses and drab feather ticks we are bedded under, and there is the sun above Portland. To me it is a message in the sky. My parents paid for the airplane tickets so we can come to California for two weeks, recover from surgery, and see the baby.

I am with all my children. I am so weak that Matthew has to pull me in the big red wagon to the park. But, I am with all of my children again.

April

The radiation field is set up with delicate precision. Behind one of the CAUTION: RADIATION signs is the simulator room, where the treatment area is calculated on a large machine with the brand name, Picker.

I am helped onto a table next to a panel of buttons. Arching over me is a hood, looking like a green praying mantis, with dials of numbers for eyes. Its face is square, with lines called X and Y. There is a note, which reads, "Target to surface 40.3 centimeters."

The table centers its patient, and the lights dim while the technician takes refuge in a lead-lined room of dials. Bells sound, and I can see my bones on a mounted TV screen.

These procedures are repeated with pieces of lead string marking certain spots, and then the boundaries are painted with flow pen. In this manner, I am prepared for my next series of treatments.

I take the bus with the children for the first radiation treatment on my abdomen. Returning home, I wait to transfer busses in the downtown city center. I feel altered, but not sick.

An enormous red double-decker English bus, carrying advertisements for local stores makes its way down the street. The attached sign says FREE RIDE, with a map showing the circle of stores where it stops.

Of course, we all scramble up the spiral stairs to sit on the tweedy plaid seats at the top. As we turn the corners, I begin to feel a low level of nausea.

The bus pulls into Import Plaza and parks as the driver blithely announces that this is the end of the line today.

I am beginning to feel very nauseated and a long way from home. "I'm sick, stay with me," convinces Matthew that the merry English bus ride is indeed over. I pull the children with me through the run down Burnside district. Matthew is excited at seeing all the empty bottles along the sidewalk. "Let's collect them and cash them in!"

I reply, "There's no refund on wine bottles, son."

We cross by the casual labor office, and I know I am going to need help. I try to call a friend, but even the print is blurring in the phone book.

I begin to vomit in a garbage can. A part of my mind can feel people driving by thinking—"Look at that ... an alcoholic ..., at her age, and such little children ..."

A social worker from the labor office comes over to me. I say, "It's not what you think, this is radiation!"

He is polite anyway and directs the children and me to our bus stop. I sit and lean against the building, instructing Matthew to look for the Number 40.

The ride is a long-suffering journey. I know that I'm going to throw up again and decide that the most unobtrusive depository will be my purse.

I become the bus ride attention center. I am passed one Kleenex, someone opens my window, and another moves as far from me as possible. The bus driver refuses my transfer as I finally ring the bell two blocks beyond my stop. I climb down the stairs and my purse spills all over the sidewalk. This is the journey from Hiroshima to my bed.

The medications lessen the nausea; but I am always wading through it, and I can hardly eat. I say the word, "food" backward. It is now "doof" and I don't want any.

"I am turning into the bones that walk."

The doctors have a solemn assembly: a staff member, my radiation resident, and two technicians. I join them. They sit straight as arrows and first suggest reducing my dosage. Then they speak again, "We feel you need marijuana."

It is unreal. All of a sudden, it is like a Peter Seller's movie, set on Telegraph Avenue in Berkeley, with enriched brownies for refreshments.

They stop my expanding meditation by referring to an article from the *New England Journal of Medicine*. They tell me about another young Hodgkin's patient that stayed stoned and well.

Cris Maranze pitches a copy of the article to me on her way to family practice clinic: "Antiemetic Effect of Delta-9-tetrahydrocannabinol in Patients Receiving Cancer Chemotherapy."

Dr. Moss begins to take a new interest in my case. I give him the article to read, and he personally administers the Rad reduction. He doesn't feel that any "extra" medication is necessary.

As my strength decreases, an empathy grows in me for the elderly. I suffer from many of the common geriatric problems. I have to watch other people take over jobs that in health I could do more efficiently.

One of the continents in my mind perceives not in words, but in shifting images. I feel like I am driving around in an old junk Studebaker body, where in health I am a four-wheel-drive Jeep that climbs mountains.

I am sick. I am weak. I have fevers and weight loss. I am again admitted to the hospital.

May 10
Hospital

There are no hospital beds for females available in hospital North, so I am sent to hospital South, where I have never camped. I am taken to the twelfth floor and assigned a bed next to a young girl in what looks like a body cast. She has her television going and sings along with all the commercial jingles as I change into pajamas. She asks me if I like Jesse James and shows me how far she can sit up, all in a matter of minutes.

I decide not to cross the sheets with my body and go to find a nurse in the hall. I ask for mercy. It is as if I am hitchhiking, and I don't want to get in that one car with a crazy driver.

They put me instead in a Cadillac, a large single room with a view. I rest in bed, so grateful, feeling as if I have won a daytime TV prize. It is quiet.

Weakness is like being in another gravity zone where there is just not enough energy for activity. I have to plan my moves.

Pictures are always extra windows, and I have none. From the pediatric floor, I choose six different quilts and hang them on the wall and put them on my bed. I take plants from the lounge and put them on the windowsill. I do all these things with the permission of the nursing staff. Then I roll up the bed to enjoy the view.

The nurse brings me a note to sign. It reads: "Consent to take full responsibility for bed to be in high position. The hospital is released from all responsibility for any accidents resulting."

Here I am all day, except for radiation.

The weekend schedule has reduced personnel and observation. My first Saturday back in the hospital, I make a secret arrangement with Stu Levy and Cris Maranze. I walk out to the main driveway between North and South and sit on a curb.

They are coming to get me for the afternoon. They pull up in a junky white Chevrolet, the kind of car that looks like it was born in a drive-in movie.

Stu's hair hangs down to the steering wheel. The tassel from his high school graduation cap (1966) hangs down from the rear view mirror.

Once Stu told me people could accept him as a craftsman who built furniture, or a farmer, but not as a medical doctor.

We go to the civic center. Stu wants to see an exhibit of photography equipment. Cris and I go to a funky junk show of neat old groovies.

I tire so fast, I cannot last. I sit in a chair. Cris sits with me there. I take out my embroidery thread and teach Cris how to make a herringbone stitch. She takes off Stu's corduroy shirt, and builds a line of teepees in thread until we leave.

Their house is in the hills by the Portland Rose Garden. On the step of their front porch is a foot scraper built out of two horseshoes. In their library is a tree growing from a pot all the way to the ceiling. "That's Arthur the avocado," Stu explains.

Over the fireplace is a rock 'n' roll band picture of the Sacred Mushroom boys. Stu's amplifiers stand like watchdog giants in the living room. They show slides of their Arizona backpacking trip.

Stu tells me a special summer guest is coming from New York. "Dr. Lipkin is a sage," says Stu. I visualize a Dr. Sage looking like he's from the Himalayas with long white hair.

I fall asleep on their couch, and they have to tiptoe around. It's not me; it's just my body that is acting like this.

I keep writing in my hospital journal, but I can create only a skeleton of experience with words.

Help is just somebody else's plan for you.

I have a phone call from someone I do not even know, who gives me the address of a Dr. Contreras and his laetrile clinic in Mexico. A lady brings me two books advocating laetrile. They are too late. I am too tired to read them.

In the shower one morning, I find more swollen lymph nodes in my groin. A biopsy is scheduled with Dr. Temple to determine if the malignancy has spread.

I talk with Richard, and he speaks such a graphic phrase that I have to walk around it very slowly:

"Have you ever seen two dogs and one has been hit by a car," he says.

"The other just circles and howls not knowing what to do."

The night before surgery, I want to write. I choose a small office on the floor that various physicians use during the day. It has a desk and a chair. A medical student is there, wearing a baroque parquet-floor tie and reading three books.

One book is a jumble of crazy images, never coming to any conclusion, but nonetheless having power to play tag with the mind. It is called, *Even Cowgirls Get the Blues*: "The brain that pound and a half of chicken colored goo, so highly regarded (by the brain itself), to which is attributed intricate and mysterious powers, that slimy organ (it is that self-same brain that does the attributing). The brain is so weak that without its protective casing to support it, it simply collapses of its own weight. So it could not be a brain."

It's a new generation of doctors and mailmen, but the bankers always seem to remain the same.

Friday, May 21
Biopsy Day

It isn't an early priority surgery, but it's to be done before noon. I decide that the lymph enlargements are guilty of disease and have to be proven innocent. With this attitude, I can have no letdown from pathology. Only the pubic hair on the right side is removed, and I am given enough medication so that I can be relaxed during the incision procedure.

The first effect of the narcotic is that I begin staring at a quilt that I had mounted at the foot of my bed, becoming wrapped in its design, and bold colors.

In this state of mind, I am taken to the surgery floor, hospital South.

First, I am wheeled behind a curtain, where one other girl is also waiting for her scheduled room and hour. Between us is a sleeping baby in a crib. The girl asks me, or any passing nurse, if we are the mother. I just think that she got more dope than I did.

Then I am wheeled into surgery and transferred to the table. I am draped except for my face and entire groin area. Above Dr. Temple are two large lights that seemed like large bug eyes, but not of a menacing species.

In this x-rated position, the staff surgeon walks in, looks at me, and asks Dr. Temple, "On which side are you performing the biopsy?"

Our minds can bring forth data in less than a second. I am immediately reminded of my first biopsy, when all the betadine preps were done on the left side of my neck, and without comment, the node was removed from the right.

So I sit up on the table, look at the staff surgeon and say, "The side where they shaved."

Then it is obviously such a dumb question. The nurses and doctors look each other in the eyes, but the surgeon's position prevents us from laughing.

We are the only two that have spoken, and without another word, he leaves the operating room.

Dr. Temple makes the incision. I can feel the blood run down my thigh.

Mike Mainer once shared in detail how a cesarean section is performed. I remember all the steps and begin to abstract. I allow free play in my ideas and decide that I am having a minute cesarean. I am about to give birth to an infant the size of my thumbnail. I sleep the rest of the afternoon.

A hematologist examines me. He has a closet of pet lions, and his recommendations unleash several for my contemplation. Their mouths are open and saliva drips from razor sharp teeth—

> Although she is clinically, in Stage III, the severity of the symptoms makes more widespread involvement a possibility. Because of this, chemotherapy (MOP) is in order. Normally, patient would be rested four to six weeks, completing radiation. However, because of the aggressiveness of this disease in this patient, that time may not be available.
>
> We are waiting staff's opinion as to this.
>
> Suggest:
> 1. gallium scan
> 2. bone marrow
> 3. bone scan
> 4. liver function
> 5. liver function test
> 6. surgical consultant for biopsy of inguinal mass

These lions stay in my room. At times they are very big, and I tremble. Sometimes they are smaller, but they are always present, with teeth.

Death is the last enemy we face.

The biopsy report confirms the spread of Hodgkin's.

I think, STAGE IV IS THE EXIT DOOR.

There are days to wait before Dr. Bagby and the staff return from their convention. It is a time for me to consider chemotherapy.

Dr. Ritzman sent a friend of his with fourth-stage Hodgkin's to my room. He says the only reason he is alive is chemotherapy.

But once Dr. Hood told me, "I've killed people with chemotherapy."

One text wrote, "Significantly, the sites of major toxicity of these chemotherapeutic agents are not all the same: although most are myelotoxic, some primarily affect the nervous system or gastrointestinal tract" (Cancer Journal for Clinicians, December 1975).

Besides the concern for the cancer-fighting agents, I do not want the top of my head to look like my knee. A disease and its treatment can be a series of humiliations, a chisel for humility.

My room has been an ice skating rink. As I sat and wrote, I glided through the hours, leaped over barrels, and was exuberant. Now there are holes I have to maneuver around. My feet can get wet and cold, and I shiver on my bed.

I have an official pass for a weekend afternoon. I plead with Richard to take me for a ride in the country. I am starved for helpings of spring on the great dishes of landscape. I get dressed, but he never comes.

I feel like a sociology thesis I once read concerning the unwed mother. Often she vests her expectations of security in a boyfriend who never comes to see her in the unwed mother's home.

Later I reach him by telephone, and he explains that he had taken Matthew, Anna, and two other children hiking.

The same weekend Mike Mainer asks me if I would like to go for a ride with him. Immediately, I phone Richard, and he agrees that it is a good idea.

Mike has a small German car with a window in the roof. We drive west through sloping farm fields. One meadow had a track of red flowers.

"It's clover," I declare.

"It's not clover," argues Mike.

He backs up the car to settle the horticultural question. It is a crimson clover variety.

We wade out and I lay down in the scarlet verdure. It reminds me of my childhood in Illinois where I used to make imprints of angels in the fresh snow. One has to wave arms and legs into wings and dresses.

"Mike, there really is a Heaven," I say.

"I don't believe that," he answers.

"If we stood back in history 300 years and I brought you a report of a continent I found with animals so incredibly different from those on your farm, you wouldn't have believed me then, either."

We eat tacos in a drive-in and go back to the hospital. I share with him one square of my worry about Richard's attitude towards me.

"Stay as close to him as you can," Mike tells me.

Friends manage to bring my children for a few hours. I am so excited. I go up to the pediatric floor and walk past the mural of Snow White to get to the game room. I explain to the volunteer that I want to borrow some toys, and I will bring them back. I fill a wagon with mechanical wonders, stories, and 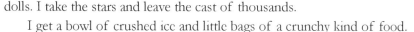 dolls. I take the stars and leave the cast of thousands.

I get a bowl of crushed ice and little bags of a crunchy kind of food.

The children come; ever moving, ever talking bursts of energy. Matthew and Anna have a style of appearing to explode into an infinity of perceiving parts. We flow together.

When they leave, I am so exhausted that I can hardly move or speak. A sadness permeates my being. I ache for my baby too. She left me at only six weeks old.

I have to get rid of the toys. Maybe all the storybooks have tragic endings. I hit the wrong floor button and wander around, a stranger pulling a crazy, red wagon in her nightgown.

As I sleep, a nurse took the cloth wrapping off a sterile instrument. He smoothed out the material. He painted with a flow pen a moon face with wide eyes and an enormous crescent smile.

He climbed over my bed. He climbed over my plants and hung this banner down from my window, using extra wide masking tape.

It is the first thing I see in the morning.

The day comes when some of the hematologist's six recommended points will stick me. They are planning to do a bone marrow. I wait.

The hematology chief of staff has returned; he comes into my room with Dr. Bagby and Mike Mainer. He says he is not convinced that chemotherapy or any of the tests are at all necessary. The inguinal nodes were an untreated radiation port, thus their enlargement does not mean I have progressed to the terminal Stage IV.

His recommendation is a discharge from the hospital, with a further course of radiation on an outpatient basis.

He takes every lion with him. I roar for joy.

On my very last day, a man comes and introduces himself as the technician who once gave me a barium swallow. "Look," he says, "these are the stains all over my pants from when you spit out the drink."

I take down the quilts, put the plants back and go home from my seventh hospitalization.

May 27, Thursday

Home is said to be the one place you can go, and they have to take you in. If I'm a rock thrown in the water, home is one of the first rings from the weight. It is a glimpse of me, through things.

I walk into someone else's house at my old shoe address. The living room is not the grandmother-lace card where I once curled up on the couch and read classics of British literature. Now, displacing my desk is a television set against the wall.

Bob Ellis/The Oregonian

My kitchen counter has been a visual pleasure with its small collection of antique tins. Now it has been turned into a beach of cheap practicality: a silver toaster has its electric cord hand under a blender umbrella; an electric can opener is wearing a green plastic bikini; tacky vendor stands of canisters advertise *FLOUR* and *SUGAR*.

"This is how it is going to stay. I couldn't find anything!" says Richard.

"And that stove," indicating my antique blue enamel queen on its ornate legs, "has to go. It makes the pans black."

So I walk through my house and the floors all slant uphill.

May 28, Friday

Richard took the children to the baby-sitter.

Saturday

He helped the baby-sitter take her dirty clothes to the laundromat. She was a young girl raising two children alone, and her car didn't work.

Sunday

This was the day my house fell down.
Remember it brown,
Like the ground.

I always operated under ordinances. I was allowed Sunday school, and that was the boundary of my formal religious training. The children went to their classes, and I sat in the back, listening to adult admonitions.

The pastor's wife asked if I would stay and share from the pulpit in the main service. It was like a new application of working out my salvation with fear and trembling. An elder escorted me to the platform after the congregation sang:

Storm clouds will come
Strong winds will blow,
But I've got a Saviour
And He's sweet, I know.

The faces spread out before me. There was a television camera for the auxiliary room. It's a large congregation.

I made paragraphs. I left the rostrum. I left my Bible. I left the church. I was tired.

Later, I call the baby-sitter. They are there. They had all gone hiking together. Thoughts fly around my head. I understand that to him I am dead.

At night, we talk. "We really are in two different kingdoms," he says in a loud whisper.

How can two walk together unless they be agreed? The *feeling* of love that promotes tap-dancing down supermarket aisles, leaping over bushes, catching blooms between the toes; that goes. But the *fact* of love becomes a code of behavior.

"Love suffers long and is kind, seeks not its own, is not easily provoked" But there can only be rest, when every eye stays in the nest.

Richard uses a quiet voice to ask for a divorce. The baby-sitter might be pregnant with his child, and he wants to marry her.

As I put the children to bed late that night, they lean out of their bunks, built from plate glass packing crates, to sing. They have Sunday school songs. They pound their fists one on top of the other and the lyrics run:

> The wise man built his house upon the rock
> And the house on the rock stood firm.
> The storm came up,
> And the rain came down,
> And the house on the rock stood firm.
> The foolish man built his house upon the sand
> The storm came up,
> And the rain came down
> And the house on the sand went squish ...

They spread out their fingers and sing it again.

Monday, Memorial Day

Richard starts all the legal paperwork to dissolve our ten-year marriage. Friends open their homes for me. I move in with a family feeling like their house is another kind of hospital.

I am in the wilderness of my life. I am a Gretel without a Hansel, lost in the woods. There is a wicked witch who will eat me, if I listen. There is always a bread crumb trail to safety.

In my thoughts are my wars fought.

I rent the upstairs of an old house. I turn each window into a greenhouse. All the children will be coming home. My parents are going to bring Mary Elisabeth to Portland. My mother says she can even pull herself up in the crib to her feet. I'm going to have to create places for the three children to sleep within these two small rooms.

I finish my journal. Instead of putting it on the shelf with the other twelve volumes I've kept since Alaska, I spontaneously loan it to my friends at the medical school.

I have one more radiation treatment. I'm about to complete all the medical course possible unless the disease recurs.

In Oregon, the salmon run from the sea to their spawning ground. There are nets. There are sporting men. There are rocks and ascents so steep that some die from the journey itself. But some silver salmon make it home. It's a matter of percentage; it always is; I could grow old.

My last treatment is the very day family practice clinic has a farewell dinner for its graduating residents. We eat on the roof in the sunshine.

Stu can only grab a hasty plate, as he still has tables up and down the hall to serve, like a Doctor Waiter.

I meet another guest at the clinic, Stu's sage, Dr. Mack Lipkin from New York. He says that Stu Levy gave him "my hand written account of my experience with a lymphatic cancer."

Long ago, I had borrowed a copy of Mack Lipkin's book. I was impressed that he had served as a consultant to the Surgeon General.

I share one of my favorite paragraphs, where Dr. Lipkin was speaking with the head of a major medical center. He told him he thinks it should be required that every graduating doctor first produce a bowel movement in a horizontal position with three witnesses present.

Later that week a secretary phones from the family practice on behalf of Dr. Lipkin. She asks if I'll come to his temporary office next Monday at nine in the morning. It's a puzzling request, but of course, I agree. I know every turn in the street from the northeast part of the city to the clinic in the West Hills. I want this to be my last knot on the whole year's embroidery of going to the hospital. I am very tired of dark threads.

July 26
Monday

I have to hurry to make my appointment. I rush out to the early morning street and wait for my bus. There are many that would be glad to give me a ride, but I want to do it myself.

An antique store has been closed for a long time. This is the day they are loading the furniture into a large rented truck.

"Oh," I sigh, knowing I should wait for the bus, but I enter the shop. The owner sells me a wooden cuckoo clock for a quarter. It has a filigree of European carved wood; there is great detail in bird wing and vine. I figure that even though it is broken, it still has to be right twice a day. Turning its face into my dress, I look like I am carrying a large birdhouse.

The owner goes out with me and stands by the curb, overseeing the hoisting of his furniture pieces.

I see the orange bus at the top of the hill. "Look, I didn't miss it at all."

I enter Dr. Lipkin's office on the third floor of the family practice building. He says he found some charm in my book and asks to send it to an editor friend in New York.

I feel like I am a very homely girl, and someone actually thinks that I can be in a beauty contest.

I must have jumped up in my chair, or made some sudden movement. The clock in my lap activates. It goes "cuckoo, cuckoo," over and over until I think this is probably my theme song.

What can I give Mack Lipkin, wise sage, great doctor? I have a little sketchbook of watercolors I have made to illustrate Thoreau's Walden. I rip out a favorite page:

"The essential laws of man's existence do not change just as our bones are indistinguishable from those of our ancestors."

My book goes to New York. It is like a piece of paper a child floats out into a stream. It is soon out of sight. It will get caught in some weeds, I think. There are holes in it. It will fill with water and sink. But, I lift up and fly on ...

SEPTEMBER 1976

Portland

Nights became the longest train ride. Mary Elisabeth always throws her bottle out of the crib. She cries like the lonely whistle as it crosses the 2:00am of Kansas. Everything is dark and flat.

Her sister Anna, now four, sleeps with me. She requires all her stuffed animals to be packed around us. These assorted lumps can make it feel that my passage is in a mail car.

Matthew is above us for the night. I turned the wide boards of the closet shelf into his bed. Just having turned six, he calls it an authentic Amtrak sleeping berth. He climbs up with a flashlight, and I've covered his interior walls with a collage of locomotive pictures.

I'm riding the single mother express; the now completed divorce was my instant ticket.

When my parents learned of my circumstance, they had driven north to Oregon like a kind of ambulance. They had helped me pay for the apartment. After providing the hundred dollars for the first month's rent, my father helped me go through the motions to get on welfare. We both knew the court ordered child support would never materialize.

I wondered, but I didn't dare ask, if he regretted all that college tuition he had paid investing in my future. My mother had always told me I would be a lawyer because I liked to argue. They used to banter on my future profession as if it were a line of golden chairs just waiting for me to pick my seat.

No one ever thought of *waitress*, which at random times, throughout our marriage, had helped pay the rent. Now I'm part of the state's statistic for receiving aid for dependent children. I think I'll skip any pending high school reunions.

"When is Daddy coming?"

Anna looked up at me with eyes that are brown pools. They remind me of a nature poster with an alert baby seal alone on an ice floe. I pause before the answer. My emotions feel the harpoon, knowing I have to say, "He will never live here."

The glacier breaks away. I don't want this avalanche to cover her. Don't let your heart freeze. No matter how much I yearn for it to be different, I can't

postpone this reality any longer

Oh God, please have for us some future and a hope.

Matthew is an unusual boy. He doesn't have one cell that loves slapstick comedy. Once I took him to a circus and the clowns never made him laugh. He just sat there trying to figure out how the little red car could keep rising up on its back tires.

He assimilated our move and his father's absence as steadfast as the little tin soldier. He could be a boy guard at Buckingham until the day he found some scrap lumber. He dragged it to the porch and asked me for the hammer and nails.

They were among the male gender possessions that were bundled away. I couldn't bear to tell him I have to regard tools as something one borrows from a neighbor, with an immediate return. My fiscal priorities are rent and milk.

I have to go to church. It's only a block away. I think of it as a one-stop shopping center for the soul.

2nd floor, MISSIONS / 3rd floor, CHOIR

Secretly, I sift through its population of over 3,000, members looking for a potential husband. Hope can't stop looking.

I'm very aware that it's too soon and a mistake to be yearning for marriage. It's funny how fashion touches everything—not only the width of men's ties and the height of automobile fins, but invisible things too. There would be a general consent and sympathy if I wanted to go to graduate school and learn to design house turrets.

I can hear the snicker everywhere, but in the church, for occupation, *homemaker*. It is such a familiar job; I just spent one third of my life in that very role. I can tie every kind of apron knot. I liked earning a merit badge by making soup with one potato. Through my illness, the wood just got too wet to keep alive with any kind of campfire. By my last hospital discharge, there wasn't one warm ember to blow. He was gone, and my temporary baby-sitter with him.

A friend, Barbara, takes inventory of me as a candidate for someday becoming a bride. I explained how I chose my husband before knowing salvation, when I was still a student at Berkeley. I had looked for someone who was willing to homestead in Alaska.

"I've revised that to scrutinizing character. Obviously, he has to also love children. I've become a package deal."

She actually studied me from across the table. With her chin resting on her hand, she closed her eyes to just one degree above a squint.

"You would look a lot better if you would get rid of that gray in your hair. Buy a dark brown hair rinse."

I'm amused that she's so blunt and frank. I like the spots of curly frost that's been forming at my temple and above my ears. The oncologist told me it could grow back a different texture and color. I want to make a joke about cultivating dread locks, but she jumped up, and returned with some small pierced earrings. I haven't worn any for years, but the holes punched in once by my college roommate are still tiny, intact port holes.

"Why are you a size eight, and wear sixteen or higher?"

I explain it's all I have, and I've always put more value on comfort than being pretty.

Without any extra comment, Barbara tells me to buy something smaller. She's a Value Village thrift store shopper too, and her instruction includes for me to look for something off the racks, and not just the bins. That's the difference between having a budget of bills verses coins.

"Laurel, this is all an opportunity to expand how you see God. It's a personal relationship; you must move closer. He can be Father and Husband.

I've known for a long time that "God is love" and "He provides" are more than just cross-stitch embroidery slogans.

At the grocery store, I slowly went down the cosmetic aisle. There were as many kinds and colors of hair rinse as cereal boxes. I felt self-conscious and hid my alchemy box of Rich Walnut Brown under the carrots and cello lettuce package.

I felt flushed at check out. Food stamps could pay for everything but the chemicals. It was in the excluded status just like alcohol or cigarettes.

When I went to use it, I quickly read down to see how long the lotion had to be on my head. I ignored the gloves, and to my later dismay found that my fingers had turned a distinct golden tan. It wouldn't wash off, even with cleanser. I just looked like someone who had spent her entire life hand rolling moist tobacco into cigars.

There were a few men who came calling. When alerted, I could clean our rooms like a contestant for the land speed record. I had different versions of the *Mr. Single Fire Drill*. I had a basket of original embroidery pieces that I could show, and there was always my homemade jam showcase.

"Have some," I would say. "The children helped me, and we picked all the blackberries ourselves."

I felt completely pathetic in my yearning for someone to stand with me in the yoke of pulling this cart full of family. I resented it as if my circumstances were forcing me to go backwards in life. I'm too old to lean against the wall of an eighth-grade dance and be wishing for a partner.

There was Martin Conway who raised bees and was a single father to a young son. Even before the ten-minute mark had struck within our evening, I knew that any possibilities with him were all *Stop, Red light, Turn back, NO*. He was a man whose speech hardly exceeded single-syllable words. When I used a simile to explain myself, he asked for a translation.

As a woman who knows what it is like to be battered, I will have to meet anybody by the great Yellow light of CAUTION.

One Sunday I was introduced to a Dr. Andrew Rodell. Somehow, he had found his way to my door that same afternoon. I had not yet bothered to pick up the early morning debris from getting us ready for church.

I winced while watching him step carefully to a chair. There were so few spots where one could even see the floor through all the litter of laundry and toys.

"Want me to get your jars of jam?" asked Matthew.

I could only shoot at him my laser look of "No."

My guest surprised me when all of a sudden he altered his voice to a slow southern accent. "Pardon me ma'am."

Andrew now introduced himself as "Mack" who was just opening a corner gas station. Calling me, "Betty Sue" he asked me to come in and pour coffee for these truckers.

I love instant theater; to make a play can turn any stuffy sedan into a convertible. It's an art to rearrange the letters that spell *routine*.

I now pretended to be an aristocrat that had fled from Russia before the revolution. Andrew became a count that had the hope of getting his estate back from the new system of collective farms.

Picking up Anna's shoe, he spoke into the scuffed toes as if it were a microphone. He asked me to tell his national news service what it was like to live three months on the moon.

I stifled my impulse to jump up on the couch as a demonstration of other world gravity.

It was so good to laugh waist deep. The real facts were my guest was in his last year of residency at the University of Oregon medical school. He was making a specialty of tropical medicine and eventually wanted to practice overseas. Danish by background, he had thick blonde hair and a round face that was more amiable than handsome. When he finally left I felt lighter, as if the room's air had been infused with helium.

Whenever he called, it was like we were playing catch with words. He could put ideas on swings, and we took turns pushing them. I liked how he had genuine muscles in the language playground.

Andrew came one Saturday and bundled the whole family to our favorite park in his Volkswagen van. His vehicle was the age and model of preference when the youth of the sixties took to the open road. If Anna were given some cans of paint, she could make her signature daisies on its side. Like her brother, she had learned to draw during church services. I had always kept my purse full of colored markers, and my formal period of religious instruction became their backdrop to meander with art.

"You know," said Andrew, "it's just been a few weeks, but you are the kind of woman I could get very serious about."

Moving his eyes away from my face, he continued his thought after a slight exhale.

"I could handle the children if you had never had Hodgkin's disease, or I could handle you in a Stage IV illness if there were not any children."

I mumbled back that I understood. It took all my strength to keep the self-control mask tight, like a dam over my threatening flood. Sometimes the hardest thing is to just stand when you want to fall on the ground and cry.

"You're awfully quiet," said Andrew on the drive back to my apartment. "Is anything wrong?"

It was then that he lost his status of being one of the *Green Light* men of the world. The litmus paper that measured "sensitivity" was hardly damp.

The endorphins that had loved recalling, in special replay, all our interactions had to die in one heap. They had lived a short life from doing the can-can to their funeral march.

I saw Dr. Andrew Rodell sitting with another single mother one Sunday. She looked like the picture of health, and only had one young son.

I started making a peculiar collection in one drawer of my mind; I wanted to know people's biggest problems. It was like a new hobby of collecting shades of black.

1. One category was things that were lost. I heard about a new puppy, car keys, and one friend got moist eyes when she confided that she lost her wedding ring.

2. There were relationship problems with children of all ages, and husbands that somehow turned to cement in front of a television.

3. Financial problems were also a common answer. Dollars were lighter than air and easily floated into the atmosphere, or the money was too skimpy to cover the giant block of want.

Maybe the audience from which I drew my sample was too young, but no one replied with any medical problems at all. I deduced that one could handle physical infirmities, but no one could bear the assorted strikes that knock against their spirit.

One night I lay in the dark, sorting the gray cards from the black, with my own shuffled into the deck. All the children were asleep. Anna occasionally scissored her feet, and I could hear Mary Elisabeth breathing through both her mouth and nose. It was as close as I could get to being alone.

An idea came that wasn't my own. It was as if a capital letter headline was imposed over all my thoughts: *You are not wise when you measure and compare yourself with others.*

It was only the top of a whole scroll of thoughts. It was as personal as seeing a graph that has measured my tears, like rainfall. I know the bits of my broken heart are all numbered.

Your problem is not being alone with three young children, or divorced. It's not that you are poor, can't work, and the inadequate size of your apartment.

Your real problem is clear. It is your attitude to all these things—

How could there have ever been a David without a Goliath?

How can you be counted in the group of the overcomers without things to overcome?

It was as if I had been outside, numb with cold, and then the sun came up. Peace is a shaft of light. I wouldn't forget it, even when again, I would be thick with overcast. C. S. Lewis was right, "God whispers to us in our pleasures, but shouts to us in our pain."

Matthew was enrolled in the first grade. He had a short-sleeved, blue-shirt uniform and dark pants that I had bought from the mother of a bigger second grader. He was especially thrilled with his choice of a new lunch box. It was a bright yellow tin picturing a school bus with all the Disney characters waving out the window. To my sandwich and fruit, he added

Bob Ellis/The Oregonian

a couple crayons, toilet paper, and a candle stub when he couldn't fit in his flashlight.

There are lines across a life just like the rings of a tree. I felt the paradox that it took so long, and it was so fast that my baby boy now goes to school. I believe there's far more feelings than words to identify them. The very consideration of Matthew becoming a man, and him having a child that will go to school makes me want to cry. It's just melancholy from a glimpse at the warp speed of generations.

Anna was envious, and every day she packed too. There's no variation. She gets my old robe because she likes to rub the yellow polyester lining while sucking her two middle fingers. It's brought to me in a bag with a gray stuffed elephant and the very bear that she pushes up by my pillow. I decided to look for a reasonable nursery school for maybe a couple days a week.

One Sunday after sitting seven rows back and across the aisle from Dr. Rodell, who now keeps his arm around his steady date's back, I'm approached by one of the congregational leaders. He asks if I would like to go to Bible school, as there's a full scholarship if I'm interested. I'm thrilled for this offering of a metal girder that will give some more shape to my life. Taking me to his office, I'm given a schedule of the beginning classes.

It's odd to sit in an auditorium of students that are either eighteen or nineteen and take notes on the book of Exodus. I am a million years older; I am a dinosaur in a room of chicks that still have some eggshells in their hair from such a recent hatching.

I wonder what's in the notes that they sometimes pass to each other, or in their occasional exchange of whispers during class. I suppose it's who likes who. Every month this church has a schedule of weddings. Sometimes I go just to get the free cake.

I'm playing with the two girls on the floor when the telephone rings. They love for me to build towers out of blocks so they can squeal and knock them down. The woman on the telephone identifies herself as a literary agent from New York City. It seems she had received the hospital journal. I thank her for saying she will show it around and go back to my spot on the rug.

It's such a funny call. It is like someone who works for a state lottery phoning to say they received my personal inscription of numbers, and they will carry it over to the drum where the winner will be drawn. The odds are an exercise in improbable math.

Within the same week, I rotated the baby to my hip to pick up the ringing telephone. It was also from New York and from a man who identified himself as a publishing house senior editor. He says he wants to put my story into print. "Your title, *Laurel Lee Goes to the Hospital Book* is going to have to be changed."

I don't tell him I adapted it from *The Bobbsey Twins Go To The Mountains*. I was talking loud because the children were making noise. I was also talking fast because he's calling from across the country at the highest day time rate.

He asked me to increase the account, and bring it to New York for a four thousand, four hundred dollar advance. My agent, who was the woman who phoned, will be drawing up the contract.

Screeching, I ran and looked at myself in the mirror, announcing to my reflection, "You are an author!" I saw that done once, long ago in a movie and had no idea I had carried that chip of recollection to imitate.

Bundling the girls into sweaters for the October air, I had to take to the streets. First, I quit Bible school. I was having a hard time memorizing books and prophets anyway, plus there was a pending test. Then, we went around to the side building that housed the primary grades. I wanted to tell Matthew. More money meant he could have his own hammer.

His response to the news was sober.

"You know what this means, Mother. I'm now going to have to learn how to read!"

I could only work on the edge of time. In the very early morning, sometimes when it was still dark, I would creep into the bathroom and pull out some dirty clothes from the basket. These, I molded into a backrest. Some people have a lucky pen, or a desk with a view, but for me, slouching was my best position. That was how I worked in the hospital.

I got a date and ticket to fly to New York, and organized baby-sitters for the children. At my favorite thrift store on 82nd Avenue, I bought some clothes off the hangers instead of the cheaper tables where the goods are tangled together. One was a rose-colored corduroy suit, and with an almost matching cinch belt, I could cover its missing wood button. My favorite was a long floral piece that could be used as a nightgown, or with the right decorative pin, a fancy dress. I put everything in an old mint-green Samsonite suitcase that was once a high school Christmas present.

The neighbor who was taking me to the airport came upstairs with a cardboard box of Hood River apples.

"Do you know what our relatives in New York have to pay for fruit?"

Before I could answer, she snorts, "89 cents a pound!"

To keep from carrying the carton I decided to distribute the red apples between the clothes in my suitcase, and my purse. I wondered if they would look like bombs when going through the X-ray machine.

After being dropped by the airport's departure doors, I was astounded when the United clerk said I was too late for the nonstop flight. It had just finished boarding. She could route me through Chicago where I would now have to transfer.

I felt sick at this self-caused delay. I'm best at soft time where one can just float in the day's waters and not use the exertion that's required for exact appointments. I can feel the need for a watch closing in on me. It started with Matthew putting his first foot into school.

After alerting New York of my schedule change, I boarded the new flight still grumbling at myself.

How long will it take me to learn there is a purpose in things; there is no such thing as luck, or coincidence.

To my surprise, I recognize many of the new flight's passengers from the hospital's senior medical staff. Some had to look twice to confirm it was really me. A few of them probably had a hazy recall of my bony face resting in a pillow.

Once airborne, I began to move around so I could talk to each one. First, I learned they were all going to an oncology convention. I had to laugh at their response to the reason for my trip. Vanity always floats to the top. They carefully worded it, but each wanted to know if I wrote about, *his personal role in my medical management.*

One actually asked if I'm the school bus driver's wife; he must read the biographical data on charts. I'm really a step lower than that. I'm a dumped school bus driver's wife. Richard often told me, in those last days, that he had found someone much better. I know the new Mrs. Lee, unlike me, can sing and play a guitar.

The flight attendants have been distributing snacks and drinks. They see me frequently moving across the rows just ahead of their cart. One, while giving me peanuts, commented on how I had sat with so many different men.

"You are certainly the flight's most friendly person!"

I have to laugh at my demonstration of unusual behavior.

I managed to harvest over fifteen bags of Virginia peanuts that I can later take home for the children. I scan the waiting room, but there's no woman agent or my new editor. Like someone lost in the woods, I just stay in one place. I hope the security is good on my waiting suitcase.

Finally, a couple, with the man leading, bustle around the corner. Slightly out of breath, they identify themselves. Henry Robbins, rumpled in tweed, looks like a British literature professor. My new agent, Harriet Wasserman is all in black. With her large cowl turtleneck and silk-like pants, she could use the outfit as exotic pajamas.

I feel like the country mouse that has come to meet the city mice. They explain that I'll be staying at Harriet's apartment and working each day with Henry in his office.

My bed is an orange Castro convertible couch in the midst of piles of books. The room's topography is mountain ranges of literature. I'm as happy as if I were living in a candy factory.

To get to my editor's office I climb the stairs past all the original Winnie the Pooh stuffed animals in a glass case. To me there's a magic quality about the publishing house. There's an alchemy of taking 26 letters and spinning such straw into gold. We bend together over this rubics cube of language, moving adjectives and verbs.

I see the city as a kind of ocean that washes onto my shore things from the deep. One morning a call came from London for Harriet. It's another agent telling her she just got the official word from Stockholm that their client, Saul Bellow, has been awarded the Nobel Prize for literature. As Harriet dials him in Chicago, I bite my knuckle in anticipation.

He was under a sheet trying to escape the house painters in his apartment. "So you're reading an essay about Jane Austin."

I made a picture with each of Harriet's phrases. Telling the news, she floats into mystery; "All these millions of years our souls waited to come here."

One afternoon as I was nibbling from a children's magazine, I found a poem that bounced like a pogo stick. I called over to Harriet.

"Maybe it's not the same man, but when I was seventeen, I worked in Yosemite's highest Sierra camp. It was 1963, and my first complete summer away from home."

I told how Jack strolled into camp talking song and verse. To me, finding out he was Jewish and from the Village in New York was as exotic as the edge of the universe. I only knew the exact square yards of suburbia. He was the first man to kiss my hand, and when I went to college, he wrote every day.

The night I turned eighteen, Jack Prelutsky phoned and asked me to marry him. He wanted me to find out what the bus would cost, and whatever the amount, ask that many people for one dollar. That way my passage would be free. My practical streak dominated, and with my refusal, he disappeared for fourteen years, until now.

From his editor, Harriet learned he lived in Seattle, and she urged me to the telephone.

"He's never married," she said as I walked to the offered receiver.

"Yes," said Jack. "I do indeed remember, and I'm coming to see you. I have to wait until my friend, Mike, comes from New York. We are going to drive down the West Coast, and first we'll come to your house."

Within that week, I learned the major difference between this East Coast culture and my world back in the West. It was *RESTAURANTS*. They flow into them for almost every meal. It's as if these dining establishments exert a special force field and the citizens of Manhattan cannot resist their magnetism.

Harriet's refrigerator had nothing substantial but a few condiments. There was plenty of room on her shelves for me to store my collected airline cache. To me it was supporting evidence to a lifestyle of public dining.

Maybe at home I would go out to eat once a year, and then it was usually to a pizza restaurant with a coupon. It had seemed special if we could watch them throw the dough up into the air.

For my last night in the city, Harriet had a cocktail party. Most of the social gatherings I have attended in Portland progress to where we sit and sing. Here they all remain standing, and talk in groups of two or three. At home, all the visitor's coats are piled on a bed where here each is hung on a hall rack.

While floating in my bubble of observation, I heard the word, "Hodgkin's" from the other side of the closed kitchen louvered door. It was a physician talking to my editor.

"Confidentially, Henry, she may not live to see the book in print. Her remission may not be long lasting. With the aggression of fourth-stage involvement, I would recommend rushing publication."

With his words, I could feel realism growing a head taller than my optimism. Its mean face made me shudder.

The infusion of money meant mobility. I could cancel welfare and move. I bought the house right across the street for seventeen thousand dollars, but we had to wait until the end of December for them to vacate. I led the children in a parade through the new backyard and around the apple tree. Mary Elisabeth's portable stroller was our only float. We would have bedrooms for each one of us.

My glimpse of a two-story floor plan exaggerated the smallness of our quarters. I felt I was Alice in Wonderland swollen to an enormous state. Wanting one night to sleep alone, I put Anna in the bathtub with a sleeping bag. Matthew climbed up to his shelf, and I tucked Mary Elisabeth into her living room Port-A-Crib.

I counted the quiet. Alone in bed, I enumerated the silence. Before reaching number six, the baby threw her bottle out onto the floor. At number eight, Matthew said he was too hot. By number twelve, Anna crawled into bed with me. The cast iron tub was too hard for her.

I quoted for myself the lines of Lewis Carroll:

> *Twas brillig and the slithy toves*
> *Did gyre and gamble in the wabe*

Laurel and Jack Prelutsky

I was nervous about Jack coming. He represented a now long ago time in my life. I would have to tell him how I left college, rose and fell in marriage. I had a past that was several train cars long and been on a journey through some dark tunnels. In contrast, my children are shiny engines and are just starting to pull their own AUTOBIOGRAPHY.

They came in the evening. Jack bounded to the front porch, lifted me up and twirled me around in his arms. No one had ever done that before.

"Let's get married," he said.

I was very conscious of Matthew and Anna who had followed me down the stairs.

"These are our visitors from Mars," I said, breaking away for introductions, and leading everyone up to the apartment.

Mike Thaler was introduced as someone who had been publishing for sixteen years. Jack said that he had designed "Letterman" for "The Electric Company." I was impressed until he began to walk around the tiny apartment. His intensity made it feel more like an inspection than just casual observing.

From a top shelf, he pulled off my pile of thumb-sized drawings that I had been working on for my editor. They were going to be inserted in the text as the original water colors were too expensive to reproduce. I told him the best books should have lots of pictures and a happy ending.

"These are scratchy, tight, and just generally terrible. What kind of pen are you using?"

Shocked by his rudeness, I just fished from a drawer my Bic, 29-cent pen, and held it up. I bought it at a drug store, just one block away.

As he heaped ridicule on my tool, I phoned my friends to come who had volunteered their extra bedrooms for my guests.

In the morning, I escorted Jack and Mike to Matthew's school, where they offered to give a program as a gift to the first grade class of Temple Christian School. There was no rain, but a characteristic overcast. Some of the church families had pounded *I Found It* signs into their front yard.

Both men were amused, and I could feel their cynicism as if it were a river that long ago had overrun its banks. It seemed impossible to plant there even the smallest seed of belief.

One week before Christmas, we had a whole day parade of crossing the street, like box turtles, with all our goods in cartons. Our first night we slept together in the living room. It was too dark to try and organize anything else. The departing tenants had taken every single light bulb.

Our new home did look as if it had been in a number of street fights. Its paint was scratched. The garage had no door, giving an impression that its front tooth had been knocked out. But I was delighted with the maximum space. I stenciled Pennsylvania Dutch hearts on the backs of the treads going upstairs.

1977

I had never known prosperity. It felt like chirping birds looping through the sky to my shoulder—birds with colored bows around their necks and bills in their beak of large denominations. I tried, but really didn't know how to spend money. I stopped turning off the heat at night, bought sales clothes for us in department stores, and introduced the children to ethnic food. From a showroom of appliances, I first bought a washing machine and then put a dryer in my basement. I began to look at car ads and assess which friend would have the patience to show me the rules of the road.

One Sunday the chil-

dren quarreled over which restaurant chair to sit in. They took soy sauce and spilled it on the table so they could draw the liquid out with their fingers into rays, and each made a brown sunshine on the Formica. Matthew, on his way back from the bathroom, saw a container of fortune cookies at a water station and confiscated a fist full for our table. Anna pretended her chopsticks were swords and started a double-handed duel with her brother. When he grabbed them from her, she yelled, and Mary Elisabeth began to shout just to be like her sister.

It felt like a long haul ahead to get each one to a responsible twenty-first birthday. Just the consideration of scaling the heights of those double-digit years ahead could make me hyperventilate.

My New York publisher was an avid pen pal. I found an alternate world waiting for me in my mailbox.

One note explained that I was being scheduled to go on a tour at the time of the book's release while my parents would watch the children.

I thought of it as the side work to writing. Waitresses have more to do than bring pork chops to the table. They have to pour catsup into the used bottles and keep the saltshakers full. To give the publisher my diary wasn't enough. I had to fill the napkin holders in thirteen cities with TV interviews. Portland would be first.

To me it was a great opportunity to tell the truth, "Nothing is impossible with God."

Waiting just outside the set for "A.M. Northwest," I never realized how nervous I could get. Already the miniature microphone had been pinned on my shirt, and in minutes I was to walk out into the fake living room. My heart felt like it had turned into jungle drums.

As the camera moved in, I wondered if there was any residue on my teeth from lunch. Spots of spinach salad could look like I needed immediate dental repair.

By the host's questions, I knew he had never read the book. When asked to talk about my battle with illness, I couldn't remember the name of my disease. I felt compelled to try and fill in the blank.

"In the sixth month of my pregnancy they found that I had ... leprosy."

Instantly, I knew I had uttered the ridiculous. Paralyzed further, I couldn't even correct myself.

My interviewer assumed it was true; I had a reputable publisher. He seemed to scoot slightly away from me on the couch.

"Movies come from books. If this is ever made into a film, who should play Laurel Lee?"

My mind was a screen without a picture tube. Desperately I searched for some image, and finally blurted, "Elizabeth Taylor."

We finished quickly as the next guest, scheduled to talk about treating neurotic pets, was just offstage.

I was so disappointed in myself. It was the one program all my friends had watched. On the telephone I had to explain the origin of my error, "People today fear cancer with the same intensity that generations before feared leprosy." The missing word was "Hodgkin's," and it was just too late.

Clipping the front page picture, I had already addressed the envelope to my parents. *The Oregonian* had done a feature interest story on the book. I knew the truth about fame; it lasts like high-fat ice cream in the sun. Tomorrow our newspaper image will be used to line birdcages or keep the linoleum clean while painters change the color of kitchen ceilings.

My seventh city was New York. A morning news program sent a limousine to pick me up at Harriet's apartment. A whole Girl Scout troop could unroll their sleeping bags in the back. Sinking into the leather marshmallow seat, I saw that my skirt had been buttoned wrong, and it took me all the way to the studio to fix it.

The program's budget was obviously well endowed. It was the first time I sat in front of a hairdresser since the junior prom. After makeup, my reflection was a way it had never looked before and never would again. Finally, I was escorted into a lounge where there were trays of catered breakfast food, and a big screened television showing the already ongoing program. Except for a secretary, I was alone.

I knew this *national* program was the peak of my whole tour. I was so nervous, I was even breathing funny.

Across the screen flashed a bulletin: "Stay tuned and meet from Oregon *A*

WOMAN OF COURAGE." I was glad there was another guest from my home state. I kept looking over at the door, but the only person that came through was the art and entertainment critic. He had hair like a Brillo pad.

While flicking his mustache, he must have evaluated my near panic state, and decided to ease the tension with a joke.

"I read your book and want you to be my wife."

Completely lacking discernment, I politely refused and then was ushered out for the interview.

Waiting on one of two stools was Jane Pauley. Behind us was a giant replica of the book cover. It was so large that if it tipped over we would be instantly crushed, and our deaths would be replayed on the night news.

She must have been warned about my anxious state; I wasn't asked anything. Instead, she showed some of the illustrations.

I could watch everything on a side monitor. I was amazed that my weak jumping rope like poem had its moment of attention;

Hospital visit, hospital visit
Number seven.
When you die,
You can go,
To Heaven ...

When asked a question, the camera shifted to me, and I could see my face completely twisted to the side. As I swiveled to reply, a line of music filled my head; it was neither faithful nor triumphant, but the theme song to the 1950s police program, *Dragnet*. That sound, and the *I Love Lucy* series, molded my childhood.

Once finished I must have been summoned to be somewhere else. Quickly ushered to a taxicab, I had a child's feeling of not really being able to understand or control any events that were in the stature of these adults around me. I didn't even know my destination, only the floor and name of the person I was to immediately contact.

It turned out to be the Time Life building and a film producer that had a flying saucer view from his wall of windows.

He was quick and blunt. He gave the feeling that he had to wear six watches on each wrist. Time, to him, was everything.

"Mrs. Lee, sweeps week is when the networks compete for ratings. As you can imagine these results are extremely important in terms of sponsors and programming. We want to make a TV movie of your story. It's imperative we start now with a script writer, and we are preparing for you a contract."

There are a lot of good things about being poor. Besides learning not to waste anything, one purchases clothing and goods from garage sales. It's

America's floating bazaar, and here I learned the important art of bargaining. I've practiced for years.

"No," I said without breaking eye contact.

"I really don't care about the money, but I do care how the story is portrayed. I'll only sign if I can be a script consultant."

Saying nothing, he stared back at me for a long time. Finally, he agreed if I could go to Los Angeles for the weekend and tell the writer my story. It meant I would have to leave that night, but CBS would pay for it.

I was exhausted by my schedule, but I was free until Monday.

It was first class. Compared to coach, I had double the seat and would soon have double the dinner. I was still feeling a kind of hysteria from the speed of events. I was used to the very slowest lane of living, being home with tiny children.

My seat partner liked jewelry. To accompany his rings, that had stones like planets, he wore a gold band inscribed with his name, *Angelo Vannuchi*.

I thought of something funny and could barely say it without dissolving into laughter.

"You must be in the Mafia, being Italian and flying first class!"

I expected him to laugh, like anyone would on some inter-Oregon flight, but instead he scowled and shot me a look with eyes like gun barrels.

Can stumbling blocks become stepping stones?

I mumbled that even people in the syndicate have a front job and then asked about his profession.

"I install air conditioners," he replied. "And what's your work?"

I didn't mention I had been a pancake house waitress and once sacked coal in a fuel yard. I simply stated that I was doing some consulting for a movie. His whole attitude changed like closed Venetian blinds that now jerked open. He wanted me to get a job for his girlfriend.

In our descent, Los Angeles looked like it had been spilled out of a bottle. It was carbonated with lights.

My hotel was on Rodeo Drive in Beverly Hills. I walked the block in the hopes that my back would stop aching from being curled five hours on an airplane seat. The prices of the window goods were exorbitant, and I imagined the shops being run by tailors who once collected gold for weaving the emperor's new clothes.

On the way to the associate producer's house, I stared at the mansions passing by my cab's window. Each one got a number that represented how many of *my* houses would fit within its walls. We stopped at a *25*, which adjusted to a *40* when I walked inside.

Invited for a meal, I was surprised when my hostess, Elizabeth, took a mink coat from a closet. The scriptwriter followed her in jeans, and Mr. Hough offered me his arm. I thought of another joke, but now knew to keep all my comedy central lines to myself.

What do the very rich make for dinner? (RESERVATIONS)

The menus were packaged in rich leather bindings. Elizabeth Hough's hands were a fire field of diamonds. I bet to myself that future cosmetic surgery could include additional fake fingers grafted to the palm, just to increase the show place for rings.

The meal conversation resembled the flight patterns of birds. Mostly we flew together. There were some updrafts where two or three locked into a subject, and touched wings. Once when Mr. Hough and Sue Grafton were gliding alone over some script details, Elizabeth whispered to me, "Keep writing for us who are so miserable."

I was stunned by the pathos.

Later, Sue confided, in the restaurant bathroom, that Elizabeth had once been the actress Jean Peters and married to Howard Hughes, the richest man in the world.

By morning, I just wanted to go home. I couldn't wait to be finished with the tour. It seemed to me that books were nothing but a diving board to film makers. They leap off that platform, but are unable to fall straight into the water. Instead, a twist of a one and one-half gainer is added to the plot. I didn't want a cannon ball or jack knife.

The back of the hotel door listed prices for a night's lodging that matched the block's shoes and handbags.

As I finished the thirteen cities, I found my frequency of thinking about home increasing until it was my incessant concern. All my interaction with the media felt as if it had as much depth as living in a receiving line. My last entry in my expense account was the taxi ride home from the Portland airport.

I like tying shoes and pouring pancake batter into the pan and letting my children tell me what their breakfast looks like. It's an edible Rorschach and they find smiles, several versions of the sun, and winking eyes on their plate. Matthew likes to pull two pancakes together and make sunglasses. Sometimes, Anna still sees daddy's hat.

I now owned a watch that could work thirty feet under water. On my desk was a brand new appointment book, which had to be retrieved twice from my middle daughter who wanted it for a coloring pad. I was being invited to a number of conferences and had to also note quarterly tax payments and my twice a year checkups at the hospital.

Mary Elisabeth learned to talk. She developed a cassette player tongue; she recorded new words and played stored data. Encouraged by the family, she counted numbers, colors, and the alphabet. At bedtime, she copied Anna's prayer list. Mary Elisabeth asked God to bless the family, naming us one by one.

One night she discovered she had a picture in her mind for every word except *Daddy*. In response, I could only hold her close.

My appointment at the Oregon Health Science Center was in the radiation department. Mary Elisabeth was disappointed with the patient's lounge. She kept repeating that they have no toys, unlike the more familiar family practice clinic.

I thought of the patients as coming to get snakebite treatment. Cancer has fangs and a poison sac. Some had the distinct lines drawn as border guides for the radiation fields.

In a stark evaluation room, one physician began to feel under my arms for swollen lymph nodes.

"Tickle, tickle, tickle," said my daughter from her chair.

"I feel fine," I said, even before he asked. I had already done the blood work and just had the chest X-rays left to complete my exam.

"Well, sometimes my back aches," I confessed. "Mary Elisabeth is a big pork chop to carry around, and I always manage to have extremely heavy suitcases." My agent had filled my arms full with free books.

"It probably is just weight strain," he agreed, but added my spine to the X-ray order.

Phone calls are usually a braid of greetings, news and plans. They have hours for use, and a late call was unusual. I was already in bed, and upon hearing the voice of my doctor, I felt the first chill.

"In dealing with cancer, Laurel, one vocabulary word is *remission*. Another is *relapse*, and there is damage on the cortical border of the fourth lumbar vertebra. It looks suspicious in your X-ray. If we confirm the Reed-Sternberg cells, consistent with Hodgkin's disease, you could be in a Stage IV, bone involvement, and relapse."

"What does this mean?" I stammered.

"We would be looking at another radiation cycle and an aggressive course of MOPP chemotherapy."

After asking me to make an appointment to come back to the hospital, he hung up. It took me a long time to get the telephone receiver back to its cradle.

Like a slap where that incoming hand made its way through eighteen months of health, I felt the sharp, stinging contact of one thought—WHAT ABOUT THE CHILDREN?

I cried, but not too loud, because I didn't want to wake them. Instead, I made the pillow wet. The bed became Gethsemane. There, among the olive trees, Jesus made a cry that I completely understood, "Let this cup pass from me."

I didn't expect a reply, but a counter thought sang back:

"All hard times are a chance to grow closer to ME."

The Disciple Should Willingly "Take the Cup" From the Lord, Giving Thanks For the Privilege of Entering Into the Fellowship of Sacrifice and Suffering.

I advertised for someone to help me with the house. A twenty-one-year-old farm girl applied. Her glasses slid down her nose and she squeezed blemishes on her cheek as she told me about her work experience. She had been fired from a nursing home when an unannounced state inspector found her not wearing a hair net while cutting chicken parts. She said she had been using some of her wages to supplement the diet of the residents. She added that if she were to move in with us, she would also bring her collections.

I asked Becky Dobbs what they were. "Plastic horses whose bridles I made myself. They were once exhibited in my hometown library. I collect games, stuffed animals, posters, and tropical fish." I decided she was a character with character and hired her.

She moved into the basement and spent most of Friday night setting up her fish tanks with Matthew.

The next morning I found two tanks stacked upon each other in the bathroom. The top one held giant goldfish and the bottom one had more exotic species, including two black Congo knives. My dining room had a tank of angelfish. She explained that her real water giants, who at times required live food, were in a five-foot tank in the basement.

Every week, when I paid her, she bought either a game, a stuffed animal, or a living thing. She bought three hermit crabs, kept them in a basin on the fish tank in the bathroom, and fed them peanut butter.

Becky had a habit of buttoning her coat over her large shoulder bag. This meant I never knew whether I would be shopping with someone looking as though she were in the last trimester of pregnancy or with an unfortunate hunchback deformity.

The Alley Cat pet store gave Becky a real buy. She could purchase goldfish in bulk for only a few pennies apiece. She came home with three hundred goldfish. She explained that mostly they would be for feeding her giant Oscars in the basement.

Becky lined cardboard boxes with plastic waterproof garbage bags. My basement had several such random dwelling places for the new fish.

Each child put a mayonnaise jar in their room to watch these cold-blooded creatures use their gills for breathing. There were two bowls in my kitchen and one on the mantle. I encouraged myself that it was living science and that Becky was the children's new friend.

December 1977
Hospital

Hospitals are known for their drama. Upon being admitted, I was brought into the *Bone Marrow Play*—a murder in one act. They drew a curtain around my bed and stabbed me; the results showed no Hodgkin's disease in the bone marrow.

It had been explained to me that the hospital needed a better sample to absolutely confirm the return of my cancer. The door in my spine was so hidden it meant a surgical extraction for a biopsy. I went into the anesthesia blur wondering if it would be thumbs up, or thumbs down in this new arena. What would come out, the lady or the tiger?

December 29
Surgery Day

Once the operation was over, I felt I had been stuffed back into the wrong body. Nothing fit, and it was laced so tight that I had pain everywhere—I was born, I slept, and, upon waking, cried until comforted. The nurses spent the night giving me morphine and changing my catheter bag. I could not turn over. So passed my infancy.

December 30

I was aged beyond the nurses' knowledge. They made me sit up and then pulled me to my feet. I shuffled along, leaning on a supporting bar.

Fever and narcotics make dreams. I dreamt I was bent under the window near my hospital bed, deftly removing loose plaster and old studs. I used the plastic wastepaper basket to hold the debris from the wall. In my fervor, the floor was littered with grit. I used more of the standard bedside containers for my demolition. I filled the bedpan with crumbling timbers. I kicked out the last layer of the hospital wall; I wanted out into the cold night air.

A young resident from Boston finally brought me the results. Doctors have to learn how to be mailmen, in white coats, that deliver bad news.

"It is Hodgkin's," he said. "You know you are the same age I am, and I want to write a book."

He was a man with a future, and I was all past.

It was now a documented relapse after being disease free for eighteen months. He began to explain the chemicals to be used the next day in my treatment therapy. He abbreviated all the drug's names to one word, "MOPP."

I started the poison IV and found the head waters of all nausea. I practiced the fine art of vomiting to where I could perform without making a sound. I spent New Year's Eve feeling that I was carrying the collective hangover of a nation.

1978

Once home, I found that Becky had visited her friends at the retirement home. One lady had given her a blue parakeet, and she put Kiki in a cage on top of our refrigerator. Due to the January cold, Becky would often move the bird inside her sweater. It was disconcerting to guests when her chest would twitch and move about.

I need everything that I can find to laugh about.

Almost every invitation to speak or be part of a conference had to be canceled. The ports of the world slipped away to being as distant as stars. My world shrunk from seven league boots to bedroom slippers. I lived mostly in the horizontal dimension.

I had to have some part-time additional help in the house. Molly was one of the students from the Bible school, and a full-blooded Eskimo from Kotzbue, Alaska. She didn't clean very well, but she was worth it for her interest in the children. She had stories of summer fish camp, where she would separate herself, and yearning to feel like a normal teen, try to find rock 'n' roll on her portable radio. She would dance alone in the woods. One night, from my bed, I heard her teaching the children all the names that her village used for the different kinds of snow.

One afternoon Matthew and Anna came into my bedroom agreeing on an issue of my negligence. Matthew was their spokesman. He had kept his school uniform on as if formal dress was appropriate to match the dignity of their request.

"We own a car now." He was using logic and not passion. "We have never put on a bumper sticker!"

They did not care what it said. Reviewing some of the categories, I outlined politics, religion, humor, and the environment. "It's a short way of saying something one believes."

The children were silent. They had not thought of a cause. Matthew suggested, "GET WELL, MOM"

Anna objected, saying it was the kind of message that went on a card. She wanted to have one printed that would read: "PLEASE MARRY OUR MOTHER; I WANT A DAD"

Bob Ellis/The Oregonian

"That is absolutely too long," I said. We decided to wait until we could all agree.

The course of drugs perpetuated nausea as if I were trapped in some high-speed spinning ride. Yet there was one invitation I had not refused. It was to visit Moscow and Leningrad for only one week, with university teachers and tour schools. It was months away, and probably impossible, but I needed the hope of it, even if it were a mere pinpoint of light.

I hated that I bought a house with stairs. It was such a short time ago, they didn't seem to exist. Now, it took real effort to change floors.

To everyone but the doctor, I minimized how I was feeling. I would wave some, "I'm all right" flag from the tip of my tongue.

I sent a letter to the organizer of the Soviet Union tour. Outlining some of my medical situation, I asked if I could sometimes rest in my hotel instead of participating in every excursion. The reply was my participation now required a physician's permission.

Like an interlocking chain, I could remember the rite of asking permission. From first wanting pets, to sleeping at a friend's house, I had made my pleas. By this time I had years of practicing tone, pose, and logic. Reluctantly, my doctor typed a letter of assent on the hospital letterhead.

No one knew that my real plan was to smuggle Bibles into a country where they are strictly prohibited. It was my idea of a last hurrah. After writing to a Los Angeles organization, I received a carton of slim contraband books printed in Cyrillic Russian. The paper was one degree better than parchment, and the words required magnification, so both testaments were in a slim volume. A letter also accompanied the Bibles, giving directions for distribution. I memorized the summary points:

1. Don't give them to any official church worker. Both priests and pastors are currently appointed by the state.

2. Only give them personally to individuals. If you pass them out in a group of two or more, there's risk of an informer reporting who received one.

It was obvious that I was under suspicion too. There were no names or addresses, but just a parting line to let the Holy Spirit lead me. I wanted instructions like the pulp of spy novels: "Wear a red hat, go at midnight to the Communist Pioneer Monument, and stand by the statue's left foot."

There was a chorus of well meaning people sharing their objections to me taking such a journey. Stopping by or phoning, they had reasons like the quills on a porcupine.

How could I translate Thoreau's idea, "To live deliberately" to every practical point? It can only be sensed.

I didn't hide the books, but layered them between my cold weather garments.

Having to refuel at Shannon International Airport, we were told to discard all periodicals that would make mention of western life.

It was then that worry first rooted the thought, "If I'm caught," led to an assortment of imagined penalties like prison, or an immediate fourteen-hour return flight. Also, there was the concern that the whole group might be punished for my single act.

Once in Moscow, a hybrid group of soldier/policemen entered the plane. Using flashlights, they searched the overhead bins and around the seats. It all felt like a grade B movie sequence until I got inside the terminal. There, by a ten foot painting of Lenin, was my suitcase piled with the other luggage.

On the opposite side of the same large room were lines waiting for inspection. It didn't look like a polite massage of contents, but instead each garment was being removed. Even purses were being emptied out on trays. It was obvious I could never escape detection. Removing the Bibles, I stacked them on the bench beside me.

The oil eyes of Lenin seemed to accuse me of being the great enemy of the atheist state. In junior high, I first heard of Khrushchev promising to bury us. There were old women throughout the terminal bent to the task of sweeping with short handled brooms. I couldn't stand up and just walk away; I pulled every book back into my bag.

Thoroughly nervous, I picked one of the lines that had a mixture of eastern bloc passengers and Americans. I retied my scarf knotting it under my chin to match the local lady janitors. Responding to some barked command, the man at the front removed his shoes for examination. One bottle of pills was also poured out, and then repacked in its vial. I could feel the sweat between my shoulder blades.

About to drown in anxiety, I searched for some idea that would act like water wings and keep my mind afloat. I remembered a quote from a paperback telling of a Berlin checkpoint and a van with religious materials hidden behind its panels.

"You've made blind eyes to see, now make seeing eyes blind."

I kept repeating it like rosary beads that I was trying to click louder than every apprehension. Yet, the smell of mildewed cement walls in an imagined KGB prison cell permeated my petition.

I had been looking around the room, trying to monitor the progress of the other members of our group. I'm sure it looked like furtive glances. We had been told that once through, proceed directly outside and board the red Intourist bus.

At my turn for inspection, I stood with averted eyes, afraid to even wipe away the perspiration from my cheeks. The inspector gabbled at me some short command, and the sound of it was reminiscent of a cough swirled with syllables. I took the clue from her hand motioning me away, and just hoisted my bag and walked over to the outside doors. My escape felt like the ax head thrown into the river, and the miracle was it could float.

Yet, as others joined me, I saw how I contrasted with their brightly colored down jackets. I had on an old fur coat that I found in a trunk left beneath the stairs. It had a slight odor from being locked away, and some of the thread must have rotted. There was an enlarging hole where the sleeve was attached to the shoulder. I didn't look like anybody who could possibly comprehend the Fourth of July.

Our hotel was exclusively for foreigners. With the exception of employees, not one Soviet citizen was allowed inside. There was an enlarged picture of Brezhnev, the current president, with hound dog jowls, standing among children holding flowers. No one was smiling. My room had a black and white TV with one channel that showed nothing but the long-distance labor of a single threshing machine.

The tour was organized to keep us busy and separate from any interaction with USSR citizens. I had borrowed a guidebook that had highlighted where the best French fries could be bought in Moscow. My interest was in the religion chapter that detailed an old seminary that had been converted to a museum. But, among the buildings, was a chapel "still in use today."

It was easy to convince others that a journey to Zagorst was preferable to viewing the Pavilion of Economic Achievement. It was good to see the prevailing of our national paradigm, "majority rules." The guide seemed surprised that we would even want to challenge and change their schedule.

It was a long drive through birchwood forests. Upon arrival, we were given time for toilets and water. We were told that if any of us became separated in the labyrinth of icon exhibits to meet at 3:00 by the bus. This announcement was like a gunshot for my personal race. I scurried, with my pack of books, to find the chapel.

On a back acre, I entered a sanctuary, which was extremely cold and dark. Mostly older women were inside, bundled in coats, with their breath visible at their lips. There were no benches or pews. In the Orthodox faith no one is to sit in the presence of God; one can either kneel or stand. Now bare of decoration, I could see numerous smoke spots on the walls and pillars from a history of candles.

The priest concluded his service by swinging a censor of incense. This was my moment. Avoiding all eye contact, I passed out the Russian Bibles. Everyone behaved exactly the same. It was hidden immediately, thrust into coat or bag, and the recipient hugged me and cried.

It was one of the few moments of my life where I lost all sense of past or future. I was exactly in the cross hairs of the present moment. It was worth all the argument and anxiety.

Laurel has just handed a Bible to a Russian woman

Like when I die, I only wish that I had done more.

I begged off going to another Moscow school. Even though this one featured the study of English, I was weary of the well-rehearsed classes that we had visited. There was always the feeling of memorized lines.

Instead, I slipped away to visit the nation's largest department store.

It was the soda dispenser that fascinated me. It offered three real breakable glasses for a carbonated sweet drink taste. Neither Pepsi nor Coke had gained entrance to the Soviet Union. There was a water ring where the inverted glasses could be "sanitized" between thousands of users.

I knew I was being offered a drink by the tall man who spoke while tapping me on the shoulder. It was his act of charity, as he could see the holes at my shoulder seams. I had been staring at the machine for some time with my ever present scarf knotted under my chin.

As I politely refused, he exclaimed that he could speak a little English. Saying his name was Victor, he was obviously excited to meet a real American, loose from a tour chain gang. I was just as happy. We both had questions.

Seeing me stumble, he threaded my hand over his arm. My first autobiographical data, after answering "Laurel," was not going to offer the explanation that chemotherapy had done some damage to my feet. Let him just think I'm clumsy.

Weaving me around long snaking lines of customers waiting to make purchases, he told me he was an officer in the Red army, as an engineer whose specialty was designing bridges.

"I've been to Cuba many times," he disclosed while smiling right into my eyes. His parents, both university professors, were probably getting concerned that their oldest son, age 33, was still unmarried.

There was an elixir to our meeting. With each exchange, I felt an increased intoxication. It was a magnetism from a whole constellation of impossible poles. Moscow and Portland are not exactly sister cities.

"What do potatoes cost?" he asked. "What about civil rights?"

His questions tumbled out like a crowding of acrobats; one was always standing upon the shoulders of another.

I had to slow his pace. I was completely out of breath. Maybe, I'll never again be able to walk fast.

After asking where I was staying, Victor began guiding me in the direction of my hotel. He apologized that his afternoon was not free, but invited me to dinner.

"I'd like to take you to my officer's club that is close to the Kremlin."

That was a part of his life and was the equivalent of me inviting him to a church potluck.

I felt bad that he had to wait outside where it was now snowing. The ban on citizens entering the hotel was strictly enforced. Each floor even had a monitor at a desk that held all the resident's keys.

Victor was surprised at my apology.

"But, you are exactly on time," he protested.

"It's just that you had to wait where it's cold," I said.

"We know how to wait," seemed like a rather grim reply.

Besides the waiters and my host, all the men were in uniform. Above their pockets were rectangles colored with medals.

Out of our window was a large red star mounted above a wall. In its light, I

could see how heavy the snow was now falling. Anywhere else in the world, the scene would have looked like a Christmas picture.

My parents are capitalists," I said.

Victor leaned forward. He had a fork full of liver pate.

I told him how I decided against graduate school because I wanted to homestead in Alaska. I married Richard because he was the only man I met when I was twenty that agreed to such an adventure.

I explained how I had doubted if there even was a God: "I agreed with your Lenin that it was an opiate for the masses, a buffer against the fear of death. Then, I read some of the New Testament. I started the paragraphs thinking it was interesting and became convinced it was true." With that said, I pulled out of my purse my last Bible. He can read English.

"Here's the part," I said, while showing the pages.

"Look, all the words are in red."

He put it in his brief case, and promised to read "this most subversive book." There's always the curiosity for what is not allowed.

We rode the subways, talking through most of the night. Now and then, I would exclaim over a particularly beautiful station.

Victor explained that in Communist philosophy the public places were designed to be the palaces for the people. If only I could stay one more night, he wanted to take me to the opera house to see a ballet.

In the morning transfer to the train station, many in my group expressed sincere concern that I looked so weak. They just had no idea that I saw every subway stop in Moscow, and several times for some in the hub. Even guilt for my deception takes energy. I was just too tired and slept most of the way to Leningrad. One more stop, and I will get to go home.

Portland

Mary Elisabeth was sitting on my lap. In the church pew in front of me, a man was helping his wife take off her coat. Such small acts of kindness remind me, with sometimes painful intensity, of my own singleness.

Time quenches some of the fiery darts, but not all.

I need the salve of a communion service. Hymn books have been replaced by large lit screens and projected words. They are playing one of David's psalms, *Create in me a clean heart, and renew a right spirit within me.*

There's a quiet hush as the thimbles of grape juice, replacing wine, are being passed down the rows. There's the necessity of personal inventory.

Taking the tray, I take my portion and pass it quickly to my left. Mary Elisabeth first snorts and then shouts, "I want dip and chips too!" She is now three years old and back from visiting my parents. I hope that I'm really well, and never have to have chemotherapy again.

SPRING 1980

Portland

It's funny how phone calls can radically alter the course of my thoughts. Several times now, Jeremy Foster has called from Los Angeles. Now, he wants to come and see us. He is Mr. Sweet Voice and talks without conveying that he has any other life but our paragraphs. Yet, he owns an independent film company and has a religious movie in theaters right now. I took my children to see it, and watched the credits just to see his company name spiral down the screen.

I remember how I met him two years ago at the national Christian Bookseller's Conference. Wandering the aisles, I was in shock at the variety of goods displayed by religious publishers. There were crazy things like a giant coffee table book of what the twelve disciples might have looked like. Jeremy, with a ready laugh, had agreed with me. Who wants 8 X 10 colored pictures of guys holding fishing nets?

He said he had read the *People* magazine article and would like to stop off in Portland on his way to Seattle for business.

May 23, 1980

Everyone wanted to come to the airport and meet Jeremy's flight. We were running so late, I wished for a clock with an elastic sweep hand in order to stretch our time.

First, we were hemmed in by slow city busses. Red lights caught us in their net at intersections. Pedestrians stopped to tie their shoes at crosswalks in front of our automobile.

Thomas Victor

Consulting my watch in the short-term parking lot, I could suspect every lowering jet with landing gear in place to be his.

"We must run!" was my cry to the children.

Having exhorted them for years, in a like voice, not to run, they galloped forward. My sentence must have cut out all their programmed restraints as they began to whoop and laugh entering the terminal. Trying to keep up with them, I could feel my bangs turn from a well-brushed wall into damp spikes of hair on my forehead.

I didn't see Jeremy standing by his suitcase watching our approach. Once upon him, I was startled and came to an abrupt halt. He steadied my arm with his hand. I had to struggle to get my breath. The children, also, could only inhale and exhale deeply at their introduction.

Standing at his side, I thought again that Jeremy Foster is a large man. His height would defy all the imaginable extensions ever created in a woman's heel.

Storing his leather bag in the car, I felt slightly ill at ease. None of the men I know wear gold chains around their necks. Maybe none of the women he knows wears an embroidered dress from a southern Mexican market.

Jeremy wanted to know about the volcano, which had erupted five days earlier. He knew the statistics, having watched night and morning news about the big eruption. The mountain was reduced to a flat-top, having lost 1,300 feet of peak with an explosion five hundred times the force of the atomic bomb at Hiroshima.

"Mount St. Helens is only fifty miles away from Portland. When it finally exploded I took the children to a viewing point, and watched a sky filled with boiling cauliflower heads of ash and steam."

It's never easy for me to drive and talk. I began to cut through company parking lots instead of using main streets. Matthew put his head over the front seat and interjected a command for me to stop.

"Bottles," he cried.

I braked sharply as he opened his door and ran to the bushes. He had spotted two empty soda six-packs.

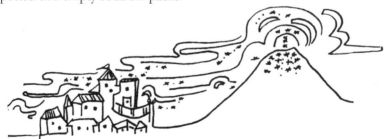

I explained to Jeremy that the state bottle law requires merchants to pay a nickel for every can and glass container that is returned.

"Matthew just turned ten two weeks ago, and this is his new enterprise. He even takes a wagon to work our neighborhood park."

Matthew interrupted with specific detail:

"I go through the trash cans."

His sentence created an image of an arm risking the perils of old hot dog crusts, and blobs of unused catsup.

I went on to add that we don't have a grocery store in walking distance, so this car is the final transport to a market.

Jeremy seemed amused. I remember he has three children that are already young adults.

"Once Matthew and Anna loaded forty stout malt liquor cans in my car and forgot to tell me. I found them only after opening the hatchback for a pastor and his secretary, having just promised them a devotional book. There, in front of the church office, their pupils seemed to dilate in surprise. I quickly protested that they were not mine, but belonged to my children."

Once in our house the children wanted to occupy the same eight square feet we shared on the rug. Matthew abstractedly stroked the hair on Jeremy's forearm.

Studying Jeremy's face, I could tell he was pleased. When the children went outside, he first referred to Matthew by saying, "He likes me." I said nothing, knowing that each one of them loved every man who came to our house.

He chose the next moment to say he had brought me something from Los Angeles, and pulled a rectangular box from his jacket pocket. He gave me no time to ponder the idea of a gift itself before he lifted the lid. On a uniform wedge of cotton was a gold bracelet.

I never have had jewelry. My Timex watch was a single band of practicality. It was as if I had completely forgotten that hands could be decorated. I turned my wrist watching the gold mesh slide until any slack was filled by my arm. It seemed like a serious moment; he had just performed an absolute act of courtship.

We rose so I could take Jeremy to his city center hotel. Just before dropping him at the door, we set a morning meeting time. As I took the Hawthorne Bridge back, I tried to sort my curious mixture of emotions. It all felt so fast from meeting each other, to lots of telephone time, to a visit and gift. I felt drawn and scared at the same time.

May 24

It was dark when I woke up. By my watch, I could see it should be lighter. A gray dust blew across the porch and filled the flower beds. A chemical haze covered my windshield. The wipers and small jets of window-washing solvent caused it to darken and streak. With such visibility, I felt like I was driving with Venetian blinds. There was little traffic on the route to downtown Portland.

Jeremy was waiting outside under the hotel's green and white striped awning. He was wearing a raincoat. The general public only has clothes for when the sky drops snow or water—it was the first time we saw the horizon filled with uniform spots of ash.

Once home, I fished out a small portable TV from the back of my closet. Standing in front of a mini volcano, the anchorman announced the fact of another eruption. The result was an ash plume, composed of pulverized rock, blanketing Portland. The airport was closed. The announcement added that all city residents should stay inside, and if automobile use was necessary, vehicles were not to exceed twenty miles an hour.

Bob Ellis/The Oregonian

Matthew wondered why it couldn't happen on a weekday; he already had Saturday off from school.

Anna said, "Now, we can't go and see our friends."

Health warnings were verbally given and simultaneously went across the screen in a typed yellow band: "Inhalation is not recommended for anyone with less than full lung capacity."

The screen filled with enlarged particles of ash. Twenty percent of its composition was ground glass.

The telephone rang and it was my friend, Arlene. She said she was going to honor the day by rinsing her hair with a new box of prepared coloring, *smoky ash brown*.

Matthew, with his sisters, now had new plans. They wanted to go outside and get some volcanic fallout so they could do certain experiments. I agreed if Matthew, alone, covered his mouth with a scarf, and held his breath while collecting a small sample.

While asking Jeremy to tell me about his own family, I could see Matthew at the periphery of vision spooning gray powder into bowls.

Jeremy didn't dig into his wallet for a photo section. Instead, he told the tragedy of his youngest son who died playing with a hunting gun while visiting relatives. The year before, the mother had deserted the family, preferring her own apartment. "I tried reconciliations for years, but she finally filed for divorce."

He didn't talk as someone still in pain. There was no change in voice tone or a kind of quick look that asks me to reply with a sentence from a sympathy card.

"How long ago?" I asked.

"One year," Jeremy replied.

"That's all," I said, surprised.

It had been my strong feeling to avoid any possible romantic relationship with a recently divorced man. So much of what they did was often a reaction to the phenomenon of being single again.

"Laurel," Jeremy said, while briefly touching my arm. "There were five years of complete separation before that."

Standing up to go and prepare some refreshments, I saw that the children had been bringing out containers of household condiments. Anna was holding an open peanut butter jar while Matthew was spooning some jelly into a saucer. There were several bowls around them already stiff with concoctions of grit.

As the afternoon faded into evening, the children became increasingly restless. They began to walk around Jeremy, eyeing him as a potential jungle gym. Mary Elisabeth showed the least restraint. She lay on the floor, raised her hands and feet, and asked, "Do you know how to give a swing ride?"

"That I do," he replied.

Anna wanted to ride in circles suspended by her hand and ankle.

After Jeremy called a taxi to take him back to the hotel, he held both of my hands while thanking me again for the day.

Climbing upstairs, I thought of my heart as a complex labyrinth, but not one without a passage to its center. While a gift of jewelry was genuinely appreciated, and stories of career exploits interesting, neither was the avenue of access. A man had to care about his family as something to be tended.

After brushing my teeth, I picked up an assortment of dirty clothes left in a pile by the tub. Leaving the bathroom light on, I turned off the one in the hall.

I considered that my past dating experiences resembled the Greek drama masks of tragedy and comedy. All the leading men had always seen my house as full of extras.

May 25

The rain of glass-like silica had stopped during the night. The same public vehicles that rescued the main streets from snow would now be collecting ash. The radio news predicted that the airport would be open by midmorning. Jeremy would now be free to catch his flight

As I drove down to city center, I could feel that I was in the grips of a bad attitude. It was my own need I was resenting. It propels me to sit by a suitor and listen to a language of colored tissue paper. Fragile and transparent, courtship words are easily folded into fans and flower petals. Having known rejection, I don't want to be led forward only to suffer it again.

I wanted to try and explain it to Jeremy as he seated himself in the hotel dining room. He removed the lid from the coffee pot and regarded me through the steam that rose between us.

I condensed for him one long and one short significant relationship—my marriage and the physician in my church. "I let myself follow their sugar trail and both times fell off a cliff." My husband found a girl friend, and the doctor knew too well the grim cancer statistics for a Stage IV patient.

"When they went through the exit door it swung back and hit me in the face."

"You must have been devastated, Laurel."

Jeremy dropped his hand, touching the edge of his mustache on its descent to his lap. "Obviously Laurel, I'm finding myself caring deeply for you, but I'm learning in life to be patient with all that is unsolved in my heart."

He continued saying he was learning to love the questions themselves. He called "questions" those locked rooms or books in foreign print that we are not ready to know, because we cannot live them now.

"Laurel, let's embrace the questions. Then gradually, without noticing it, we'll live along some distant day into the answers."

Jeremy pulled the airline envelope out of his pocket and read to himself the time of the departing flight. While he hailed the waiter and played solitaire with his credit cards, I thought I matched his analysis. On the right hand, I'm completely charmed by him in an ever warming affection, and on the left have questions. I thought of the *caring* as sheep, and the questions as a flock of *goats*. They were freely roaming over all the indentations of my mind.

As we drove to the airport, we noticed that most pedestrians and all employees whose jobs required outside exposure were wearing face masks; I saw one salesman at a corner selling white industrial nose and mouth covers for a dollar. A small elastic band secured them tightly in place. My ride through the streets reminded me of grim future photographs. The captions would read, "Toxic Air Pollution," or "Germ Warfare."

A small circle of land planted in a ring of rhododendrons is a hub to four directions. A life-size Joan of Arc sat on her metal steed at its center. Someone had tied a face mask across the damsel's cast iron mouth and another on her horse.

Our wait in the flight lounge was mostly mute. He asked me to write him from England, gave me a quick hug and was gone. At the last possible moment for visual contact, Jeremy turned to wave. The silver in his hair seemed luminous in the dark passage.

Out in the parking lot, I sat at the steering wheel with the ignition key in my hand. I watched the enormous tons of aircraft lift and land. I saw cars creep along the parking aisles looking for a stall.

I sat there wanting to redesign nature. I just wanted one more handful of mercy to alter humanity. I thought that only those with a cupboard of food should feel hungry, not anyone with a swollen abdomen and an empty bowl. I thought loneliness should be the portion of well-matched couples when one is waiting at the corner for the other.

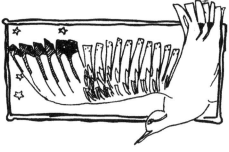

Starting my car, I could answer my own thoughts. I can't push earth closer to an orbit of heaven. *Yet there is a comfort promised to those that mourn. It is the doxology for any who suffer.*

May 26

I pulled the ancient and modern suitcases up from the basement. Carrying them upstairs in two loads, one in each hand, I thought how Jeremy's visit had marked our last family weekend together.

Mary Elisabeth took the blue tin case from me. I could hear her knocking it through the portals of her closet. She will fill it with select toys to take to her grandparent's house, and I'll intervene with sensible slacks and underwear. While pulling Anna's case by her chest of drawers I could feel the old internal bruise caused by the rubbing of two lifestyles. The problem was my belief in the old order. Mothers should be available for every childhood bad dream, wearing aprons with whole-wheat cookies in their pockets. Yet, with some pleasure, I had committed myself to a full schedule in England for the British release of my second diary. I didn't even have the excuse of going to earn our support. I had been careful with our bursts of income, securing it into interest-yielding certificates. I know the adage of making the time I do have with them a quality experience. All the working mothers I know could inflate beach balls with that sentence, and toss it around. But, I do always try to take one child with me, and these next weeks will be Matthew's turn; later this summer the girls will come, while their brother stays with my parents.

I went into Matthew's room to inventory his piles of shirts and underwear for his backpack. Along the top of his dresser was a lopsided row of plastic sandwich bags filled with volcanic ash. Even as I lifted one, a mist of powder was deposited on the veneer.

"We are not taking this with us."

Matthew explained, in a louder voice than what was necessary, that he had plans for it. He thought to sell it in England. He wanted to stand on a street corner and hawk it. He even prepared a slogan: "One British pound for a Mount St. Helen's ounce.

I refused to argue. Seeing my "It is final" look, he shrugged, and took the ash outside.

Once on the plane, Matthew buckled his seat belt and bent over to stow his knapsack. Unzipping a side pocket, he pulled out a portable yellow plastic fan that I didn't even know he owned. Activating the battery's energy, he blew his hair up from his ears, then opened his mouth to cool his tongue. I regarded his

Bob Ellis/The Oregonian

gear with fresh suspicion, but it was too late for the issue of a new audit. I would have to check the contents in London.

There were a lot of things Matthew wanted to know. To him questions were like small, empty cups. A little answer filled a cup quickly, and he would begin to set up others.

After a series of queries about our journey, I explained that once we get back home, we'll have one long weekend in Minnesota, as I'll be speaking at a library meeting. Matthew was unusually silent and then asked me to tell him about the time he was born. Even his voice had a slight hush; it was his own genesis.

Looking away for a moment, I wished over the unending cloud cover that the truth was something stable and ordinary.

"Your father and I waited for you. We were excited to have a child.

"We had been given a ride to Berkeley when I was six months pregnant, leaving a house in rural Washington where we had been caretakers. I had not even seen a doctor. I remember how we had less than twenty dollars, no car or job. We lived in a red pup tent at the back of a friend's lot.

"I was so big your father had to push me up hills, and I would arch over my stomach, swinging my arms in imitation of an elephant."

As Matthew laughed, I remembered how Richard got employment just six weeks before the delivery. We became managers of a decrepit house that rented single rooms, with community bathrooms and one kitchen facility. Our facility was so tiny that we had to share a twin bed, and that seemed luxurious after sleeping on the ground.

"Your first bed was a wooden box that your father had built and hung by ropes from the ceiling."

Matthew seemed satisfied with my narration, then he asked, "Will I ever see Jeremy again?"

My pause was so lengthy, the child asked me again. I simply stated the truth that I really didn't know. "He has lots of summer appointments," I explained. "Maybe your sisters will see Mr. Foster when I take them to Los Angeles later this summer.

Matthew's only reply was "Lucky."

June 1980
London

When possible, I never check luggage, but cram my canvas bag under the seat. We didn't have to lose time by waiting on the airport conveyer belts. Being so portable, we were first through customs and out into the pedestrian mall. I explained to Matthew that someone from our British publisher would be meeting us.

Towering above the crowd was a man holding a sign inscribed with our names. Edwin Quimby escorted us to his car apologizing that his really posh vehicle was in the shop. "Oh crumbs," he said. "Let's just stow these bags in my boot."

While Matthew, looking bewildered, checked our host's footwear, I whispered, "trunk."

Our arrangements were to stay with a family in a suburb so we could see a local festival; Edwin explained this, while declaring various drivers to be "dumb, dumbs."

Once on Rochester's High Street I woke up Matthew to see a man strolling in a velvet Prince Albert tailcoat accompanied by a woman in a billowing purple gown. The whole avenue was filled with people in nineteenth century period clothing. A boy ran by the car in pursuit of an iron hoop held in locomotion by a stick. Seeing his bare feet, short pants and the square collar of his sailor middy, Matthew declared it was all "weird."

"Oh, my giddy aunt," crowed Edwin, "It's Dickens Days. Since Charles Dickens lived in Rochester during his childhood and later years, the whole town celebrates its historic resident in an annual three-day program."

I agreed to join Edwin Quimby that night for a musical in Chatham, at the town hall.

Once alone in our room, Matthew took delight that we were living eight hours ahead of his sisters. Settling into bed, he wanted to chew the wad of our time change. He felt we had pierced into the future. As he fell asleep, he muttered that we could know all major news events first.

Edwin came to the door wearing a top hat. It made him look like a historical tower that had been turned by some enchantment into a man.

Over his arm was a red satin frock. Bulging from the skirt's folds was a muslin half slip. It had two seams constructed to hold circular hoops at mid-length and around the hem. Passing me the bundle, Edwin explained that he had borrowed them from a friend who works in the costume department at a theater in Kent.

After buttoning the back of my gown, I felt like the kind of gaudy lamp that is won at carnivals by tossing a quarter onto a plate. In the car, Edwin handed me a bonnet from the back seat. The hat was a vehicle to support a mass of red feathers, which quivered as if charged by an electric current. Edwin addressed my self-consciousness by restating that everyone in Rochester has some kind of costume.

The music hall was at the very edge of town where narrow streets beckoned to my every cell curious about old architecture. Having arrived a whole hour before the performance, I excused myself from my host who was engaged talking to friends.

Turning corners I exclaimed at quarry stone foundations and a clock built into an arch. My thoughts began to take the voice of one engaged in conversation. I explained things to a phantom Jeremy as if he were floating by my side with a listening ear. I wondered if my desire for a relationship had been accentuated by my illness. Sometimes I felt a compulsion to absorb a lifetime into a single hour.

"Jeremy Foster," I thought, "there is in me a haste to know everything by noon, as I wonder if I'll live to see the evening." Stopping by a large open gate with gargoyles on the top, I concluded that I had become a *time junkie*. I absolutely crave more years.

Entering the old churchyard, I began to read the multitudes of inscriptions carved in stone. Besides the ancient dates and old poems etched in moss was a freshly dug mound. The largest floral wreath was designed to look like a dart board created with tightly packed blooms. Propped against the mums was a card that read: "From the boys at the Scarlet Bear Pub."

I didn't see the small crowd that had gathered behind me. As their number grew, the sound of them made me turn. None were in costumes. My recognition of their presence set them free to laugh and call out at the Victorian apparition in the town graveyard

Instantly I remembered that the night's music program was in Chatham's public hall, not Rochester. I wondered how far I was from the town where people were supposed to be wearing Dickensian dress. I didn't want to explain anything to the spectators because one spoken word would identify me as a dumb American. It became an issue of national pride to keep quiet.

A full hoopskirt is not designed for speed. Its length and the tension of its expanded circumference kept me from bounding back to the sanctuary of the town hall. As some of the crowd followed me, I sought comfort in philosophy. I thought about Thoreau's statement on fashion:

We all stand like shipwrecked sailors on a beach and laugh at the old fashions, while religiously following the new ...

July 21

I was so excited in our taxi ride to the Chelsea district of London. We had been invited to have lunch with P.L. Travers, author of all the *Mary Poppins* books. They had been the favorite novels of my childhood, which is much more memorable than a favorite food or favorite color. I refused to see the movie; I didn't want anything to be superseded over my own personal pictures made from paragraphs. The Mary Poppins in my head was neither sweet nor pretty.

Matthew was not at all excited—if anything, he was irritable. Before we left Oregon, I had made him read every one of the books, and he didn't like them.

My agent told me a story that the city of New York had contacted P.L. Travers with a proposal of putting a statue in Central Park and needed her permission to erect the life-sized figure. She had agreed until she found out it wasn't to be her likeness but her famous protagonist instead. She retracted the agreement.

The houses out the window were brick and pushed together, sharing common outside walls. As the taxi slowed to check addresses, I could guess which one it was going to be. Only one on the left side had a bright pink door.

As we climbed the stairs, Matthew began to declare that he actually hated the books. "They are stupid and written for girls!"

I don't believe in threatening violence, but I pointed to a sticker bush and promised to push him in it, once we leave the house, if he breathes anything like that at the author.

A housekeeper let us in to a narrow hall and stated that Mrs. Travers would be right down. Behind her was an enormous wooden rocking horse with flaring nostrils. We waited in the living room. Above the fireplace were colorful letters written to her from children. Matthew muttered he was worried about my manners, as I wanted to see everything up close, even in touching distance.

Mrs. Travers bustled into the room and explained that there were two menus for lunch, as her physician had put her on a very special diet. We followed her through double glass doors to a large table set for three. The portions had already been distributed. Every place setting had a green salad and a baked potato, but at that the resemblance ended. While Mrs. Travers had lamb chops and steamed vegetables, we had a single slice from a grocery store's frozen pizza.

Just as we began our meal, a side door slowly squeaked open. Our hostess put down her fork and turned to stare at it. I began to spring to my feet in order to shut it for her. She rebuked me saying, "Never do that! Whenever a door squeaks open on its own, someone you cannot see has just entered the room."

I somehow felt I had been translated into my own chapter, and this un-usual woman was our new governess. I want to float to the ceiling; I'm ready to drink soda pop out of the kitchen tap. But Matthew's expression was a look identical to a bank employee that doesn't have time for nonsense.

I also noticed that my son was beginning to pile lettuce leaves on the table. He chose the side of the bowl that was the maximum dis-tance from our hostess. I scooped them onto my plate. Turning them with my fork revealed several veins of English mud still within the dark green folds. By the end of the meal, it appeared that everyone had cleaned their plate, but me.

P.L. Travers patted him on the head and pronounced him a "good boy."

As we prepared to leave, she wanted to get Matthew a present. He bright-ened until she returned with her arms full of leaves. Handing it to Matthew, she exclaimed it was rosemary from her own garden.

Once outside, my son suggested that next time we visit someone famous, let's stop by for Colonel Sanders or maybe Betty Crocker.

"I bet you've read her boxes all your life!"

My recurring impulse had been to translate Britain into letters for Jeremy Foster. I had wanted to breathe the old bookstores and the view from the top of double-decker buses into print. But, I only sent simple post cards, as I felt our communication should equal our commitment. I had even hoped for a certain extinction of my feelings for him in the weeks that separated us from even a phone call. Yet, the thought of him persisted.

June 26
Portland

In the drive to our house from the airport, my senses could rest in remembering and predicting the familiar configurations of stores and homes. It was soothing to drive by my church on Glisan St. and my neighborhood grocery shop. The products for sale were spelled out in black magnetic letters and hoisted to a billboard over the parking lot. I sang to myself, "Tomato sauce is seven cans for a dollar." I wished that I had not committed myself to go to Minnesota; I was ready for home. A neighborhood dog at the curb was all the committee of welcome Matthew needed.

The deposit of dust was to a degree that messages could be scribbled on furniture. It seemed to be in excess of what was usual, and I wondered if I could suspect the volcano. It was Matthew who went right to a phone and dialed a friend. From upstairs he yelled down to me that he was invited for their family camping trip and please, please, could he go. Picking up the extension, I talked with Mrs. Urbanski, and consented. Matthew loves swimming, and they were going to a lake. I wanted him to have a week on the planet of his choice.

I approached the mail that had been stacked at my desk as if it were a deck of cards. Four letters with a Los Angeles postmark were from Jeremy. I sorted

Bob Sisson

them in my hand by the dates wondering if they were going to be hearts or clubs. Every envelope had the word, "Personal" underlined above my address.

I found the contents to be disappointing. There was no hint of dreams or sunrises. Instead, he thanked me for the hospitality. It was sincere, but the formality reminded me of an era that prescribed leaving one's calling card on a hall table. He wrote of office projects, certain goals and ideals. Each letter was signed, "Your loving friend." The fact he had written four times seemed more significant than the contents.

I decided to telephone Jeremy's office. The secretary sang the company name and the fact that Mr. Foster was not available. She added that he was in Minneapolis on business, and gave me his out-of-town phone number.

June 27
Minnesota

I didn't wait long to call Jeremy. As soon as the morning hour reached the breakfast zone, I phoned his hotel.

Letters have certain inherent controls, as there is time to choose a vocabulary that reflects restraint. Telephone conversations are spontaneous; Jeremy suggested he could meet me in the hotel lobby. He added he had picked up a few things that he had wanted to give me. I knew that probably meant books.

I still had the bag of European candy bars that were bought in a London dime store. Impulsively, I decided to give him the whole sack. On my way to the elevator, I saw that some of the wrappers had discolored in a way that suggested the bars had been melting and solidifying regularly.

Once we were together, the length of the separation seemed to fall down a hole and was sealed over in the power of friendship. His first line seemed to match my last sentence spoken weeks ago. Jeremy wanted to see what I had brought him. We were sitting in a kind of central garden that the hotel was designed around. The artificial landscape could be viewed from the balcony of every single room.

He thanked me for the chocolates, but I noticed he stacked them without reading the variety of labels.

Jeremy opened his brief case saying, "I thought of you when I saw these things," He pulled out five small containers embossed with the label of a Los Angeles antique store. Raising one of the three perfectly square boxes, he revealed a delicate gold pin. Its face was etched in the kind of scrollwork that monks used in decorating ancient manuscripts. Next, he lifted out a bracelet of pearls connected by a single gold chain. Another bracelet followed that was sterling silver on one side and gold plate on the other.

I was wondering how jewelry could remind him of me. I always thought I was best associated with camping equipment.

Jeremy said that the last two boxes were very old rings. The first one held a single green stone. The last box was introduced as his favorite, six rubies arranged around a single diamond. Both of them must have belonged to women with large fingers as I could shake them off my hand.

Feeling the heat in my cheeks, I knew my face was flushing. It all seemed too rich and excessive. Seeing my offering of candy, my emotion turned towards embarrassment. The Cadbury's fruit and nut bar was on the top.

"Much of my family," continued Jeremy, "live four hours from here, due north."

Before parting, I agreed to make the drive with him in one day by leaving before dawn. We could return in time for my Portland flight, which had been organized to connect with my daughters.

After speaking to the library association, I was finally alone. Taking the jewelry out of all the boxes, I laid the pieces across the surface of the hotel room table. It cannot work, I thought. Our cultures are just too different for any relationship more than friends. The two of us represent a kind of multiplication table of opposites:

My state park campsites equaled in number his king-sized bed hotel suites.

It was one old station wagon against one shiny Mercedes-Benz. For every flannel shirt I wore, he had twenty with designer labels.

The pillows on the bed were stuffed with feathers, instead of the standard particles of foam. With my fist, I could beat out a hollow for my face. My words were muffled in such a close range of bedding. "You, Jeremy, need some other woman than me. She should have fat fingers to wear all your rings," and I cried, "Goodbye."

June 28

I never knew that Jeremy could sing. He lifted up verse after whimsical verse about a group of Irish musicians. His voice boomed between the windshield and back window. If our hours in the car were a tablecloth, he spread it with light dishes of childhood stories and music. After my cares of last night, I felt it wasn't the right time to spill things and make dark blotches.

The apartment his mother lived in was a part of eight connecting ground-floor units. It looked like a small rural motel surrounded by long solitary fields.

Mae Foster walked out to the car. She didn't waste any minutes on the formality of waiting for company to knock. The upturned corners of his mother's face held a number of connecting indentations, which supported ample cheeks. Mrs. Foster brought us through the door intending to escort us to a chrome and Formica table set for lunch.

I didn't want to go past the baskets of quilt scraps. Treasures of stitched colored cottons were tucked in the few feet between the couch and her kitchen. Mae talked old sewing lore. Tapping her head, she said, "It was those who were not quite right that were first given crazy quilts to make. That pattern of irregular scraps sewed together was for the woman who couldn't be trusted with scissors."

The chief decoration on the walls and along any furniture surface were family photographs. Years could be traced from the black and white shots of fedoras to the slick colors of the great-grandchildren's school pictures. The boy, resident within Jeremy, began to spoon through his mother's bowl of homemade noodles looking for those that had clumped together while cooking in the steaming broth.

Once sealed back into the quiet of the car, I turned to Jeremy and exclaimed that he had never told me he was reared in a pioneer farming family of Norwegian immigrants.

"At one time, Laurel, we lived in a house constructed of roughly hewn logs, and I can remember feeling lucky when we got orange crates to put our clothes in."

Out the window, I saw acres of corn. The speed of our vehicle made the cultivated rows have the moving perspective of wagon spokes. The air smelled as if it were filtered through the fields.

"Jeremy, I left the suburbs for college knowing that I didn't want to spend my life acquiring ever enlarging houses, to fill with even more things. I hated the practice of evaluating people by what they owned. I wanted ideas, and I was excited to go to a university where there were real Nobel Prize winners on the faculty. I was disappointed to find it the same, only now the currency was degrees, honors and publications.

"That's when I decided to drop out and homestead. I married a man that wanted to go with me to Alaska.

"I see many of those same values in your mother, which helps dissolve some of my fears I've had about our relationship. Frankly, Jeremy, you are just *down-home folks*, even wearing those designer initialed socks." I pointed at the floorboards. "And owning your Dyco oil stocks."

Jeremy laughed, and turned his face from the road to lock his gaze momentarily with mine. "Well, so are you, even with that *People* magazine profile."

I had been very embarrassed because the story featured all the money I had made, including a record high paperback sale, the TV movie, magazine rights, and foreign translations. My agent had supplied all the numbers.

"Look, Laurel, these are my priorities. God—first, family—second, and work—last."

It was what I needed; I felt a freedom to wear one of those new bracelets around my arm.

July 2
Portland

I didn't want to wait for Jeremy to call. Having just had my July medical check up, I feel the necessity to be very direct and not charmed into some pleasant conversational galaxy. Having never been sick, Jeremy can't really understand the flash floods of some diseases. The telephone is today's instant letter.

I automatically dial his office line. With no family in California, it seems he is always there. His desk must be like the command center of a space ship. Making and distributing family films means he knows all the time zones of the planet.

I quoted Dr. Moss's warning today that my whole skeletal structure was prematurely aged and damaged from the aggressive treatments. Remissions can be brief.

"Jeremy, I have spent time with the families of many cancer patients. Often, I find a defense against reality is in their denial of the disease."

His only response was cheer and confidence that I will continue to be well.

July 11
Los Angeles

Once we landed at Los Angeles International, my eyes scanned the terminal windows in my eagerness to see Jeremy. The flight attendant interrupted my intense sweeping gaze. She had a pencil and wanted to make a notation of Mary Elisabeth's seat number. She explained that the maintenance crew would replace the bottom cushion with a dry one before the flight continued to Phoenix. My daughter spilled her drink, got another one and spilled that too.

Jeremy's face had tanned since I had last seen him in Minnesota. After hugging Anna, he picked up Mary Elisabeth, then stiffened and set her down quickly. Her wet dress made a number of dark splotches on his blue cotton shirt.

At the car door, Anna spilled some of her red stirring sticks onto the asphalt. She had gleaned them along with bags of peanuts. While watching her and her sister climb into the back seat of the Mercedes, my pervading concern was that neither girl would get carsick.

Jeremy mentioned Mount St. Helens. He shared that the evening news had carried a bulletin about the fresh build-up of a pressure layer that would release another volume of ash and steam into the atmosphere.

I told how our local grocery store printed "Volcano Alert" onto their paper sacks. Stamped in red was a list of safety precautions, which included the necessity of food storage for the days of being shut inside by an eruption.

"Stores are now stocking souvenir ashtrays, constructed with a layer of volcano dust encased in glass. Matthew wanted a pen with a chamber that shakes the ash into fresh turbulence as one writes."

We pulled up the circular driveway to the hotel where I had reservations from the woman's fellowship that had scheduled us to come south. The children saw the room as only a passage to the swimming pool. Alone for a few minutes, I tried not to rush while changing my blouse for one with shorter sleeves. Wanting to calm myself, I slowly pushed the buttons through the fabric openings and straightened it in the mirror. It was my white shirt that I had spent a winter embroidering with birds on vines. One wing took days to color with thread. My feelings seemed too high. It was as if ecstasy was on a trapeze. I couldn't bring it down, but I could somewhat calm the wild swinging within me.

Jeremy was waiting out at the pool in the central plaza. The heat had baked together chlorine vapors and perfumed tanning oils. Most of the patio inhabitants had the pose and look of deck chair apathy. I pulled over a Mexican tooled-leather seat by Jeremy. There was no hurry for speech, just a certain camaraderie of sitting together on a hot afternoon. His chair was in the sun while I had utilized the shade of the eucalyptus tree. Jeremy began to speak of loneliness as an emotion of isolation, as if it were a separate ball in space.

"I've always had my work." With almost a drawl, Jeremy seemed to suggest that one's labors can keep it in orbit and at a distance.

"But now, the depth of our almost daily dialogues just exposes the pain of not sharing things together to a greater degree." His statements required no response from me. To talk, even in agreement, would only subtract from the empathy of the moment.

"Laurel, we really know a communion that adds a significance to every-day life ..."

Somewhere my daughters were jumping up and down the pool's stairs, a gardener was watering flowering plants in large clay pots, and people were adjusting their bodies to catch the rays of heat, but it all seemed very far away. Jeremy leaned toward me. He said quietly that he wanted me to be his wife.

I felt a physical impact from his words as if he had unexpectedly thrown a solid object at me. I was immediately out of breath and my face flushed. The question seemed too large for me to catch or hold. The exertion lay in my own longings for intimacy, and this was buffeting against my sense of careful prudence.

When I looked at Jeremy, I could tell he was only feeling my caution as a reply. His face reflected the extra brightness of someone near tears. Within a moment, that wave of moist luster seemed to roll back within his being. In the deepest part of me I cast the whole question of matrimony up into the courts of God. And to Jeremy I quietly replied, "I don't know this yet," while putting my hand on top of his.

July 12

I couldn't sleep. Maybe the folds in my brain that cross its surface like riverbeds had moistened with rest, but they never knew the real tides of sleep.

I couldn't let go of the solemnity of Jeremy's proposal, along with certain memories.

At age twenty-nine, I had filled jars with strawberry jam, iced them with sealing wax, and thought I would always be married to Richard. I assumed I would grow old in his kitchen, and my last act in life would be to fold my apron into the triangle of a retiring American flag. I wondered if all I had lived through was to prepare me for marriage or warn me against it.

On my flight back to Portland, I knew that my heart's impulse was to say, "yes" and make a commitment. I wanted to sign my name, *Laurel Lee Foster* on my airplane napkin above the script, "Fly the friendly skies, United ..."

July 15

A dewy gathering below Mary Elisabeth's nose was the first clue of an influenza invasion. I bought the child her own miniature package of Kleenex to substitute for her sleeve, and all the orange juice that the Lee family could drink. After lecturing Anna to avoid using her sister's drinking glass or toothbrush, I, in turn, tried to dodge some of the close-range confidences of a four-year-old. Even with these precautions, my throat became scratchy. My physical decline exceeded Mary Elisabeth's experience. She never curtailed any activities, while I lived between the bed and couch.

"Is it Hodgkin's disease?" Matthew stood over me. Having come from the kitchen, he rotated a carrot between his thumb and finger.

"Go to the doctor. He may want to do an autopsy."

"Biopsy," I said, raising my voice. "And they don't do it for a flu."

The child was wearing two contrasting pajama pieces. His bottoms were imprinted with football players, while his shirt extolled the American space program.

"Jeremy-Foster has asked you to marry him, hasn't he?"

The name was uttered by stringing together the given name and family name into one sound. I guessed that his ear had just been around the corner from one of my phone conversations when I had been asking for advice. He continued in a rambling sort of voice, "If you don't marry him, you'll make the mistake of your life."

I wondered which call he had overheard. My parents had been hearty in their endorsement. Jeremy had flown to Fremont, taken them to dinner, and written a thank-you note, which Mother had read to me over the phone.

Arlene wanted me to be happy, but advised me to go ahead only when I was absolutely sure.

It's what I didn't know about Jeremy that constituted the risk. I thought of how every person is built with certain fault lines, crevices within their

Thomas Victor

character. Some they know about, while other finer cracks lie hidden, not well defined, yet with that separation between what they should do and what they don't. It was Jeremy's twenty-year lifestyle that I pondered.

I questioned him once if in the past he had chosen in his priorities the nurture of his business over that of his family. We had been sitting in a restaurant, and I can't even recall the menu or decor, but only his answer. First was the confession that he had been often absent because of his projects.

"I now know that was a mistake, Laurel.

I want to adopt your children. Give me the gift of a second chance."

My telephone is forest green. One year after its installation, the cord comes out of the receiver with a number of sagging loops because of being stretched beyond its power of elasticity. There's a subtle grime surrounding the three digits that are the numbers for local calls.

I pulled the phone into my room and shut the door. Having once proposed, Jeremy never repeated the direct question of marriage. Across all these days, I could finally reply, "Yes, I'll be your wife."

Now, it was a line, clear and drawn. Jeremy asked me to open my calendar to see if we could establish a prospective date. He closed in on October 20. In three months, Jeremy said he could find us a house in Los Angeles, and I could use this time to prepare a wedding and the transport of all our things to the south.

August
Silver Creek Falls, Oregon

What will it be like when we're married, Mother?"
Anna was waiting for me on the bank of the stream. She had piled several flat rocks in front of her tennis shoes. Pulling off my knapsack, I sat beside her.

"I think it's going to be really good. The pictures of the house can't show us what it will be like to live on the side of a mountain, and only six miles from the ocean."

Without looking up at me, Anna had one last question.

"Will Jeremy Foster leave us if he doesn't like us?" My daughter reached

156

out and stripped off some of the pink blooms from the clump of wild foxgloves and put them on her fingertips.

"Anna, the night we get married, you and your sister and brother will be sitting right up in the front row. We want you to see and hear everything. Jeremy and your mother are going to make promises to each other, and to God, not to leave the other, no matter what happens." I chanted sickness, health, richer, poorer, better, worse.

The child visibly brightened.

"That's it!" she said. Anna began to think of all her friends who lived in one-parent families due to divorce.

"Everyone that gets married should make that kind of promise." Anna felt she had a solution for one of the ills of the world.

Christian Renewal Center Chapel

Pastor Hansen wanted to make room for the numbers of people still standing in the back. He invited all the children to the front. We were married in the midst of little people sitting on the stairs, touching their shoes, playing with their pockets.

Once we walked out as the Fosters triumphant, Mary Elisabeth followed us. Marching behind us in the aisle, she waited until we stood yards from the church and were engulfed in the shadows from the woods. She brushed Jeremy's leg for attention:

"Are you my Daddy now?"

"Well, yes," he said, surprised as I was to see her.

She ran at his legs with both hands extended, then pulled back shouting, "Catch me then! And ran towards the church where my mother apprehended her.

I saw a number of single mothers sitting together at one of the reception's round wood tables. Their plates were dappled with second helpings from the spread of meats and salads. One speared a shrimp and said laughing, "You're not one of us anymore."

Oh, I am, I thought. *I am everything I have ever been. It's as if several lives make one. There is a time and season for every kind of understanding.*

Jeremy's son and two blonde daughters sat in a row to eat. His youngest girl, Jessie, had stayed in Minnesota. Having just met them a few days before the ceremony, I yearned to sit with them. Watching them talk among themselves, I thought how literature has been unfair in its traditional definition of "stepmother."

There's a lot of bad press for stepmothers and alligators.

As we drove to our Portland hotel, I thought of how we'll be leaving for Puerto Vallerta in the morning, then meet again as a family together in our new Topanga home. I kept repeating in the confines of my mind, "I'll be 35 years old tomorrow, and I'm a married woman ..."

October 24
Mexico

To me there is something about water that has some of the same properties as sleep. A night's rest is the passage between exhaustion and stamina. Likewise, all bathing has a quality of renewal. It seemed appropriate that we were either in bed or in the sea for the genesis of our marriage.

I ran back to the hotel room to get some fruit to eat with Jeremy on the beach. Pausing by the door frame, I surveyed our room. One small, harmless lizard clung to the wall by the ceiling.

Our toiletries at the sink, garments, and shoes are like two distinct fingerprints. His swirls didn't match mine in the care of our possessions. I have what I call *middle clothes*, which worn once are not dirty, and are about to be used again. I put them on the backs of chairs and bathroom hooks. All of my husband's garments hang from hangers in an even row. His shirts are all together, followed by another unit of trousers.

At the sink was Jeremy's brown leather box with a zipper lid. He used it as a miniature medicine cabinet. We still have two tubes of toothpaste; his was returned after use, while mine lay on the tiles as a work of sculpture. It has distinct twists and folds created by my pressure points. Always losing the cap, I have to transport it in a sandwich sack.

I take the time to gather up my left sandal from the couch and the other one by the bed. While picking up my jacket from a chair, I think how the sharing of our lives cannot help but reveal my rough edges too. If I'm a board, then I bear certain stains, like watermarks from carrying certain pressures. There's no doubt that parts of me need refinishing. Wryly, I thought how life provides all the grades of sandpaper.

Taking some mangoes and bananas from the dresser, I feel our adaptations consigned to the future. Some, I think, were disappointed in their honeymoons, but I wasn't. I had waited a very long time for intimacy.

October 30

After checking our luggage, we sat in the departure lounge for the flight to Los Angeles. I watched a tour group from Japan pat their souvenirs. Most had purchased exaggerated felt sombreros embroidered with gold spangles. One brushed his thumb over the end of bull horns mounted on a board.

My husband had gravitated to his briefcase. It was a time to reorder his mind for going to the office. Jeremy was engrossed in some papers. He had taken out his reading glasses and abstractedly clicked their ear extensions together before putting them on.

Moods are the weather of the soul. Although I was anticipating being in our house with the children, I felt some anxiety about the transition. It was almost a tiny knot of distress about reemerging into regular life. He will join the morning freeway club as I start learning the tracks to Southern California supermarkets. It had been so nice to live with just the lines and prose of a romance novel's cover art.

I wanted my husband to make a gesture that he understood, or give me some look of reluctance at ending our first days where there were no diversions but the other. Instead, once on the plane, he moved over to the aisle in order to utilize the middle seat as an additional filing cabinet for his works in progress.

November 1
Topanga, California

"Now think, Laurel," said Jeremy, "how the name of a residential street rarely reflects the essence of the avenue. Melody Lane can be the entrance to the city dump. Towering Oak Drive doesn't even have to have a tree."

I agreed that Valley View wasn't a title that merely conjured an image, but was in every way appropriate. There was no section of the road that wasn't engineered over a steep incline, giving view to a deep bowl.

Clicking off the digits of addresses, I wanted to determine how close we were to our new home. Once I saw it, I shouted an exclamation of delight, which was more of a sound than a word. The stucco siding and tile roof were Spanish. There was a mass of flowering vines that led to the front door. Cactus grew in a bed between the walk and drive.

I didn't throw a bridal bouquet, wear a blue garter, but I really would have liked being carried over a threshold. Once in the entrance hall, I surveyed a solid wall of empty bookshelves that was the backdrop to a staircase that flowed down in a dramatic width from where we were standing. At our side was another short flight that went up to a closed door.

"There are five levels," said Jeremy.

It was the kitchen at the bottom of the stairs that I liked best. The ceiling was crossed with the kind of hewn beams that are found in ski lodges. I went and sat on the window seat, measuring from memory my number of antique cans to the length of oak shelves at the back wall.

Lost in the galaxies of pending decoration, I enumerated my varieties of dried flowers that I wanted to suspend with dried herbs.

"What?" said Jeremy, "I don't want any dead plants hanging from any ceiling."

Surprised, I stood up and said nothing more about interiors. Slipping my arm into his, I looked out of the window to a meadow at the distant base of our hill. A large flock of goats was in view resembling an illustration from a children's book. One man stood in the midst of them holding a shepherd's crook. The animals all had their necks bent to graze the wild grass.

"I love it here," I cried, "and you."

November 7

I was irritable. All the straight lines that form my logic were somehow being drawn into angles and corkscrews. I hadn't woken up that way. Some early morning thoughts had concealed in its fold a kind of black marking pen that was now shading all my perceptions.

Jeremy knew it. We stood in the backyard looking out at the hills and not at each other. I marveled at how we were learning to read the language of the other's face. One could translate the wrinkles at eyes, and decipher a lip's compressions.

I felt I should offer an explanation as a disguised apology. I had thought of several, of which he could select one, or combine a number of them together. I proposed one of my theories of conduct that I call, "Newton's Law of Behavior."

"What goes up has to come down. It's the principle of emotional gravity."

I thrust both hands into my denim pockets.

"All that energy of preparing for the move and the wedding had to eclipse from that full-moon strength to this crescent."

It was a way that we were different. I had a tendency to emotional highs where I could be in the flight pattern of birds, or conversely request the moles to move over to make room for me.

My husband neither flew nor knew caverns. He was a straight line. We had gone through the house again together that morning, maneuvering around piles of cardboard boxes that needed to be unpacked. The larger pieces of furniture had been lowered into temporary locations given in haste to the moving men.

We each had our own proposals of what needed to be done to the home. My plan of priorities was perceived by Jeremy as ideas that challenged his, like a knight with a jousting stick. The issue had been the living room paneling. To me it was cheap looking—too dark and too slick. I stood, now remembering the passion of my sentence and exaggerated gesture:

"Jeremy, these walls don't imitate wood at all, but kitchen counters!"

I went on to mimic chopping onions on a space above a chair. My experiences in remodeling old rooms had given me the knowledge to cover the plastic paneling with stucco.

Somewhere deep inside, Jeremy had closed himself to me, leaving me to imagine the damage I had done. He reminded me of a sensitive fern whose leaves fold together when touched.

Now we looked out at the California hills, bleached by the sun until they resemble cantaloupe skins in the distance. There were no goats or other animals to be seen in the meadow landscape. I was wishing our heads were set on one side with hinges so they could be opened and allow a fresh breeze to stir through the coils of brain matter.

I wondered briefly how much of a mistake it was that we never experienced being cross with each other before marriage. One thousand hours of telephone talk had never revealed our conduct when irritated. I wanted to analyze every detail while Jeremy was practicing a silence that now reminded me of shades pulled to the sill.

"It's the children, too. I know you delayed their coming by a week to help me, so I could get everything put away, but I miss them."

My husband drew me over to his side. The gesture and the weight of his arm absorbed my feeling of being upset. Our shadows merged behind us into one figure with four legs.

November 10

It was Anna who first spotted us in the airport lounge. She broke rank from the flight attendant and ran with a small hiking knapsack knocking against her shoulder. Her permanent teeth looked large in what was still a small girl's eight-year-old face. Matthew and Mary Elisabeth followed in a burst for first place, turning us into the finish line. There was a blur of small, new details. Matthew seemed taller, and Mary Elisabeth's legs had a number of Band Aids.

Jeremy was "Dad." They must have been practicing the word in their minds, as it came out alone and not in a stammer with his name. After we had stowed the luggage in the trunk, Mary Elisabeth leaned out in the space between us to again touch her new father. Jeremy had just adjusted his seat up closer to the steering wheel to give the children more room. The four-year-old put her hand on his shoulder, sliding it down his arm to his stomach. She patted it and turned to observe to her brother and sister:

"It's just like a water bed."

Once the children were in their new rooms for the night, I began to think how we are now taking our places in our home. Once Jeremy was asleep and deaf, I slipped out of bed to push off all the television buttons to make the room dark and quiet. Unlike me, my husband likes to pull some television dialogue up to his neck. I'm not accustomed to that sound he seems to require as a prerequisite to slumber.

I prefer to paddle in thoughts, like rhymes of a new family where our success will be maintaining commitment to the other's well being. A sleepiness began to bend my poems further apart until I was finally without a syllable.

November 11

The children had lost the ability to walk in a house and talk in any modulated tones. Once they were dressed, I sent them to the car while I went to fish out an old radio microphone head from one of Jeremy's storage boxes. I had promised to show the children Topanga Canyon and decided to imitate the monotone professionalism of a tour guide.

"Coyotes abound in these coastal range mountains, along with other small animal species. The size of a dog, they run in packs and can often be heard throughout the night."

While Matthew pronounced that was "cool," Anna began to imitate the coyote's high-pitched yelp. Mary Elisabeth scanned the roadside, demanding one to come into her view.

Our road is so steep I have to keep pressure on the brake all the way down to the highway. We pass several houses that are posted with signs that they pay a patrol service for professional surveillance. Some say, "ARMED RESPONSE," which I don't mention to the children, or the car will be filled with them imitating popping noises.

"I want you to note that the junction of our street with the main road is marked by that small health-food store out your right window."

Matthew deciphered, "Freshly squeezed carrot juice," and "We have DMSO" for his sisters.

"To reach the elementary school, you will be passing this post office." I told them about the cat named *Zip-code* that lives under the counter.

Since they were going to be walking to school, I wanted to underline their route and get their enrollment forms. Matthew groaned when I turned up a steep hill named *School Road*.

Topanga Elementary School is a long, one-floor ranch style structure with the office in the front. The secretary was fitting a plastic lid onto a lunch container. Her appearance looked to me like she could be valuable to birds, if only she would eat outside. Select crumbs had landed on her lap and the shelf of her bosom. Even her straw purse was unraveling, leaving long pliable fibers that could line nests.

Anna answered her question that she was transferring from a Portland school. "We're not going to live by the volcano anymore!"

"That reminds me," said the receptionist as she pulled out more forms from a file cabinet, "You'll need to fill out the catastrophe forms with the children's emergency name cards."

I read the paper on top of all the information sheets:

Topanga residents have been through enough calamities to know that disaster is a way of life in the Canyon and that fire and flood and land movement are probably inevitable. (My mind substituted the correct synonym, *earthquake*.) An emergency tag will be used when students have to be evacuated. It will be fitted to the child's arm. Please, fill out the necessary information. Delay is a luxury we cannot afford.

HERBERT MINKER—PRINCIPAL

I looked up wondering if the enumerated dangers were being exaggerated. I noticed the crumbs that had been attached to the receptionist person were gone. I spotted them on the clay tiles between her chair and the cabinet; she's a friend to the small scavenger insect.

A short man opened an office door at the corner of the room. Above the door frame was a plaque inscribed, "Principal." Below it was a simple paper sign recording his zodiac birth month symbol.

"I'm Mr. Minker," he said, eyeing the children.

"We do have a dress code at this school. All the students must wear shoes."

I didn't know what to say, since we were all properly shod.

"Have you told them about the rattlesnakes?"

"Just about coyotes," replied Matthew.

"We have a lot in this area, and the children should freeze, not bolt, when they hear one," instructed the principal.

"Oh," he added, "Mrs. Foster, you'll need to purchase an official identification card for access into the canyon when the road is closed. The California Highway Patrol sets up roadblocks forbidding all traffic except for those with a 90290, Topanga zip code card. I think it's ten dollars."

It all began to feel like a bad comedy hour.

Mary, Matthew and Anna

Should we paint the roses red
While the earth quakes, rattlers shake
And calamities knock us all dead?

"Last year," said Mr. Minker, "we had floods and mud slides, which washed out the road along with a number of residences."

Behind Minker, on his office door, was magazine cartoon. A caricature figure sat at a desk with three containers in front of him. The labels on two of them read, "IN," and "OUT."

The third simply said, "WAY OUT," and I ushered the children back to the car.

December 24

I stood in the kitchen stirring the cheese soup that would be part of our first course for Christmas Eve dinner. I made patterns with the spoon by scraping out an alphabet in script as if to amuse my hand and keep it from quitting in the monotony of its task.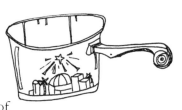

It was good to have Jeremy home. He was upstairs in our bedroom watching the news. It was the earliest he had ever been able to get away from the office.

Our guests were due to arrive within the hour. Dr. Jean LaCour lived across the street; my door faced her door. She taught social sciences at a state university. I had never been to her house without finding a different configuration of text books on the rug.

It was Matthew who met the goat shepherd and asked him to come. He had met him while exploring back trails on his way home from school. He had described Gus McFadden as a bearded man standing in the midst of three hundred animals. Dogs were following his commands and running around the circumference of the herd. Matthew accepted the invitation to join them in their walk to the winter pasture that proved to be directly below our house.

I never knew which wall concealed the doorbell. It had a power in its chimes to penetrate all five architectural levels. I heard my husband invite Jean LaCour in.

Our neighbor looked as if she had dressed for the night in the back of an art gallery. Her jewelry was from a display case of bent wires soldered to pins. Her clothes were the vivid hue of primary colors. I had observed that the average Los Angeles woman in her fifties weighs fifteen pounds less than a counterpart matron in Portland. It was an earmark of living in a city where one didn't wear a coat.

It was Matthew who saw the flashlight first in the backyard. I walked with my son down the stairs to the kitchen door marveling that our other guest had climbed up the steep brush trails to our deck.

The shepherd stood smiling. While shaking his hand, I noticed that he was missing one of his canine teeth. His countenance was the hardy health of those who work outside. He wore army surplus clothes where the wool was embedded with hay and bits of branch twigs. He washed his hands in the sink while asking if this was really the right night. A faint odor of goat cheese mingled with the warmth of the kitchen.

Jeremy seated us at the table. The world has grown old while generations of fathers have pointed children to their right chairs.

Gus McFadden talked through the meal about his profession. He had a contract with the state of California for his herd to graze the firebreaks along the rim of the Santa Monica Mountains. Most of the months he roamed with his flock over a designated route, keeping it clear of all vegetation. He told us he was the highest paid shepherd in history.

Jeremy was interested in the wooden crook that he carried into the fields. Gus explained it was a tool that he laid over himself at night when sleeping in his canvas bag. One of its purposes was to provide visibility so the animals would not trample him if startled to flight by coyotes. As I got my platter of baked confections, I could hear Anna ask to hear more about the canyon's rattlesnakes.

Once Dr. LaCour and Gus had left by doors at the opposite ends of the house, the five of us sat together watching the last of the fire's embers. After a few minutes, Jeremy stood up and excused himself. He wanted to go and watch the ten o'clock news upstairs.

"Stay with us," I protested. "Let a plane fall from the sky and a diplomat disappear without you knowing it."

He laughed while climbing up to our room. His humor helped deflect the sting of his abrupt departure.

The children and I turned off all the lights except for those on the Christmas tree. We lay on the floor squinting, in order to blur our vision and alter the color patterns until the tree had the quality of Tokyo's neon. I told the children the story of the Christmas shepherds. When the angels came with the message, it all had to be prefaced with "Fear not."

Matthew paraphrased it for his sisters as, "Don't Freak."

I thought through the next line, *I bring you tidings of great joy, which shall be to all people.* They seemed like words that could be embroidered on capes, which when worn, would confer the power of flight. I wanted our family to dress like that.

January 3, 1981

I chose a fresh carton for storing the Christmas decorations. It was my night's work to sweep us into January and clean the hearth of candle wax. I folded away the children's wreath constructed entirely of breakfast cereal pasted on plywood. Some of the Cheerios had flaked off, but the outline of a bow in red Fruit Loops was still intact.

I was in the grip of the kind of sentimentality that triples the weight of the heart. It made me yearn for a woman to talk to, as if sifting with another through feelings could diffuse my peculiar melancholy.

I turned over Anna's creation of Joseph to wrap in the *L.A. Times*. It resembled a pizza crust struggling to stand upright. After closing the box flaps, I went into the kitchen and dialed the area code for Portland.

Once Arlene knew it was me, she was quickened with the facts of math.

"You've been married for two-and-one-half months!" Her queries about our life were without pause, as if each question mark was instantly swallowed by her next curiosity.

"The Christmas weather here is like a July picnic. Almost all of the store merchants paint their glass with snow scenes as they have to simulate winter."

I confessed how I missed Oregon at odd times, like when I saw the winter coats at the back of the closet.

"How is Jeremy?"

"Fine. He works maximum hours with the energy of three men. I've told him that if he manufactured tires and was this absent, I couldn't bear it. But I believe in his films, so I keep myself encouraged with that.

"What exactly is his work?"

I had come to compare Jeremy's office to the surface of a stove. "He has a number of movies for production that are in different stages of production. While some simmer at the back, another is boiling and needs to be constantly stirred. Scripts are like the recipes."

I also explained that Jeremy does a lot of film distribution.

"Are you ever sorry, Laurel?" My mind instantly filled in the words that Arlene left out.

"Sorry ... that I married?"

I started to quickly answer in a reply I would use to everyone. The word "never" was at my tongue. But with Arlene, I had to pause.

"Sometimes I feel abandoned."

It seemed such a lack of loyalty to Jeremy to say it. Yet, I realized that the cause of my depression wasn't the end of Christmas, but his perpetual absence. I could feel my cheeks burn. The flush was more from my realization than my disclosure.

"Every couple ..." said Arlene.

I finished the sentence for her. I knew her thought, her paragraph: marriage adaptations eventually provide more than a solid relationship—they bring maturity.

"I know, friend," I said. "Marriage is our best and last chance to grow up."

We both laughed, and I glimpsed a clubhouse where spouses sit behind the front lines to encourage each other.

February 11

Climbing the stairs to our bedroom, I could hear the droning sportscaster calling out yard lines and plays. I had to hold the wood tray with Jeremy's coffee with one hand in order to turn the bedroom doorknob. Jeremy had already read the Sunday paper and now was watching afternoon football. The thought recurred that I had never known the breadth of televised athletics until my marriage. I was still incredulous that a reasonable, intelligent man could be thrilled by padded bodies slamming into each other looking for a ball.

I had tried to participate. I thought it was just a matter of knowing the rules in order to experience some level of enthusiasm. My small degree of cheering for one side would shift during a game to rooting for whichever team was losing. I felt that if football truly had some national women's audience, the commercials would reflect this in endorsing soap powders. Instead, burly men demonstrated aerosol foams for the camera's close-up lens.

Looking over my husband's head, I could see the Santa Monica hills rolling by our horizon on the land's last stand before the Pacific. I had become used to views in our occupancy. Every window framed an expanse of sky.

Jeremy called my attention back to the screen, which continued to repeat the same slow motion frames of a player intercepting a pass. I sat by him until it was over, then took my tray back downstairs to the kitchen.

The sink was full of dirty dishes, as I had spent the morning in church with Matthew and the girls. It seemed that the children's exclusive expression of hygiene was their habit of getting a clean cup for every sip of water. On the stove was a saucepan left by Matthew after heating himself a second bowl of soup. Between the pan and empty bowl were enough noodles that it looked like a message spelled out in some cryptic alphabet.

I needed to decipher a mystic's note. There seemed to be an emptiness to

Sunday afternoon. It was a vague, restless feeling that I, alone, seemed to be experiencing. Everyone else in the house was occupied and content.

I fished the dishcloth out of the sink and squeezed out the old water from its last job. Opening the cupboard, I lifted out the liquid soap that the manufacturer had dyed emerald green, and squeezed twice what I needed into the faucet spray.

My negative mood was gathering strength. I felt disappointed that what I had yearned for seemed so dull. Part of me kept marveling that my present clean bill of health didn't seem enough, whereas if I had been sick, it would have been. It was as though parts of my consciousness encircled me and took seats to watch Laurel in the central arena.

There was a simple cheer from the good attitude: *Your life goal is not personal pleasure. Embrace the maturing that comes from any self-denial* ...

Its voice was quickly obliterated by passion. It brought a quote from literature. Elizabeth Barrett feared to take Robert Browning's hand in marriage because, she said: "In that first wedded year, the men always change from being the lover to a husband." I could feel my irritation that Jeremy's only expression of leisure in four months of marriage was to close himself away with the newspaper and sports. Usually he worked weekends at the office.

"Stop," I said out loud. This was the epidemic of discontent. It resembled the bubonic plague, of the Middle Ages, in wiping out more families than history can number. What scared me was feeling such anger within myself; it couldn't be simply talked away.

I thought of thirteenth-century monks who put ashes on their heads while crying out for divine assistance to be the people they wanted to be. Scooping out some suds, I mashed them into my hairline. Beginning to feel better, I used both hands to cup more bubbles, which I wiped onto my head, above my ears. Absurdity has its rewards.

Jeremy came into the kitchen. I knew it must be halftime, and some coordinated bands were marching on a distant field. I stood by the sink of half washed dishes with soggy hair and wet shoulders where the water had run down.

I anticipated him to react, in a smile, or with questions, but he registered no response at all. He simply said that he wanted to make a snack. I started laughing and put my arms around his neck. If there were any devils hanging around whispering fiery accusations, our embrace made them flee.

March 17

After the children were asleep, I sat on my bed hoping to lose myself in some author's plot. But instead, I kept straining to hear Jeremy's motor in the sparse nighttime traffic. I sighed as every car kept climbing above our driveway.

Snapping the book shut, I went out to stand on our bedroom's back deck. "Laurel, you married an absolute workaholic."

All the mysteries of each other had been solved by the quantity of days we had lived together. We never spoke of "The Future" anymore which was constant in courtship. With him, that had been just a language of intentions, as his habits proved stronger than any promise.

I had only glimpsed beforehand how Jeremy's desk and working papers were his real living room and warming hearth. With reluctance, he took leave of them at night and rushed back to greet them at dawn. He had no concept of family time or even the necessity of a meal together.

I thought of the Minnesota boy that was father to this man. He had been molded by the constant labor of an impoverished truck farm, while I, a child of the suburbs, had had time to lie on my back making stories for every fleet of clouds.

A barking dog joined the sounds of the night. Somehow, I felt my thoughts had a long, drawn-out barking quality to them too. The fact that it was Saturday and after ten o'clock was against me. It was that time of the weekend, which removes one's defenses against loneliness, so it had begun its seepage under the bedroom door.

Returning to my room, I knew that I would have to have a serious talk with Jeremy. The thought of a pending conference filled me with some uncertainty about how to approach him. He seemed to me like a powerful locomotive consumed by pressing forward with his ministry of movies.

"Jeremy," I practiced, "the only problem is the order in which you pull your cars behind you. Your family is somewhere at the end of the line."

Maybe, I thought, I'm at the edge of adaptation and need to register my last complaints before forming whatever colors of skin it's going to take to make me blend with my environment.

April 10

It was early morning. Jeremy stood at his chest of drawers in vapors of after-shave lotion.

"Jeremy, you know the story of Old Testament Esther?"

"Yeah," he replied, turning to me with his day's choice of black socks in his hand.

"She went through elaborate preparations before telling her husband what was wrong with the kingdom. Let's pretend I did all that Jeremy."

I had his attention. He pulled out a chair and sat at the small oak table that had fluted legs like four stacks of pumpkins. His choice of seating provided the necessary conversational distance. I began to feel a deep inner nervousness that potential confrontations produce in me. It was my peculiar vulnerability. There is an old twinge of insecurity that strikes through my bones, like joints that ache in certain weather.

Yet, I was blunt. "I need to see more of you. *We* need to see more of you."

"We? I?" he replied in a kind of non-answer.

"The family has to be given more priority."

Jeremy stood up and started moving back to his dresser, reaching into the corner that held his handkerchiefs. He was going back to his occupation with dressing. I felt it as a dismissal. His silence made me join the hand of frustration to that of reason.

"I think in these past five months we've had three meals together as a family, two at Christmas, one at Thanksgiving." It was a fact and not an exaggeration to make a point.

I was sorry, but not surprised, to see my feelings rise and the beginning ground swell of tears. In the past, one of the things that I had blamed was his expense account, which opened for him every restaurant door without personal cost. I was done making any kind of excuses for him.

Jeremy's continuing silence set loose enemy soldiers that moved in rank from my thoughts to my mouth. They were the hosts of resentment, with each unit wanting to attack with its own accusation of his broken promises.

Jeremy was controlled. He didn't raise or quicken the tempo of his voice, yet there was an illusion that he shouted at me.

"Laurel, will you stop being so intense!"

I knew I was handling it wrong. I was throwing my message for help into the sea and had failed to get it into a glass bottle.

I walked over to the chair that Jeremy had vacated. He sat on the bed.

"I used to think of you, Laurel, as being much more professionally motivated than you really are. You don't travel and speak at all compared to what you did before marriage."

It was said to me with a slight tone of reproach.

I had always feared that once married I would be guilty in a husband's tribunal because of my wanting to accept invitations. Now the hour of the issue had come and my censure lay in the fact that I received so few.

I looked out the window realizing that I had disappointed him too.

"Exactly what do you do during the day?" His question was without sarcasm; he simply seemed curious.

My impulse was to detail every stage in the scrubbing of carrots. Instead, I held up three fingers.

"Nurturing the children, housework, and I keep notes in a diary."

"You need more personal time," he concluded. "I want you to call an agency and start interviewing for a live-in housekeeper. Look for numbers in the want ad section under *Domestics*."

To him the issue was solved, and Jeremy walked to the closet to select a tie. He rolled the green silk strip into a knot. The pattern was of small, evenly-spaced black whales.

I realized he was trying to provide for my needs by duplicating what he himself required. He was putting Band-Aids everywhere, but on the sore.

"Laurel, you can come down to the office, and write there in a room." I nodded an assent while thinking how that would allow us more time in proximity.

I followed my husband to the door. Holding his briefcase, he turned and kissed my cheek. The rear tire of the Mercedes drove over the daily paper that was folded in thirds and bound with a string.

April 16

Julia sat next to me on the front seat. I remembered to pronounce her name by saying, "Who," for the first syllable, according to the language of Central America. Each of her front teeth was framed in gold. It was a distinct style of dentistry where the enamel looked gift-wrapped. The agency counselor told me that my new household help was from El Salvador and didn't speak any English. She, herself, had just learned of my lack of vocabulary. I could only ask her name, age, and the time.

I stopped at the large grocery by the intersection of Sunset Avenue and the Pacific Coast Highway. All shoppers can look to the water's horizon from the parking lot. Taking a cart, I read the dual advertisement embossed in plastic on the toddler's seat. Only in the Pacific Palisades is the store paid a fee to exhibit a phone number for a limousine service.

Once through the open doors, Julia took the cart and held it back, intending to walk behind me at a servant's pace. When I slackened my speed so we could be abreast, she took half steps to keep a few feet behind me. She felt compelled to intercept any tin or bag of produce, and be the one to stow it in the cart. It made me quote Dorothy; we were both a long ways from Kansas.

May 10

There was no sound, or glow of light coming out into the hall from beneath Matthew's door. Over an hour had elapsed since I had positioned his blankets and heard his prayers. As I thought of it later, there was no real reason why I had ever opened his door.

I found him looking straight up with the entire circumference of his cheeks wet from crying.

Quickly, I sat by him, asking what was wrong.

"Dad," he said. "I don't even feel like I have a dad. I never see him. He comes home after we're asleep, and when he is home, he just stays in the room and acts like it's his private motel."

While Matthew talked, I remembered Jeremy's promise to adopt the children. Yet, I knew if all their names had been legally changed to "Foster," he still wouldn't be any different. I suspected that his conduct with my children was no different from how he had once related to his own.

I held him, but had to use my tough voice to speak Matthew's name. Self-pity is a lake, and I wanted to get my son back to shore.

With my arm around him, I asked, "If Jeremy were a blind man, would you expect him to go hiking or play sports with you?"

"No, but that's different."

"There's all kinds of blindness, Matthew. He isn't meaning to hurt you; he just doesn't see."

"Okay, I'll try to believe that," he replied.

Once Matthew slept, I indicated to Julia that I was going out. The parking lot of Jeremy's company seemed empty except for his car parked in the stall closest to the door. His drawn curtains were the only rectangle of light at the front of the building. I knocked and waited for him to unbolt the door locks.

"Long distance," he said, and retreated back into his office. From the receptionist's desk, I could see his back drop of bookcases and filing cabinets.

My assigned room was smaller and across from the accounting offices. From my door, I could see the minute glowing light indicating Jeremy's active line. I switched on the flourescent overhead panel and sat at the old library table. On my desk were some slogans of encouragement while my paragraphs of complaint were buried in my journal. At random, I opened to an old entry and read out loud:

> *Today we have been married two months. The days are like garments that we wear, all cut from the same bolt of fabric. It looks like a pleasant design, but I'm beginning to sense something is missing—as if there is a lost button, or some secret worn spot.*

Restless, I snapped the notebook shut, and seeing that Jeremy's phone light was still on, I wandered back to the warehouse where the computers and packing supplies were stored. Passing by desks, I noticed that their surfaces were empty, as if their keepers had to straighten them at night in counterpoint to making their beds in the morning.

The Xerox machine was emitting a low-powered hum. On impulse, I raised the lid and laid the side of my face on the square where the papers are put for duplication. Pulling the cover back over me, I shut my eyes and punched, "One Copy." The machine shifted, carrying the weight of my head across the photographing light. The etching was deposited into a mesh basket. I examined the Xerox image of my skin folds and eyebrow hairs. I began to experiment with degrees of pressure on different expressions.

I didn't know that one of the accountants was working. I straightened up and found him staring at the president's wife who had been photographing her flaring nostrils. He was a somber man, wore glasses, and had some lesions from what was once troubled teenage skin.

"It really works, Len." I said this while showing him a sample from my series of photos.

"Try it," I urged.

Len first put his hand on the machine, and the print duplicated his palm. Encouraged, he cast one look to make sure there were no spectators to his folly, then put his face flat on the machine. His glasses came out the best with the rest of him receding into darkness. He took his pictures with his briefcase and left by a back door.

I took a selection of my new art into Jeremy's office. He swiveled around and took them from me, smiling.

"Conference," I said. "Topic: Matthew."

I was mimicking a business sheet by stating my agenda. It was a costume for my approach. If I cried, Jeremy would be a lot less apt to hear me.

"He wants more interaction with you. It's a deep need as he hasn't had a father since the age of five."

I could feel the control in Jeremy's answer like a stick shift pulled back for a steep hill.

"You've got all the time you could want for him now, Laurel."

Ancient as caves is the rage of a mother bear who will stand in front of her cub. I wanted to shout, "You're making the same mistake with us as you did with your first family."

But instead, my reply had a slightly higher pitch: "People are more valuable than these unending projects!"

"The office," and "the family" could each be a hilt in our two swords, raised and crossing each other in tension.

Following Jeremy's taillights back into Topanga Canyon, I talked to myself.

"Don't be dumb, kid. You're not ever going to string together the right words that are going to bring your husband enlightenment."

I knew one solution would be to squeeze out for myself drops of the same fortitude I had developed during the years of being alone with the children. I made up a song, and made the tune to be something like the lilt of an Irish jig:

The princess met Prince Charming,
They rode on his white horse.
But in every castle dungeon
Is some dragon of remorse.

September 3

Matthew was laughing. He held his hands to his shoulders, demonstrating for his sisters next to him in the back seat of the car how to play "Jell-O." It was a style of riding up the street where gravity alone directs the body mass. No muscles or bones are allowed to be in operation. Three children rolled against the door while I turned into our driveway.

Anna heard the telephone first. I ran inside, counting the rings and shouting to Julia that I would get it.

Jeremy's greeting came through the receiver from his Minneapolis hotel room. He explained he had been in a lengthy conference with his ex-wife. They had been in the office of a state agency that counseled in family services.

"She is completely unable to cope with our youngest daughter and is demanding that Jessie be sent back to Los Angeles to be in my custody."

All that I knew of Jessie Kay Foster was that she had an established pattern of being a troubled youngster. At age fourteen, she had even had a baby that had been adopted at birth.

"There are two solutions," said Jeremy. "We could look for a well regulated boarding school, or ..."

I interrupted, repelled at the idea of shuffling away any child with such apparent needs.

"No, let's give her a real home."

Even while saying it, I could feel my heart sink. Some offstage voice was whispering, "You're really in for it now."

"Laurel, her older sister, Gloria, also wants to come out later and just be a help in anyway she can. She's 25, and has written away for some local college catalogs."

Jeremy detailed how the two of them could use the outside guesthouse. We had remodeled a large gardening shed, tripling its floor space, and added glass doors, plus a deck. A set of cedar stairs joined it to the main house. They could have the kitchen shower for their use.

I began to feel a kind of panic at such rapid changes to our home structure. I said the noble words, "I'll do my best," but my phrase was a corset, and I could feel the flesh squeezed and bulging around my declaration.

September 20

The first passenger off the Northwestern flight from Minneapolis was a mother with her infant wrapped in flannel. Already the businessmen were passing her by with briefcases scarred from constant travels.

Both Jeremy and I strained to see through the crowd for Jessie.

"There she is," said Jeremy, pointing to a statuesque girl who started waving. I realized I had been expecting the kind of teenager that lives in the corner of Greyhound bus stations. They ask for cigarettes and have visible tattoos.

Jessie Foster walked to her father and related an account of a fly in the coach section who would now find itself in Los Angeles. She raised her hands and told it entirely from the insect's point of view. I liked her. She sounded creative and intelligent.

Jessie's honey-colored hair was short, and her earlobes had been perforated for the full potential of holding a number of pierced earrings.

Once in the canyon, Jeremy put his hand on my leg just as he bypassed our street, choosing other mountain roads. He looked at Jessie in the rear view mirror announcing, "We're almost there."

I thought of it as a joke and decided he was searching through the back ways for a tumbled down cabin to pretend it was ours. It was as if he counted the exclamations from the back seat about our isolation before pulling into the drive.

While getting Jessie's boxes out of the trunk, Jeremy whispered, "I want to suggest a confusing distance between our home and the main road." I knew she had made another attempt at running away in the week preceding her flight west.

Matthew and the girls rushed out of the front door. I knew inside were signs that they had colored for their greeting of a big sister.

October 20, 1981

As Jeremy held open the restaurant door, my senses were first struck by the music whose notes suggested girls who work in tea stalls, averting their eyes and bowing. There was also a fish smell. From our entrance, looking beyond the simulated bales of rice, I could see a sushi bar.

I kept thinking, "We have been married one year tonight." I looked down at the new opal ring that Jeremy had just given me outside after parking the car. Once seated, my husband put his hand on my arm. It was as if a deposit had been made in that deep internal vault that needs romance. All displays of affection are its currency.

I had a thought about millions of couples over thousands of years. I spoke in general: "Marriage provides the much needed opportunity to surrender to something beyond one's own self-interest."

Jeremy looked up, having appraised my sentence as being specific and an initiation of a truth session.

"Still, Laurel, I'm not finding marriage as rewarding as I thought I would."

It was an acid retort to sentimentality. I wanted to respond with cynicism and pleas: *Oh, Jeremy, maybe no one does, but say some sweet things tonight.* I reflected how one difference between a good evening and one that is strained is to leave a few things unsaid.

Jeremy was deft with his chopsticks. No bamboo shoot was too slippery for his skill. After only spearing the denser vegetables, I asked for a fork. Jeremy's declaration of not being as content as his courtship anticipation had lodged in me. Even the fact that I thought on it again was a signal of its damage.

Jeremy brought up the topic of the children.

"Jessie sure seems to have stabilized. I think it's due to being shifted in position from the youngest and last at home to the oldest and adored."

I told him how I had found her earlier this week with a game she had designed and mounted on cardboard. It was a symmetrical drawing of sunglasses sectioned into squares. She had inscribed it, "PUNK IN." The tokens progressed from conformity to punk culture.

I quoted: "Get old dress, ahead 3; Wear designer jeans, back to start;

Dye hair extreme colors, ahead 6; The finish reads, "You have won these cheap sun glasses!"

"She's agreed to come one time to church with me and the children."

"Good luck." He laughed. "You are going to like Gloria too. She will be here within two weeks."

From the wedding, I remembered her as a tall blond girl who had been eager to help her father. She had sewn some buttons on his suit coat and stayed with him until the ceremony.

"I've been talking with her. She wants to assist in the office and not take any college classes."

As Jeremy talked, I again experienced some anxiety at another stepdaughter coming. She would actually be closer to my age than I was to my husband. Yet, Jessie had proved to be far less of a problem than I had feared before her arrival.

We sat in silence after Jeremy had ordered his coffee. Because it was our anniversary, I wanted to brush hands and interchange some dense cosmic rays of affection.

"I remember," said Jeremy.

I was instantly ready for that sled. My mind flew with his two words recalling Mexico ...

"When I married Patty, we were so poor that we couldn't even buy the wedding pictures."

This reminiscing would have been all right on another night of the year. I sat there listening about his first family, their trailer, baby Robert, and their anniversaries. My feelings were crushed, and my throat began to ache as I held back any cry.

I began to quietly crumble my fortune cookie, breaking off bits as he talked. I wouldn't even open its message slip, just stood to go, leaving it still folded on the plate.

Jeremy followed me to the car. I thought, *in all ways he is a most brilliant man except in his management of a wife's emotional needs.*

Once home, Jeremy fell instantly asleep. I wallowed in disappointment until humor rescued me with its own perspective. I whispered over Jeremy's deaf ears: "If I were involved in an accident, my husband would not be able to identify the body."

November 3

I was in the corridor of a dream. At first, I explained the sound of the tapping in colors that pulsed. But the sound broke through my sleep, chipping off pieces, making a hole of consciousness. The room was washed in the early morning color of pearl. As Jeremy called, "Come in," from the adjusted height of his elbow, I was ready to rebuke whatever child wanted to confide with us at dawn.

It wasn't a child at all, but Gloria, who had moved in earlier in the week. She walked over to the small table by her father's side, holding the white coffee pot and single mug.

She had come from Minneapolis with numerous taped boxes and suitcases. I had seen little of her, as she was working the same long hours as Jeremy.

My feeling of *Invasion at Daybreak* didn't lift. I burrowed deeper into the blankets wishing for the hole of sleep's gravity. I thought, it's her father's job to explain our personal territories and hours of access.

"You wanted to start early today, Jeremy."

I opened my eyes. It was the first time I noticed that Gloria called her father by his first name. My mind inventoried Jessie's vocabulary, but I could only remember the younger sister using the word "Dad."

Moving my head to focus, I looked at Gloria. She had on a long bathrobe made of a purple synthetic material. It appeared to be created from fuzz pulled off and compacted from blankets. Her dyed hair hung down with the strands indented from the single back braid that she usually wore. It was her hands that commanded my attention. Her vermilion fingernails had the artificial sharp uniformity that's only possible when glued in place at beauty shops. I noted on her right hand that Gloria wore her mother's wedding ring.

Jeremy looked up at the digital clock that he kept on his dresser.

"Thank you," he said. "It will soon be nine o'clock in New York."

"Look folks, it's barely five-thirty here," I said.

Gloria turned, casting out a "See you later," at the door. Once alone, I had to make a statement.

"I hope this won't become a habit."

Jeremy bristled. "Look, Laurel, I couldn't ask for more efficiency or loyalty. Gloria's going to be the office manager, and I've shared with you how she's helped me before.

I did remember. The first time Patty moved out of the family home, Gloria, who was then in high school, took over managing the two younger children. She had also lived with her dad when he first opened the L.A. office and helped pick the personal furnishings for his condominium.

Jeremy's speech on her office efficiency made me visualize her in the downstairs shower typing with her finger pads on the tile as an exercise to increase her words per minute. As Jeremy stood up, I could tell by his expression that he thought what was good for him should be good for me.

But, I couldn't let it rest. I was feeling agitated and uneasy, sensing the potential of a whole new sphere of conflict.

I had learned to speak as quietly as he did, but inside I was shaking my husband by the shoulders.

"I definitely feel Gloria needs her own apartment. It would be better for both your daughter and us."

He walked to the bathroom and picked up a towel from the shelf built into an alcove by the door. I suspected he wanted to ignore the subject. Gloria's shower water was still coursing through the pipes, which forced him to stand by the bathroom and wait. The house plumbing could only take care of one need at a time.

"You have your children here, and I have the equal right for all of mine to live with me if I want."

I got out of bed and walked over to the window that faces the east. I looked at the morning light beginning to illuminate the grove of eucalyptus trees behind Jean LaCour's house. I remembered when we moved in a year ago how I had imagined koalas rollicking in the upper limbs. I wondered if it were possible to graph all my whimsical thoughts and rate their decline into sobriety.

"I don't want to quarrel, Jeremy."

"Neither do I, Laurel."

Our truce seemed to be composed of one single flag that had more gray tones than white.

December 1

"Hello, Arlene. It's me again, Laurel."

I was stretched out on the office rug holding the door shut with my foot. My personal office had become a telephone booth with two WATS line buttons, allowing for long distance calls at a reduced rate.

"I think I am going crazy!" I envisioned a mental hospital built on one floor with adjacent gardens. I imagined being hospitalized and allowed to do one simple activity: I would use crayons in a coloring book, filling in one-dimensional drawings with little strokes.

Arlene's responding laughter was infectious. Maybe, I mused, I should mark this too as another sign of my mental decline—Laurel Lee will laugh at anything.

Moving into a sitting position, I put my back against the door and surveyed the room. In the months of secluding myself at odd hours to keep a diary, all office-like appearances had been stripped away.

On the floor there had been a clear plastic piece cut with kidney bean curves for a chair to roll on. It was the first thing I had taken to the storage room. In its place was a hand loomed rug. I used baskets for filing cabinets. The stock boy had helped me tack a full size quilt over a blank wall. I had found costumes left on a back rack from a movie filmed in India. I put some of the gauze and cotton pieces on my coat rack. In the privacy of a mood, I would dress in them or wear them in layers whenever the air conditioning had been adjusted to blow the coldest drafts.

"Arlene, I've decided that marriage resembles a boating excursion. During courtship the suitor takes his seat in the bow, crooning with a ukulele, while the woman smooths the wrinkles from her gown. Then comes the current. Low hanging branches swipe at them, and there are rocks right below the surface that can easily tear a craft."

I limited my long distance calls to three chosen women friends. They could be trusted. They had practiced for years keeping secrets in their church life. I only divulged a part of my difficulties to each one so it was three times as serious as anyone thought. I described my mind to Arlene as some days feeling like a table with wads of old gum pressed beneath it.

My friend liked specifics more than similes.

"How are your stepdaughters?"

"There is no descriptive phrase for Jessie other than she is in the process of becoming. She goes to high school wearing Levis and 1950 felt hats with mesh-net veils.

"Gloria is much more difficult. Toward me, her conduct is faultlessly polite, but it's marked by a tangible reserve and distance."

In turn, I listened. I like news of a life. Her children have been in music recitals, and her secret fear is that she has a receding hairline. But with Arlene, I could count on listening to advice. "Don't indulge yourself in listing the broken courtship promises. Sometimes it takes muscle to practice real love, and that means stop outlining everything that is wrong."

The fourth light dimmed on fifteen interoffice phones as I hung up. I took off my white Nehru jacket and picked up my purse to go home. Even at the door's first crack was a sound wave of typewriters. Across from the receptionist's corridor, Jeremy's door was closed. He was on a business trip to a Texas city.

Gloria's desk was in the first carpeted area behind the women's rest room. She had a diet pop and an order of tortilla chips smothered in cheese. Her preference was to have her food brought in so she could work through lunch. While we greeted each other, I saw she had mounted photos on her bulletin board. One was of herself dressed as a harem girl at a Halloween party. Another was Jeremy and Patty in blue ski sweaters, arm in arm. It seemed that all of her apparent loyalties were locked to the old order.

January 5, 1982

Leaning against the outdoor deck's rail, I could hear the humming faucets as Julia filled the sink with detergent. I had glanced at the collection of china stained from the morning's use. There were the youngest children's plates with catsup blobs from scrambled eggs, the Foster girl's saucers that they had appropriated as ashtrays, and Jeremy's coffee tray.

The fantasy of having a maid was over. I had found for Julia another canyon family who wanted the services of a housekeeper as soon as I would release her. We had all agreed to a week.

As for me, I needed labor. There was a simple therapy in scrubbing a bathtub with cleanser that turned blue when contacting water and sweeping dust into piles. There was a sense of connection in knowing the contents of every covered dish in the icebox. The children, too, were getting lazy. They needed chores far more than having them performed by a hired adult.

I had also learned that too much solitude produced introspection, and too much analysis tended toward melancholy.

I pinched off bits of bread crust for the birds, scattering crumbs along the rail. The blue jays moved between branches, their heads cocked at attention to the bounty. I reflected that having a maid had given me lots of time to write. Shaking out the rest of the bread sack, I felt an appreciation for the season Jeremy had provided. I thought of my pen at the office as an iron with which I could press my feelings onto a page. Yet I sensed that I had disappointed Jeremy. He had given me books to read with the instruction to try and turn them into scripts. In every attempt, I choked all the necessary action with metaphors.

I took the far stairs built of mortared brick to start my descent to the back of the property. Roots and ground swells gave each tread its own angle as I clumped down in my open-heeled clogs. I crossed a hillside pad of knee-high weeds to the single back pine surrounded by bushes. I had taken the time for the private quiet known to those in cloisters. No one could hear me or see me.

It was my daily need to go down to the back acre. I felt exactly like a watch that had lost its accuracy and had to stand before God for adjustment. There were days I had resentments to bring that acted like sand grains clogging my works.

Part of my care was the whole situation with Jessie. She had denied that she knew where certain items of jewelry and clothing were. The child had just started disappearing for a few days and then would show up with false explanations. To me, she was raising every flag she could find for a father's attention.

Jeremy, in telling her he wouldn't tolerate lying, falsified a home address and transferred Jessie to a high school near his office. She had to report to his desk by four and sort papers for a minimum wage.

For Christmas, Gloria had given her father a television the size of one of his office shelves. Now he could watch sports and news from his padded desk chair. The only thing he needed from the house was a shower and clean clothes.

There was a new glaze of silence to Jeremy Foster. He was a back to me at night, and by day only exhibited a sealed inner eye.

I remembered how Arlene said there were some in Portland who wished they had my maid, house on a hill, and a husband in a Mercedes-Benz. I had to give a short laugh, thinking outside appearances rarely tell the scale of the battle.

I sat next to the trunk in a mulch of pine needles. Sometimes I would shut my eyes and other times leave them wide open. I don't think there is anybody in life who doesn't need help.

I left my car at the office parking lot in response to Jeremy's invitation for breakfast.

"Doesn't the interior look good?" He brushed his hand across the leather hearth above the steering wheel. I nodded my assent.

"Gloria found some special waxes for automotive interiors and spent Sunday morning hand rubbing them in."

It was only a few blocks from the office to the Breakfast Cottage, a restaurant with an exaggerated peaked roof.

Jeremy was vigorous in sprinkling pepper grains over the surface of the eggs, while I ate my bagel with feigned appetite. It was unusual for me to be invited midmorning for a meal. I wondered if he had any reason other than us having some time together like a handshake. There was a hum of language from the dining booths that outlined the side of our room. It was the talk of toast crumbs and coffee cup saucers. I felt a drowsiness that poor air and warmth produces.

Jeremy said he had a problem.

Instantly, I was alert. It was his quiet voice where one word doesn't weigh anymore in spoken sound than another. He had rehearsed some disclosure.

"It's a frailty."

He was pausing now with one of his favorite vocabulary words that's his synonym for the weakness in human nature.

"I just—it's just a lack of emotional attachment for you." He spread out his hands; they were open and empty.

I felt myself being pierced. Physical pain can never approximate the anguish in a spirit.

"It's something I've been struggling with a long time, and it's caused me a lot of suffering too."

I could have comforted him if he had grief from any other cause but this.

Instead, I sat completely mute from the shock of his statement.

While Jeremy paid the cashier, I walked by him and out to the parking lot. Waiting by the locked door, I stood in a state of fierce aloneness. In all my high wire acts of adaptation, I had never doubted the base of Jeremy's affection—it had been a fact that had helped me to keep trying and make adjustments. Now, he had rolled our safety net away. I felt afraid.

The front car seat was miles long for our distance.

I just went from his vehicle over to my station wagon and sat behind the steering wheel. Looking down, I saw that every indention in the floor mats was filled with sand. There was also a green crayon, an orange juice cap, one safety pin, a peso, and a grocery receipt. Then I gave my first cry in one deep sound.

His words seemed like a rock hurled into water. Upon impact, successive rings were appearing, round after round. The first wave was anguish for myself; I had just wanted to love and be loved. Then, I felt sorrow for my children; they deserved better. Then, I was in mourning for everyone alive who was suffering, and those who have, and those who will. The history of the world was in tears.

The girls were in the driveway. Anna's school sack was abandoned by the door. She and Mary Elisabeth were occupied with searching for the sun lizards that darted around the clay pots. Watching them gave me some consolation that they never seemed affected by all the change. They remained essentially cheerful.

"Why don't you ever bring home some donuts?" Anna said. Once in the front door, I found Matthew had brought in the mail to the front hall table. I glanced at the free newspaper of ads. It was headlined "HOME IMPROVEMENTS NEEDED." My pain could turn everything into a message.

When Jeremy came home, I was waiting for him in the kitchen. He got some ice and momentarily went upstairs to pour some alcohol over the cubes in his cup.

I watched him from the window seat. Here was my husband who could daily calculate the rise and fall of the dollar against every major world currency. He alone made decisions and carried weights that usually rested on whole institutions. I wanted us to stand again arm in arm.

"Oh, Jeremy, let's get marriage counseling. We have both helped a lot of people, but this is the time we need help ourselves.

"You can," he hissed. "I'm going to bed."

Both heat and emotion rise faster than logic. As he pursed his lips to walk past me, his silence seemed worse than any parting word.

"Won't you talk with me?" I cried.

He used a voice that was so quiet it seemed to come from the stillness that rides in the center of a storm.

"I'm not going to cast out my pearls ..." he said.

My mind filled in the last two words he omitted. This new wound wouldn't let me sit still enough to hear a choir sing. I had run out of cheeks to turn. In less than a second, I tightened my fingers into a fist and punched his upper arm. My knuckles hit the area of flesh where doctors give vaccinations.

When I finally crawled next to his sleeping side knowing he had no regard for me, it was a Hindu bed of spikes.

There was no release in sleep. A parade of dreams began, each with its own colored float. I saw my wedding bouquet with every flower dry and flammable. I dreamed a key was being inserted in our front door lock and someone said, "Is there a family in the house?"

I was in ancient Cana running back from the kitchen to the guests at the wedding supper, saying, "We have run out of wine."

January 15

There was an early morning mist lying in pockets along the crevices of the hills. My husband sat on the bed, changing the television channels with a remote. He weaved the warp of the screen with strands from every network's news. I interrupted a foreign journalist's report on Beirut.

"Jeremy, I've designed a daytime game program. The contestants will be a panel of wives, each allowed a specific time to relate their marital problems. The audience will vote by applause at who's the most ill treated, and the winner will get a ticket for one to a luxury resort."

Encouraged by him laughing, I switched off the television. "I've been around commercials for a long time. What is it you don't like about me—itchy dandruff flakes, these horrid age spots?" I held up the back of my hand.

All of a sudden, the walls seemed to sweat for seriousness. Jeremy stood up in a valley of decision. He could begin to stitch us together or rend us further apart by his answer.

"We all have blind spots in the perception of ourselves," I said. "I'm motivated to change."

After a prolonged pause, Jeremy replied, "I cannot stand how you are always so intense, always ardent; you repeat yourself, and everything to you is a holy cause."

The hope in me began to bolt. If there were a machine that took X-rays of a personality so its structure could be visible, I was intense. It went back to the months that the amniotic waters hid my form.

"And," he added in a softer voice, "you don't have any desire for accomplishing things ..."

He was wrong. But I couldn't find the words to explain my idea of progress as being internal and invisible. Jeremy stopped looking at me and gazed out at the mountains. "I am tired of any kind of demands. Look, Laurel, I know that I'm too much of an independent person for marriage. I really knew it the first time."

His eyes stayed on the hills. "The important thing is to take care of this in a way that won't cast a shadow on either of our reputations. No divorce. We'll just separate, and you can rent a house back in Oregon. We'll continue to make any necessary public appearances together."

I knew he meant those times that Mr. and Mrs. Foster were invited again as guests on a national Christian network or to the President's prayer breakfast.

The hypocrisy of his proposal made me look hard at him. His words reminded me of a tomb. The appearance was white washed and ornate, but inside were skeleton shards. Words are always a second face.

"It's just like making movies to you, isn't it Jeremy? Everything has to be for image and nothing for substance."

I raised my voice. "You don't seem to care about imitating what is good, only how to counterfeit it!"

A terrible silence filled the room. I had just displayed every characteristic that he had enumerated, plus a few more. My voice dropped. "I will not live a lie. And I will not leave you either."

He had become as stern and fierce as I had ever seen him. He answered me in a thunder peal. "I'll keep this room then, and you can sleep on the other side of the house by your children!"

Julia's bed had been empty for just over a week.

I studied Jeremy's face, not trusting myself to speak. If "lack of attachment" were a creature all its own, it had shed its skin, revealing features marked by hostility. I stood there not knowing how to leave the bedroom. It was now a territory that was neither "ours" nor "mine."

Only by thinking of a sculpture of an Indian I once saw could I walk to the door. He sat on a horse with a spear buried in his chest, but instead of being stooped over, his hands and face were raised to the sky.

January 17

It wasn't the sound of the shower that woke me, but the silence directly after it was turned off. My twin bed was above the kitchen. Soon I could hear Gloria take the whistling kettle off the burner to pour the water through the filter. She carried the coffee tray up the stairs to her father. Every morning she used the same soft knock at the door.

I stared at the wallpaper, knowing that my stepdaughter was seeing that I had been expelled from the room. I felt my face flush that such a close range observer could see our troubles. I didn't want to imagine even a line of their dialogue. I made it a forbidden thought.

I needed a devotion, feeling starved for daily bread, feeling I couldn't get my eyes high enough to see the hills from whence cometh my help. I chose one line and held it steady while tracing the wallpaper's miniature stars embossed on blue.

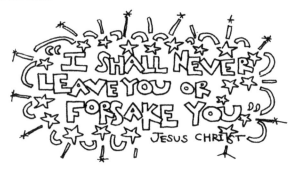

My impulse was to write, using my pen as alchemy, changing the baser circumstances into words. As a journal keeper, I wanted to divert some pain into language, but remembered that my diary was still at the office.

It wasn't until the afternoon, when I was bent in chores that I thought about the money. I was in the process of trying to roll the rubber garter down on a new vacuum cleaner bag. Stopping all work, I realized that because of my trust in my husband, I had taken all of my separate property earned before marriage and put it in a community account. It had not been done all at once. First was the balance in my checking and savings pass-books, then all the Treasury certificates as they matured. I had even wired him the down payment in time for the Topanga escrow closing.

I stood up to calculate. There were the additional cash assets from the sale of two houses that I had given my husband to deposit. It was Jeremy who asked for both of them to be sold. Abandoning the old Hoover, I went to look for our current account number in my purse.

One grief was that never before had I doubted Jeremy's financial integrity. All numbers, bills, forms, and taxes belonged to his talent. I thought of him as knowing the zip codes for America.

I didn't bother with the yellow pages, but waited through the sixty second recording that exhorts Los Angeles residents to keep better phone records. I gave the information operator our bank and branch, then dialed the seven digits into the North Hollywood Bank of America.

I imagined that the institution's officer only had to twirl a knob and look into a lighted computer screen. "Bennett is my mother's maiden name." She stated an amount less than two thousand dollars. I thanked her, marveling at the polite composure that's possible when layers of the earth are shaking. Over two hundred thousand dollars were gone. I had no alternative but to confront Jeremy at his office, the center arena of his business.

There was no color left to the evening when I could finally take my car keys in hand. Driving to the valley, I felt the sweat of an ancient soldier dispatched for battle when his town had been looted. The bulk of that money was an estate for my children. Someday I had wanted them to go to good universities, without student loans. We had always lived simply; it was Jeremy who was extravagant.

Only my husband's car was in the lot. Gloria liked to take a few hours at a health spa before following her father home. Someone had forgotten to lock the warehouse door. I walked through the darkness to the lights at the front offices. I could hear Jeremy's television, but at the doorway saw that his back was to the screen. He had on his glasses, a short-sleeved shirt and was reading a trade magazine.

"Hello, it's me." I said.

His reply was equally cordial. He rose to his feet, not in greeting, but just to face me.

I looked at his room. It was where he received many of his prospective film investors. It could have belonged to a theologian for the number of its Bible related pictures and verses. He had a number of framed photos of sites in Israel. The back wall was entirely books; some were leather bound prayers, and others, sermon principles. I knew that one devotional there had been inscribed to the two of us from Bill and Ruth Graham as a wedding present. Not wanting to forget my diary, I decided to get it first before beginning any discussion.

As I turned, Jeremy must have quickly risen from his chair, for he was right behind me.

"I thought it was best to make a change," he said. His voice had an anxious pitch.

He was right if he was anticipating my hysteria. When I turned on the light, everything of mine was gone. The quilt, baskets, library table, and rug had been replaced by standard office equipment. One desk faced the door, and another was set at the side. Both had typewriters.

"I moved Gloria in here," Jeremy said.

My impulse was to run and cry ... I wanted to put the children in the car and find an Oregon cave to call home. I wanted anything where there could be peace and order.

I knew I was shaking.

"Where is all that money, Jeremy?"

I followed him back into his own office. He shrugged, avoiding eye contact. "Laurel, you of your own free will allowed everything to go to a joint account. Even the law says it's mine as much as yours. It had to be spent on necessary things."

How I understood the anger of Christ that cried: "YOU HYPOCRITES WHO DEVOUR A WIDOW'S PURSE, AND FOR A PRETENSE, MAKE A LONG PRAYER."

I followed Jeremy into the warehouse after he had switched on the lights. I could see the coat rack protruding from a box near the door. The oval basket was next to it with the quilt folded over the top. I couldn't stop myself from fluttering with tears and taking breaths that shook my chest. Jeremy walked to the rear door and loaded my possessions into the hatchback.

I drove up into the colder air of the canyon. My rage knotted my ideas into the same cord that Jesus used on certain businessmen in the temple. He overturned tables and the seats of those who sold doves.

Jeremy Foster was now a wolf to me. He had an elongated jaw. His closet was filled with sheepskins, which he knew how to fit over every claw.

After expending myself in thoughts of outrage, I became sober and still. It was only my desire for my diary that gave me the strength to pull the things into the house from the back of the car.

I brought in the large basket last. All of my papers were gone. I couldn't find even one of my spiral theme books filled with the events and abstractions of my married months. I could now assume it was an intentional act of disposal; they looked exactly like diary records. But, my journal was safe. It had been concealed by my haphazard filing system. I always kept it hanging from the coat rack deep within a woven peasant's bag.

Taking it out, I scribbled in the margin, *That I might withstand these days, and having done all, to stand.*

January 26

I knew that my resolve was crumbling. The days seemed like seawater trying to wash out the mortar in my walls. But the damage was the dampness that crept within.

I barely saw Jeremy and Gloria, except in the mornings; it was as if they took a strict vow of silence when passing by me in the kitchen or walking past me in the hall. Their meditation seemed audible—they wanted us to leave.

I sat on the stairs marveling at their stamina for dissension. Pulling my knees up to my chin, I could feel my need for a resting place apart from the extreme tensions in the house.

Going down to the kitchen phone, I dialed the area code for the Christian Renewal Center. Within the minute, the wire of a ringing telephone stretched into acres of Oregon fir trees.

Pastor Hansen answered. He had pronounced our matrimonial vows over us. "Well, yes," was his immediate reply when I asked for a room. He explained that the lodges were booked through the winter for conferences.

I felt I had been living in a brutal boxing arena and needed the corner of the ring. There would be water and a towel. I couldn't guess the time it would take between bells.

Having forgotten to put on slippers, my bare feet were cold from standing on the clay tiles. The floor had absorbed January's air. I sat next on a stool and dialed Topanga Elementary School. I wished it were summer vacation so I didn't have to interrupt their new winter term. The receptionist used her Southern California vocabulary; she wanted to know if I were taking them with me "on location."

I knew I would have to tell Jeremy my plan. Phoning his office, I hoped he would be able to take my call. His voice warmed as I mentioned going to Oregon. He had one instruction—Work with a Realtor to find a rental house, and he would get a moving company to ship to us the personal furniture we would need.

His words made me feel like an Indian ordered from the tribal lands to some bleak reservation with two bedrooms, one bath.

Mary Elisabeth brought into the packed car a blue paper hand fastened to a foot long stick. She had created it at school, and each fingernail was a small star. Using it as a wand, she waved "good bye" to our house while I backed the station wagon from the driveway.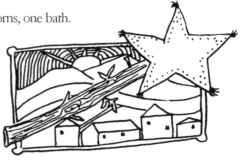

She turned her attention to Jean LaCour's carport and the row of mailboxes on the posts.

Anna suggested we make one stop in Topanga before going on the highway. She wanted to go by Gus McFadden's barn on the state park and look again at the baby winter goats. I explained that we couldn't as it was going to take three days of driving to get to our camp in Oregon.

January 29
Christian Renewal Center, Oregon

Once through Salem, the country roads were designed to go around fields, unlike the six-lane freeway that went straight through them. There was snow. It wasn't the thick drifts of winter calendar photos, but the faintest etching of white on the land that was colored by overcast skies. I wanted to drink from the view through the dashboard window.

Matthew was in the front. He was already asking if he could drive once we turned onto the gravel logging road that led up to the retreat center. There was a grocery bag crumpled at his feet and three skeleton apple cores on the small shelf behind the shift.

Our last stretch was a single lane. I could remember it in summer, rich with foxgloves and daisies. Opening the window for a moment, I breathed in the cold of the afternoon.

Both Allan and Eunice Hansen were home. Part of their greeting was to explain that the electric heater in the trailer had already been turned on. As Allan told me the exact location of our new abode, I realized it was the trailer the summer cook had lived in. It was at a point in between the house where I had dressed to be a bride and the chapel where I had taken my vows.

Once up at the top parking lot, the children ran before me. They lived with the impulse to race. Our hours in the car had only wound up the springs in their legs, which were waiting for release. The front of the trailer rested on cement blocks and ends of boards. It had a faded decal of a bull's horn near the roof that read "Trails West."

Anna, the first inside, turned to announce it had a musty smell.

"But where will we all sleep?" Matthew asked.

There was a cubical for eating, two twin beds, and a quarter of a bathroom with a foot pedal for flushing the toilet. I showed them how to collapse the table's leg and unfold the dining seats to make another width for our sleeping bags.

I looked at the slick blond paneling and orange rubber-backed carpet. I pronounced it far better than our wide home with its strife.

"You hit your husband?"

I sat alone with Eunice Hansen in her living room. Her husband had just taken my children over to the lodge to go through a box of coats and sweaters left from the weeks of summer sessions. Mary Elisabeth had wanted to inventory the toys and borrow a few from the box in the nursery.

To Eunice's question, I had to nod my head "yes." Her expression bordered on unbelief. "What are the ways you differ from the person that Jeremy Foster thought he was marrying?" She asked, meaning it as a point of meditation, and not requiring a reply.

Using my headlights was the only possible way to get back to our trailer. Clouds blotted every star. There was a penetrating dampness with the silence of the woods. It was the kind of night where fallen leaves are absorbed into the ground's wet mulch.

Once we were all zipped into our single flannel bags, I listened to the children breathing. Their sound reminded me of a factory for manufacturing sleep. Because of the number of my thoughts, I knew it would be hours before I could join their production line.

I had begun analyzing my two marital relationships. My first husband donated my clothes to Goodwill Industries and moved in with the pregnant baby-sitter. This time my life savings are gone, and Jeremy wants to force us out of state. I felt like a tree that lightening had struck twice.

Restless, I sat up and found my tennis shoes in the dark. Already wearing a sweat shirt and sweat pants, I wrapped my sleeping bag around me as a thick robe. Stepping outside, I stood insulated from feeling any cold. My strongest sense was hearing the night's sounds. There was a soft rain on all the branches receding back into the woods. I walked a few feet from the door listening to my feet shuffle on the gravel. Through the trees, I could finally see one light at a staff member's house. My breath changed to the briefest mist about my mouth. I walked down the short trail to the chapel and opened the single side door. Running my finger pads along the wall, I felt my way to the inset box of light switches by the double doors. The one I touched illuminated all the bulbs that shine down on the altar. I could see them again out the window as the instant reflection created a second church with a quality of lines like a room in dreams. There were no pews. A stack of folding chairs was leaning against one of the walls.

The rug was almost startling for its bright shade of red. It seemed like part of a devotion, that it was one of three colors by which all colors are made.

I walked to the front. The altar was built of wood as thick as half a tree. On it was a single crucifix. I couldn't stop the memory of the last time I had stood there. The new Mr. and Mrs. Foster, ready to go forth, seemed like such a triumphant union. Now we had our own nail holes, thorns and a spear.

I traced through my mind the utterance from the cross, "MY GOD, WHY HAVE YOU FORSAKEN ME?" I thought of each letter as separate and unconnected, trailing off into all the contradictions that had been endured.

I still believed, even with all the abuse, that marriage vows were meant to be a permanent covenant. Only I got the side of the contract that was "For worse, poorer, and in sickness."

I wished for a cathedral to trace the passion in stained glass. I imagined the act of refusing the bitter drink, which I pictured as a raised cup spilling over the sides with the memory of every act that caused hurt.

I had a realization: In drinking from the bitter waters of my own betrayal, it was clear that I was poisoning myself. I was always sipping on details and was ready to pass the cup to anyone who would listen.

There was no stopping Calvary's next line: "FORGIVE THEM. THEY DON'T KNOW WHAT THEY ARE DOING."

I didn't want to imagine anymore. Wrapping my sleeping bag around me closer, I turned to go outside. I had too much rage. Jeremy had come courting the week *People* magazine had printed my book's earnings ... From the beginning, he had been calculating and deceitful.

My anger compared to having a tooth that hurt from even the slightest pressure. My tongue was quick to touch it. I knew if I didn't get it extracted, all

Thomas Victor

my teeth would finally rot, and I could never smile.

So it was torn from me while I cried: "Help me to forgive Jeremy Foster!"

I felt as if I weighed nothing; I walked back to the trailer experiencing a cloud-base height above the rain.

February
Salem, Oregon

"What are you going to do now, Laurel?"

"Well, go immediately back to Topanga and be genuinely cheerful to every citizen in the hall. I will not beg, cry, or demand."

I sat with Arlene in her living room. She had inherited some of her grandmother's furniture. Every piece was arranged in such close proximity that a feeling of confidentiality was lent to every sentence.

I told her how I had called the office to tell Jeremy I was coming back. He responded by not saying very much at all. His few words seemed much more indifferent to my news than angry.

Arlene handed me a cup. It was an old flowered mug painted with English buttercups.

"I know it's going to be hard. But there is a lot of difference between the day I left and now." I thought of myself coming north, riddled with bullet holes, a seeping, bleeding woman. Now, there is ointment and armor.

I sipped from my drink after testing its temperature. Its steam warmed my cheeks as I thought how feelings can be deception's field. It had been easy for me to perceive Jeremy at first as having every virtue; and likewise, he thought he was marrying a success-oriented professional.

The real failing had already been in operation long before we met. It was simply that I had wanted to be married so much that my yearning blocked me from reason and counsel. I had cried too long and too often for a husband. It was my dream that I had clenched in a fist of discontent and wouldn't release. But time had now pried every finger open. There is peace in an open and upraised hand that isn't grasping for anything.

"Through this, Arlene, I hope I'm learning to be content in whatever state I'm in, or will be in." My friend abandoned her chair to come and sit right next to me.

"By all evidence, Laurel, it does seem that Jeremy will move away. But until that hour, there is even the possibility that his commitment can revive."

I nodded in agreement; we both knew families where dead relationships had been restored.

She touched my arm saying, "You can't carry the responsibility for what he alone decides."

It made me think of him as a clipper ship, resplendent in pennants and sails. But his direction had nothing to do with his banners, only with the hidden rudder of his own will.

I answered Arlene slowly, "By coming into my life, he could not complete me. And if he should leave, it will not defeat me."

My eye traced some of Arlene's labors at the other end of the room. A shirt she was sewing for her husband was set on the back of a chair. One sleeve in matching material lay on the table. I knew I had to go. Arlene taught piano lessons, and one of her students would soon be coming up the walk.

Once on the porch. I saw that the rain had stopped. Isolated drops from the morning's deluge fell from branches. I crossed the yard looking up at the tree limbs hanging above my head. Their lines seemed sealed into winter, but I knew that within each twig were factories for leaves. By the time I got to the car, my feet were wet. While backing out of the driveway, I noticed that the wind was blowing over houses, across streets and lawns to the south.

April 1
Topanga, California

It started in the morning; the front door kept opening and shutting. The first time, I assumed he was leaving for the office. The second time, he may have forgotten something. By the third, I knew that Jeremy Foster was putting his clothes in the car. Jessie had been sent back to Minnesota some weeks before, and I could assume that Gloria's departure would be coordinated with him vacating the house. She may already be gone.

I felt quiet relief. I had paid all the coins of mourning, day by day, dropping sorrows into the black hole of what was wrong. I couldn't afford more grief. I needed my energy to solve some practical problems.

Jeremy had had another conference with me at my return. He had picked the living room, and sat in the chair furthest from my couch proximity. He took papers from his briefcase; the house was in the first stage of legal foreclosure proceedings.

I had asked him how that could happen. The reply had held a slight sneer that I could understand so little about business. There were delinquent house payments and an overdue balloon payment. He had a quit-claim document that would deed the house to me now, with all its financial problems, as part of the pending divorce settlement. I felt full of earthquake epicenters, but didn't shake, and cry, and run. I took the property.

All the rooms were like a herd of prize dairy cows; I would find ways for them to give milk. The master bedroom could be immediately rented, and the guesthouse leased. Upon demand, I could be a Bed and Breakfast for canyon visitors. During the three months of summer, the entire property would be available for an inflated sum.

This was the day in my life where I should go lay down in the backyard, and squeeze dirt. It would be my salute to *Gone With The Wind* at the part where Atlanta had burned, and the plantation was threatened. "I'll plant the crops myself," said Scarlet O'Hara, and the Little Red Hen. Shields can be forged from literature.

April 17

I didn't have any potato soup left. Fifty-six cents fed us for days when invested in the right vegetables. I already owned all the necessary seasonings. I forgot to soak the pinto beans. My noodle casserole would take too long. The secret is in making the white sauce.

The children's solution was a unanimous request; they wanted to go out for pizza. I agreed on the one condition that we earn the money for it together.

"How many years will it take us to pick up that many bottles?" asked Matthew. "We could work the beach and for twenty-nine cents a piece buy a hamburger."

Anna loves sarcasm. She suggested we look around all the parking meters for dropped change and eat in a year-and-a-half.

"No," I laughed, and explained how the airport has a system where one gets an automatic quarter for each returned cart. Hardly anyone bothers, and they are abandoned all over the parking structure.

In the car, I suggested that we divide into two teams and compete. Once each side earns eight dollars, we can get any kind of large pizza we want, plus drinks. The winners choose the toppings.

"That's 32 carts," interjected Anna. She was tightening her tennis shoe laces, putting each foot up on the dashboard. We would be team one, and Matthew, plus Mary Elisabeth, our competition. I used the free parking and the complimentary airport bus, which took us to the terminal.

"Don't separate from your buddy, and in one hour we'll do our first accounting," I said while pointing to the clocks on the wall.

Mary Elisabeth was especially jubilant about winning. Their strategy was to follow anyone loaded with luggage, and once at their vehicle offer to return it for them. "We even got tips," she added while hopping on her right foot and staring directly at her older sister.

I was surprised at the silence when I asked which pizza restaurant they wanted to go to. We were all hungry by now. Matthew wanted to spend it differently because, he explained, it was so much money, and we had all worked for it. It was a joint decision that our discretionary funds would be used to buy a small appliance. Everyone wanted a waffle maker. We had enough cash left over to buy fresh strawberries and real whipped cream. Once home, Anna made the batter, Mary and I washed the fruit, while Matthew used the whisk until the cream was stiff.

It's a wonderful mystery how the poor can sometimes be so rich, and some of the wealthy are absolutely impoverished.

May 14

For once, I had mostly answers for Arlene. I had already picked up a lot of the puzzle pieces that were shaped to fit the questions. I was beyond, "Why?" I thought more about "How Much?" and "When?"

My parents loaned me the house debt balloon money. I rented the guesthouse to Leanne for $500, and she sends that amount to my folks each month.

"She's a computer expert, and on Sunday wears white gloves and rings the hand bells in her church orchestra." The last couple I had in my bedroom was an elderly British couple who liked pots of tea by the hour.

"I already have my tenants for the entire summer. They are math and philosophy professors from Illinois that will be teaching at UCLA."

I told how I stopped at a large grocery store with the intent to cruise the imported deli section for free cheese samples. A worker was removing all the packages that had expired code dates. He was glad to fill for me a large carton and mark it down to a mere five dollars.

Once I grasped how much is actually thrown away, I made an agreement with the management to donate any discards to my "about to be created" food bank. The local Topanga church agreed, and I brought in two brand new trash containers for the back warehouse. It is fun to come and pull in my nets.

"We have so much food that every Friday I now make an open potluck for the neighborhood."

It's like creating a time warp back to the 1950s in the world before television corralled everyone inside—and shut the door.

I laugh while telling her that my white-collar guests always devour my dishes, and I just never mention that the main ingredient came from a large, clean, trash can.

"Lots of people in the canyon now know to go to the church and get groceries." There are some hidden campsites for homeless people and laborers who sit in front of the post office with tools for doing manual jobs. These are our real guests—for all food supplements.

I'm waiting too for answers to my letters. I've been putting lots of job requests in envelopes. They are like bottles that have been cast into the waves of overseas mail. I'm asking private schools, in the countries I would like to visit, for a job.

I am well, I can walk. I like my present mobility. I may as well take my children and see the world.

1988

July 16
Botswana, Africa

I have finished apologizing. First, of course to Mary Elisabeth, and then to everyone that would voice objections. My parents would probably scream if they knew. Anna would be kissing the Oregon soil in humble thanks that she didn't have to come with me. My friends would be aghast. They think of me as normal, with a fuel economy car, and assume I'm a registered Republican.

We have no choice but to hitchhike across the desert. I learned yesterday that the one bus has broken down. With a good vehicle, it could be only five hours to the main highway. We have just finished our one week vacation taking a guide and log canoe and camping in the animal reserve known as the Okavango Delta. It was the Africa of safari brochures that I learned about while teaching in the capitol.

Mary is cheerful while we carry our bags along the last quarter mile of asphalt. She's convinced someone will stop in a safari jeep with binoculars mounted on the windowsills. She also knows she's about to get something on me; I may have to live with something close to the orbit of blackmail.

We were told last night about a bottle shop grocery where people congregate who need a lift. It's also the last stop on pavement before the corrugation and the dust.

I actually see a crowd ahead. Without the bus, there must be over sixty Batswana waiting down there for a ride. Behind them, the white chalk road stretches into pin-line infinity. Stopping with my daughter, I want to survey this vista of one of the world's great deserts. Even the literal name of "Kalihari" means "the great thirst." Somewhere in those distances are nomadic bushmen carrying ostrich egg vessels of carefully gleaned water.

Picking up our pace, we walk through the milling crowd. There's a lot of charcoal evidence of past fires. Each footstep is also recorded in the soft sandy soil, along with horse hoof prints and tracks from small herds of goats. Most of the people are reclining on blankets folded to about the width of a cot. There are battered suitcases, along with cardboard boxes and black enamel cooking pots with long handles.

I notice one European couple in back packs, while my daughter is commenting on the number of babies. They are asleep or in wide-eyed peace, all held to their mother's back by a special wrapping of blankets. The knot that secures them is worn like a brooch above the breasts.

There's a distinct smell too, with so many people milling together. It's not unpleasant, but a blending of earth and smoke from fires.

We walk beyond, as our best hope will be in a solitary solicitation. Each vehicle that passes looks so loaded with passengers and gear, I don't even bother to solicit the drivers for help. Here, the signal of request doesn't use the upturned thumb of North American highways but the shaking of an extended hand as if seriously afflicted with palsy. The only unloaded four-wheel drive wagon that I tried it on has just passed us again—and this time in the direction back to town. I think we are going to have terrible chances, looking back at the mass of competition.

We left camp when it was early this morning and cool enough for coats, but now with our exertion, I'm going to strip it off for my bag. The clothes are equally divided now between the two suitcases, as the canned goods have mostly been depleted.

At the grinding sound of a truck coming to a halt, we turn back to stare. It's an enormous semi with a single tractor tied up by the cab in an elongated empty bed. Strips of unmatched metal are bolted together to create the sides. These partitions are vibrating with such a clanging that the noise dominates the crowd until the gears are changed and the motor is turned off.

As the driver jumps out of the cab, we continue. Ahead is nothing but sand and a flat, shimmering vista of sparse bushes. If lucky, one can sometimes pick out a distant ostrich.

Again, it's the sound that makes me turn back. People are swarming to the rig and hoisting themselves up onto the empty flat bed. Baggage is being handed up, and arms are stretching out to aid various women. The word that it is going to Francistown reaches us. That would put us on the main highway with busses and even hotels. It is a moment of decision.

Remembering how loaded every vehicle has been, I decide for the sure thing. I motion to Mary so we too can seek a place. My daughter is reluctant, and I sympathize that riding in an open truck is going to be unpleasant.

"But just think where we can be by early afternoon."

"Oh well, grit your teeth," she replies. "Or more likely, grit in your teeth!"

Mary, scrambling up first, fits her toe on the hub cap and hoists herself through a separation between the tin partitions. After giving her both bags,

I feel panic hearing the motor ignite. Everyone seems to be up there other than the few who race out of the shop clutching drinks. They stream past me, crying out in the Setswana language what I interpret as, "Wait!"

I'm actually having to slither up the metal and over the side. The front of my coat has absorbed every track. Starting to brush myself off, the lurch of acceleration makes me scramble for my own place of passage. Most are huddled up by the tractor and cab, although there are people everywhere wrapping their blankets and adjusting their bundles for backrests.

Closest to us is a rig-sized spare tire that we stake for our passenger seat. Around us is so much dirt that radish seeds would flourish. Any ideas that we could talk or even look at the view vanish in the rumbling of our first thirty feet. The metal partitions vibrate with such a force that it equals thousands of giant pot lids being slammed together. The highway dirt actually stings our faces forcing us to retreat into our coats that we pull over our heads.

There are no shocks to absorb the bumps, forcing me to somewhat recline to protect the bones of my spine. Every human being is isolated by the necessity of preserving himself or herself through what is already an ordeal, and the minute hand has made only five rotations. I peek out at Mary. She has completely covered her head in her purple down jacket. In my second of survey, I am pelted with stinging gravel bits. For once, being deaf would not be a handicap.

Back under my black coat, I can hear vehicles passing us. This means I need to recalculate our expected time to hours more for practicing wilderness endurance.

Thankfully, some men up in the control cab must have to throw up or urinate. Stopping provides a momentary reprieve for us souls in one of Dante's outer orbits. Casting off my coat, I look at my daughter. A fine silt of dirt has covered her face. Any wrinkle of skin is a shelf for an extra etching. She laughs at the sight of me. I can see my own arms are likewise dusted and only imagine my reflection.

"What are you doing to stay sane?" I ask, only daring such a question because she is in a surprisingly good mood.

"First, I recited time tables, seeing how far I could go, but that got boring. Then, I began remembering all our trips. Mother, do you remember that time on the train in Mexico?"

The motor sounds the doom on anymore interaction. There's a motion around me of everyone pulling survival wraps around their heads.

I know exactly what Mary is reminiscing. She's recalling a past test of endurance. She was only eight then and Anna was ten. Our cross-country train in Mexico had been stalled for hours due to some repair work on the tracks ahead. Too afraid to risk getting off in a small village station, I took Matthew for just a few moments to explore some of the back cars. Glancing out a window, he shrieked. We could see the front part of the train, with the two little girls, starting down the track, leaving us back in the unhooked cars.

Jumping off, we flew after them, and after breaking my own land-speed record, overtook the two hysterical sisters. We found Spanish matrons trying to comfort them in their abandonment by giving them mangoes and murmuring endearments that the girls could never understand. Their vocabulary didn't extend much beyond "tortilla" and "peso."

The memory cracks my own interior photo album. My childhood had safe vacations with no real discomfort other than parents who smoked in a closed car. Sometimes I would lie on the floor to breathe the less tainted air under their front seats.

I misjudged, by over four hours, the time it would take for us to get to the main highway. The wheels register the hum of cement. As we turn, it's already evening when the driver pulls into a gas station. Most of the other passengers are unloading their bags and jumping off to the pavement. Mary and I also move our suitcases to exit.

"You're not getting off?"

It's the Europeans, who we learned at another five-minute driving break are from a university in Germany.

"The only place you can hope for a hotel is in Francistown," he says while rubbing his beard.

Mary and I cannot face another four hours in this truck. It gets cold too, when the sun is down; in the Southern Hemisphere, July is the middle of winter.

Mary, seeing my hesitancy, has her own solution. She has seen a family having their car filled at the pumps. With South African plates, they could be returning from Victoria Falls and are on route through Gaborone and our school.

Deciding to ask for help, Mary lowers herself to the ground. This family must have uniformed help in the kitchen and a man that trims the flower beds. Even their sheets would be ironed, and their children wear hats as part of their required school uniform. The father is dressed in a suit coat and tie.

In contrast, Mary Elisabeth looks like she has rolled in a coal bin. She's wearing one of her brother's old tee shirts. It's red with a fuzzy imprint of a Kodiak bear inviting people to the Arctic Circle.

I can almost feel their incomprehension that a young, white child would jump off of a truck in the company of Africans and solicit a ride. The mother turns to her children in the back as if to distract them from such a sight, as the father refuses with an exaggerated shake of his head. It's the journey of Tom Sawyer, now cast with a female in Southern Africa.

I climb down to buy us rounds of soda pop in consolation. The station toilet doesn't have a sink, so we can't wash the day's dirt from our hands.

It's a different configuration for the last haul to Francistown. I don't see any women at all except for the one German girl. The couple has unrolled their sleeping bags on top of a flat folded tent that they can use for insulation. We move our gear to a niche created in a corner up by the cab and tractor. It's starting to get dark, which blurs any of the other passenger's features. About twenty men sit in clusters, and some have bottles of alcohol they are already passing among themselves.

By now, we know well that noise of the ignition. Suppressing a shudder, I reach out to Mary in a gesture of sympathy. The texture of her hair is so stiff with dirt that it feels as coarse as yarn. I think of the years that I showered away nothing more significant than sweatshirt lint or sock fuzz from between my toes.

Our comfort has not increased in the transfer from corrugated dirt to pavement travel. The temperature is plunging. After fishing out all possible garments to wear, we button our coats. Still everything feels like paper against the rushing cold. Together we have to lie down to cut our wind exposure.

"Maybe I should put my coat over us," I whisper to Mary as mine is full length, and it can be a kind of blanket.

My daughter refuses and in turn offers to remove a sweatshirt that we can share as a pillow. We've penetrated to a realm of consideration where all our usual objections or irritations with each other have disappeared. I know that as this ordeal ends we'll drop back into the orbit of me suggesting that she shouldn't wear all 27 woven friendship bracelets until they fray from her arms. And I'll be asked to remain in the car when I fetch her from school to lessen her possibilities for humiliation. I might be wearing my authentic pair of bell-bottoms in these years of pegged pants.

But for now, all that we have is the power of kindness for warmth. We lapse into silence while holding each other and our personal tumbling thoughts.

Unexpectantly, the truck veers off the pavement and onto the shoulder. As we roll down an embankment, I fear the driver may have fallen asleep, or worse, they are sharing their own whiskey bottle up in front and missed the highway.

We come to a halt, and I can hear men standing and a shuffling of feet.

"What is happening?" asks Mary.

I motion her to silence, wanting us to remain as invisible as possible. I've clocked thousands of hours reading news magazines. Every evil of man has been told in small print. Numbers of tourists have disappeared from parts of Africa, even close to where we are. I don't want Mary to even consider our vulnerability.

"This is probably just another toilet break," I whisper.

"No," she says. "They would never come so far off the road for that."

We can hear both doors of the cab slamming shut. I rise up to peek over the side. I'm hoping they will raise the hood or do some limbering exercises for a stiff neck. Instead, the light of a struck match momentarily reflects on the blade of a hatchet. I can see the one man trailing in the back also has an ax. They pause as one lights his cigarette, inhales and passes it to another. Just a few feet from us, they begin to quietly walk in our direction. I've heard how rural witch doctors sometimes use parts of the human body for their medicine.

Feeling scared, I pull my Swiss army knife out from my purse and remove my wallet, pushing it into the lining of my coat.

"What are you doing?" asks Mary in a voice that is more breath than whisper.

"I don't know," I mouth back.

Neither of us talks, trying to discern through their tones to what's being said. The men from the front are now calling to those behind us. It sounds like a command. We hear men jumping off both sides of the truck and a talking that recedes as they walk into distances.

I stand up, and we are all alone except for a moving lump of one of the Germans sitting up in a sleeping bag.

"Do you know what's going on?" I ask.

"Firewood," the woman replies. "My husband went to help them too."

Even as she is speaking, we can hear the ring of axes. As I put my knife back in my pocket and replace my wallet in my purse, the first of the severed tree limbs is being thrown over the side.

One carrier is her husband, and she replies in English to his German sentences, "Wonderful!"

"The driver," she shouts over to us, "is so surprised that a foreigner will come and help, that he is inviting us all to be his guests tonight at his home in Francistown."

An older man with white wool hair comes to confirm the invitation. On the way back to his cab, he stops at our corner to ask us personally to be his guests.

"Oh, thank you," I reply. "But it will be so late we can just get a hotel."

"Nothing in town has its doors open after 11:00! You won't be able to get into any hotel," he says with a soft chuckle. "But at my house, we'll have tea and a fire. And in the morning you can bathe."

This time my thanks is uttered in humility. My impulse is to sob. I can still feel the weight of the knife in my pocket.

Francistown has few lights. I didn't even see any colored neon but just irregularly spaced globes erected for area illumination. Now, in a subdivision, the houses look like they couldn't be more than four-room rectangles with a tin roof. Like Gaborone, all the yards are dirt due to the climate's lack of precipitation. Some of my students in my Gaborone school, back in the capital, have only seen rain twice in their lifetime. They told me all schools and businesses close in instant celebration.

It feels like we are just coasting to a halt, as if the driver has calibrated the exact moment to release his foot from the gas. From our corners, we gather belongings in relative silence. There's an awareness and respect for a sleeping neighborhood. Most of the bed passengers just melt away into the night, except for the Germans, and us, who follow the driver and his four helpers now carrying pieces of firewood.

I like the old man. He seems to delight in providing hospitality. My muscles are aching from the day's marathon. I'm thinking too, of the promised list for warmth, tea, and a bath. An instruction in Setswana directs where the wood should be piled and for a canvas sheet to be unfolded that was stored at the side of the house. We are motioned to sit on the tarp, as a fire is built before us. The long branches extend like rays from the center blaze. Our host waves his hand to indicate we can sleep anywhere we like.

He, himself, chooses the spot directly in front of his door for his pile of blankets.

Silently, from around the back, comes a daughter with a tray stacked with cups that she passes to each of us. She returns, and I'm dazzled by the sterling silver tea service she bears with matching dignity. It belongs in the palace bringing cucumber sandwiches to the queen. There's an ornate pitcher for milk and another with boiling water for diluting one's drink. Using tongs sculpted with claw tips, for the sugar cubes, I can see the ovals of my finger nails are encrusted with dirt. The sight of my filthy hands keeps me from reaching for a shortbread cookie. The elegance is so incongruous with our setting. Even as we take our first sips, some of the men have retreated to the far corner of the yard where they have turned their backs to urinate.

When I explain to the German couple that we lack camping equipment, they pass over to us their tent that we can use as a makeshift blanket. We'll need the extra insulation, and the dirt pours out from its folds while we adjust its broad side.

All the men, now, are beginning to spin their blankets around them like cocoons. Pulling up our canvas, I feel like a mole that scratches out some soil in the hole of its burrow. I turn to Mary in the process of seeking to match hip bones with the earth's depression.

The fire is still bright enough to see her. I can trace the track of a tear that washed a course down her cheek; the grime lets me know that only one has fallen. It was a silent passage to where her fist smudged it from her cheek. It's a feat of adulthood not to announce when one is crying.

Already we have been told that we are just blocks from the busy bus route to Gaborone, our school, our things, our airplane tickets home. The promised bath will be a bucket of water that will be warmed in the morning's ash for everyone's hands and face.

I reach over to my daughter. Mary Elisabeth has been too old for me to hold her hand, until tonight, when she has become old enough to let me.

December 1988

December 2
Bangkok, Thailand

Being so early at the airport, my flight number and return to Los Angeles has not even been posted on the mechanical board of departures. Not able to check in, I cruise airport shops, marveling how customers could just step outside and from almost any vendor buy silk ties at half the price.

It has only been a week but with a solid teaching offer in Bankok. I'm anxious though for home. In my absence, Matthew has probably left the bathtub filled with water so his goldfish could get exercise. I miss Anna and her sister pretending they are horses and overturning chairs to create a three-room jumping course.

At the Thai Air desk, I'm told that my flight has been postponed for 24 hours. I'm given a phone to contact my family and a hotel voucher packet. I have to swallow an impulse for tears as the sticker is pressed on my ticket with tomorrow's date.

To keep from further mourning, I dump my bag onto the hotel bed and dash back to the open elevator. Walking between the front door taxis, I look for the special city busses that charge the extra nickel for air conditioning. We drive past photo billboards that announce a Miss Thailand was crowned Miss World. There's a hand painted sign advertising a tourist spot where a cobra fights a mongoose.

Remembering my first day immersion into Bangkok, I decide to try again one of the temples that had been closed due to a pending visit of the king. It was listed in all the English visitor's brochures as an important city landmark.

The outer walls are encrusted with bits of sparkling glass—the inlaid surface compares to the visuals of a kaleidoscope. The entrance stairs are covered with the free-form shapes of all the visitor's shoes. Guards are stationed inside the door to make sure one immediately sits or drops to their knees. Another temple employee has his vigilance trained to the soles of visiting feet to make sure they don't point to any object of adoration.

The central feature is a solid emerald Buddha. Its size is identical to the base of a living room lamp or a substantial cookie jar. I can't stay long. Those who are prostrate with supplications have tapirs of lit incense, and the pall of the sweet smelling smoke chokes the room. It's as if cigarettes are being exhaled through filters of cheap perfume.

After reclaiming my shoes, I want to sit on a bench and let my senses recover. I choose to look down at a water lily secured in an urn then up at the sky. While stretching my neck between these points, I'm approached by one of the three monks that are also in the plaza.

He asks my name and about the state of my health according to the script on every chapter one, language book in the world.

"I am fine, thank you. How are you?"

The other two monks join us, then request for me to accompany them back to the temple and practice American English with the other resident monks.

Maybe true nurses can't help but rise to their feet when they hear of fevers to cool or cuts to bandage. I wouldn't budge, but the chance for a blackboard makes me spring up in agreement.

They begin to move towards the temple gate, but one turns with an admonition: "It's only proper for you to walk behind us."

Reducing my speed, I have to laugh that here the idea of a woman's role has hardly evolved to having the right to vote.

It's surprising that they lead me out into the street. Their golden robes are the exact color of chrysanthemums. The length of them makes them appear to be gliding through the block of vendors. I notice how my progress is monitored by quick expressionless glances. We are such an odd parade. Out of respect, the throng parts for them and me in their wake.

Looking ahead of my golden horses, I can see we are heading straight for the river. There's a dock with a crowd waiting for a water bus, which resembles an open barge. For a few cents fare, transportation looks like it is provided straight across to the other side. There are no tourists here. The ranks of them had begun to thin in the first blocks beyond the temple grounds. I decide to ride the boat, look at the other side, and then return. Anything beyond is stretching my limits for what feels safe and comfortable.

Once aboard, I see that many of the people are loaded with produce, and there are a few caged chickens like a stamp of authenticity that I'm far from Kansas. Dorothy's pet, Todo, could be a local dish.

I assume that the monks are not looking at me because they know I'm aboard. One flashes at me a quick smile that I interpret, "we are almost there."

The other side of the river is crowded with inner city apartments interspersed with an occasional market. I follow my guides for two blocks and then have to ask, "how much further?" I really want to turn back.

All three stop. One rubs his bottom lip with his thumb while regarding my hesitation. I'm not moved by his declaration that we are getting very close. One, assuming I'm tired, motions to a motorcycle driver that has a special attached cart with two long benches that could hold a maximum of ten passengers.

The fact of even needing a vehicle seems to cancel out the other's statement of the temple's proximity. Now, their robes appear to me as a shade of yellow for caution, like the color in a traffic light.

As I'm ready to thank them and turn, the one who smiled on the boat takes a small step towards me: "All the afternoon classes at our Watt have been canceled as it's a minor holiday. There are so many that need to practice English."

Opening his hands in front of him, he makes his final plea—"We could all go into one of the biggest rooms where you could do simple conversation with us."

I'd been locked against continuing, but his sincere request turns me like a key.

Climbing up first, I move to the far corner of one long bench. As the monks seat themselves, the one who summoned the driver declares that they all want me to meet their master.

If our vehicle had not jerked forward, I would have run for the boat and pounded back through the markets to the postcard racks and vendors of western sodas. He used the very words that had been told to me when I had first visited a tourist booth: "Be very careful, as one of the biggest national problems is false monks, who say they have a master and use religious robes for their own exploitation."

A slightly louder pitch from the motor renders any further conversation impossible. I am truly alarmed. As if to confirm my suspicion, we are winding through back roads some distance from the river. The men have faces of stone. I'm captured aboard, and the miles we've traveled from the sidewalk speech have already proved that the one who declared our proximity is a liar.

I think of my week and all the coins of provision that were added to my begging bowl as an impoverished traveler. First, the ticket was free; it was transferable. It was the gift of a girlfriend who had done some work for the airlines. My first night I stayed at the home of a taxi driver who took me in when the cheapest hotels were full.

While I asked directions, a retired Thai physician invited me to stay with his family while in the city. He told me he had been on duty in a New York hospital when Malcom X was shot, and he helped perform the autopsy. Next came the job offer but for too many months to be an acceptable invitation with my children.

I took the train north, and in my few days rode down the Mekong river, took elephants up steep mountain trails, and visited a nomadic tribe that had lost their written language long ago from ingesting opium.

I had swallowed enough adventure and was ready to go back and fan myself on my hotel bed with the free meal vouchers. Calculating that it's been about twenty minutes of motorcycle pulled distances, I made my plan for escape. Once they disembark, I will remain and immediately motion to be returned to the river. For them to touch a woman in public would prove to any passerby that they are counterfeit.

It appears that we have entered a true slum area. There are no sidewalks, and even the streets are in need of repair. Potholes require the driver to regularly swerve across the lane. There's little traffic, and the few pedestrians walk on some boards placed over the filthy, rubbish-filled water.

One monk shouts an order, which brings us abruptly to the side. As the driver turns off the motor, he climbs off the bike to collect his coins and goes into an adjacent shop. These three minutes of action has foiled my plan. I have to climb off.

"It's only one more street over. We know the fast way."

For the first time their configuration changes. One in front is motioning to me, while the other two have drawn back to the rear.

The smiling one ahead explains that this area of Bangkok is known as "Little India." As he talks about the im-

Visiting the hill tribes in the Golden Triangle

migrants in this area working predominately in the garment district, he leads me into a path between two buildings. I almost stumble on the irregular line of boards placed over the muck. Somehow, I let myself become manipulated to be encircled and isolated. The smell here is ancient urinal and old cabbage leaves. No one looking into this tunnel can possibly see me. It's here that I can be overpowered. I know that everyone assumes that foreign visitors have money. My Thai air ticket and passport can be sold on the black market. I just feel that something bad is about to happen.

Often I've been impulsive and foolish. Never feeling I've had much time because of cancer, I've tried to cram a whole life into a decade. I just don't want to be raped, or injured if they want to grab my purse. They can have all my remaining twelve dollars.

I'm getting the grin again from the one ahead. The same look that was once innocent and friendly now seems utterly menacing.

We are far enough from the street to be in a complete shadow from the buildings. At the moment I want to scream from suspense; it's announced that we're here. Twisting around to see who spoke behind me, both men in the rear guard are smiling. Our leader, hastening his pace, moves quickly to the end of the corridor. As he steps out from between these stucco walls, I can actually see real temple gates. The entire block is filled with the Watt, and the roofs have peaks like dollops of old meringue.

I'm so relieved that my impulse is to shake their hands and pat them on the back. Yet, now that they are established as real monks, that act would violate their core of teaching.

Behind all three, I follow them across the street and into the compound. I'm led up some cracked cement stairs to where there is a line of hut-like houses. They are obviously residences as the few by the doors wave back at my monks and at their call rouse the others. As the new group of men file out to join us, everyone keeps their distance from me. Among the crowd is one in khaki trousers and a short-sleeved shirt. He introduces himself as the "temple boy," explaining that he's from Laos.

Led by the temple boy into a room, he has me wait in the corner. There's a blackboard to my right and a large picture of a mournful monk in full holiness robes. Those streaming in look to be the age of high school seniors. Some sit on the single cot, while the majority crunch down in orange folds to the floor.

I'm brought a Samsonite folding chair that looks like it was borrowed from a Baptist church potluck. The temple boy is really the oldest man in the room and well past the required age for any U.S. Presidential candidate. Once I'm seated, he brings me a two-liter bottle of cola with a glass set over the open top.

The first questions asked of me are as simple as explaining American food and giving the correct pronunciation for colors. The temple boy is invaluable for translation. To my compliment, he modestly replies that his French is much better. They inquire about the western family structure. There's a ripple of surprise that a land with a surplus of food would have an average family size of just three children or less. One wants to know if the Easter bunny is a fertility goddess.

I'm asked if I want to talk to their master. To my nod of agreement are instructions of where to position my clasped hands in the greeting of respect. Once I complete the gesture and have it coordinated with my head being bent for a two-second look at my feet, they lead me from the room.

The committee that's to present me includes two of my original contacts plus the temple boy.

There are cement paths among the present buildings and a rubble of crumpled older structures. I can almost feel the generations of exact routines. I had pantomimed for the class what it must be like when they bring back their begging bowls and share the day's offerings, as it has been done here for hundreds of years.

I'm being brought up to the assembly place of worship. The ceiling is supported only by pillars, as there are no walls. Told to remove my shoes, I step up on the green linoleum floor. On a cement niche, painted fingernail red, are a number of idols. On the opposite side is a small desk that has no legs, so the body of it rests on the floor. Cans are in front of it with their tops slit for donations. The temple boy sits next to me as the other two monks go together to fetch their leader.

At the first sight of this older, frail man, I can't help but compare him to photos I've seen of Ghandi. Instantly, I ascribe to him the honor of internationally exhibiting passive resistance or looking like the star from a past year's big movie. After acknowledging my nod, he sits on the floor behind the desk.

To me he speaks and only at the end of his sentence looks to the temple boy for translation. He is going to have to be the mailman of all our ideas.

"You must be very brave to come here with my boys!"

I want to laugh at the memory of my utter anxiety. I was sure my execution was at hand and there were knives hidden in those billowing robes.

"Tell him that my book says, 'Perfect love casts out all fear.'"

I measure again my words once they are spoken. The garment of them is true; it's just that I'm far from that stature.

Chuckling at my reply, he says, "Tell me more about your book."

As we are talking, an elderly woman comes with a donation. Her coins are knotted in the corner of a cloth. The slit on top of the offering tin is wide enough that they can all be deposited at once. At the clang of her gift, the master picks up an object from his desk that looks part fan and wand. Not even breaking eye contact with me, he gives a few sweeps of it in her direction.

There is a silence when I finish. The young monks, the temple boy and myself are all looking at the master who has dropped his gaze down to his hands. Finally, he outlines all of the temple's facilities as an introduction to a room that they keep for guests. He offers for me to stay and explain a little more each day.

"Some ideas," he says, "are great birds—one could make them fly away or let them peck some more at your heart."

With keen regret, I have to refuse the hospitality. I realize that it's places like this I can go to when I finish raising children.

The master bids me farewell after issuing instructions for all of them to escort me back to the hotel. Already there are the first blush colors of evening.

We walk in single file to the street. I buy an assortment of penny fireworks for Matthew. Taking the express bus, I pay all the fares and give away my change for their return.

The neon in the ceiling panels is so bright that our reflection in the window dominates over any view of the streets. I'm tempted to talk to this apparition of myself riding right outside the glass.

Once within the block of the hotel, the temple boy takes charge by motioning to the brothers at the back. Most of the passengers that are left seem to be airport employees who rise with us to crowd both exits.

After the four of us have reassembled, the monks are especially animated as we cross the street to the brightly lit hotel. They are surprised that there is a door guard but no shoes for him to watch.

I lead them right to an empty elevator, but as it begins to close, a uniformed arm inserts itself, retracting the door. A policeman orders us all out and back into the lobby.

Stating I'm a guest, I'm asked to prove it with my key. While fishing it from my purse, I insist these are my friends and are welcome in my room.

"No more than ten minutes," he declares noting my room number for a later inspection.

Even though there isn't a single shoe in the long corridor but old room-service trays, all three insist on removing their sandals. I invite them in, leaving the door wide open for the security patrol.

I want to send something back to the master. In the nightstand drawer, between the beds, is a Gideon Bible. Every page is in both the curly Thai print and straight line English. While my guests are regarding the size of my television screen, I grab the Swiss army knife from my suitcase and saw out the book of Mark and a chapter from the book of Revelation. Reincarnation seems to me like the ultimate doctrine of procrastination. There's no such leisure as putting off to the next life what can't be done in this one.

I'm compelled to ride down with them in the elevator. The subdued colors of the lobby and furnishings make it look like a spaceship that has nothing to do with Thailand. It's so neutral in decor that we could be any-where in the world. My friends own the streets, but here, they are the aliens. I walk with them until we are outside in the warm night air.

"It's sad," says one, "to get a new mother and have her leave the same day."

I watch them merge between the vendor's carts. Their robes glow for a moment in the lantern light, and they are gone.

The grief in this planet is like a dark invisible sea. We all waded into its shallows to make our final goodbye.

Turning, I make myself think about tomorrow. All the children will be meeting me. I have just enough money left to take us out to a Thai restau-rant. I want to hear about their week staying with friends. It can feel like we live whole lives in just a seven-day spread.

1991

July 30
Moscow, USSR

It's a rare day when I hate to wake up. It's just this stray pack of problems that keep nipping at me. Some have even drawn blood. For the past seven weeks, I have not been able to purchase any kind of ticket to get us out of the Soviet Union.

I can hear Matthew's girlfriend, Svieta, in the adjoining room. For thirty cents a night, the three of us are staying in the Moscow Pedagogical Institute dorm. It is the sister school to the one in Kiev where I have been teaching this past month.

The fine wire mesh below the mattress makes twanging noises with movement. I can hear Svieta's bed through our common wall. It sounds like she is getting up and padding across the linoleum to the door.

I only bought us one-way train tickets from Warsaw because I knew the Soviet return portion would be dirt cheap. I never imagined a ten-month waiting list to any city, by train or bus, that's across the border. Svieta explained there are so many national shortages that people sign up to go for shopping expeditions. It's been a couple years since her family has even seen bananas.

Failing to procure transportation, we have missed our flight back to the States from Frankfurt. Then, I had to extend our visas, using the services at the school business office. Now, no one can find our passports; and it was explained that when the manager gets back from his vacation, he would surely be able to locate them. The answer to my next question was, "We don't know when he will be back." I heard somewhere that holidays in the working people's paradise are no less than a month.

Looking around, the walls have been painted battleship gray. There is one table, another twin bed, two chairs and a simple plywood wardrobe. It has the charm of an old correctional facility.

I can hear my son and Svieta coming down the hall. They punctuate everything they say to each other with laughter. Of all these present troubles, nothing compares to my concern for Matthew. He just turned 21 in May, and he's convinced, by the sheer power of his emotions, that he wants to marry Svieta. She is his very first girlfriend.

"What are you going to do today, Mom?"

Without waiting for an answer, Matthew smooths back his short brown hair and declares they are going back to Gorky Park. It's over a bridge and walking distance from our dormitory. He's so tall that for years people have asked if he plays basketball.

"You know, the Ferris wheel is less than a nickel!"

I went there myself yesterday afternoon. I saw a lot of drunk people on benches, crumbling cement, and more attractions closed than open. All the maintenance men must have bought train tickets to the border and decided never to come back.

Svieta puts out her hand to Matthew in a kind of "let's go" gesture. I follow them over to her adjoining room, which is as plain as mine, but she has flowers. Several bouquets are in glass jars on the table and in a line along the windowsill. Our money translates into piles of rubles providing flowers and café lunches for mere coins. It's a young suitor's heaven.

Svieta reaches into her bag for a sweater. Her English proficiency is perfect, but her style is to express all rage and poetry with silence, slight pouts, and deep looks. This time she says, "Bye," while Matthew uses the Russian four-syllable counterpart, but neither glance back.

I'm going to have to talk with them before their appointment tomorrow with the American embassy. For the first time in years, I wish for a father that could confront his son. It will be an enormous adaptation for me to see the children grow up and go away, but to watch them exit with the wrong partner would put barbs in my empty nest.

Svieta has explicitly stated that she doesn't want to move to America. She calls her mother, "my best friend." She's an only child, a daughter in a brown school dress, with an apron and white lace collar, winning medals for excellence. I've seen the photographs of her in red hair bows, standing under Lenin's picture, making both sets of grandparents proud. You can't take her away.

I think how Matthew has told her that he would insist for their children to just be born in the USA. He explained that her hometown, being right next to Chernobyl, would make for higher risk pregnancies. He would want the advantages of American medicine.

I can see ahead to how his wife will sit and not have any taste in those days for bowls of bananas. There's a sadness too deep to be comforted by new Nike shoes or even a husband's embrace. She's a girl that belongs close to home.

The hot water is turned off to the dorm for the summer. It's a long corridor of now silent rooms. It's supposed to be the best language school in the entire Soviet Union, so I like to think that some of the spies and mole operatives put in at least one semester here.

There's an illuminated fish tank in the lobby. Since someone has borrowed the ceiling bulbs, or they just haven't been replaced by defecting repairmen, it's almost the only light at night when we come in. Two brown fish hang motionless between the rocks. They seem somehow connected to the two matrons in shapeless dresses. One sweeps the first few steps, and the other asks to see our paid-in-full guest pass. They are like amnesia victims. They have no recall of all the times I have produced this exact card and that the first four steps alone are clean.

Outside the busses are completely crowded. It's almost a Soviet sport to be able to press in—and win points if somehow one can get a seat. I sit on a street bench next to a veteran who has pinned his war medals on his overcoat. They are displayed to obtain small courtesies from the crowds at large, and they are a part of the national conscience.

I keep thinking how Matthew has declared he will live most of his life in the Ukraine since Svieta can't bear overseas distances. They met last year when he was in the first American student group allowed to attend the university. He already has a job offer to teach English for a salary that translates to twenty dollars a month. To him, life's coin has landed heads up for love and adventure.

I see the tail of the eventual wear of life here. There's no concept of service and expediency. He'll get weary of standing in long lines—even to pay his monthly charge for electricity. No one is allowed to send it by mail. I can foresee a sadness in Matthew that even a wife can't comfort. It's a struggle here to find shoes, and sometimes sausages get stuffed into their skin with small ground bones. Maybe the only consumer advocate program has its headquarters and constituency in Siberia.

Crossing to the subway station, I begin to feel through my pocket for an extra entrance token. In my seam, half submerged in lint and denim thread, is an American dime. It's silvery and from a distant planet. It has a message to me while I'm trapped in this time warp of visiting winter in summer, glimpsing what life was like during the nineteenth century. Once again, I need to be reminded, *In God We Trust*.

The metro is crowded. I look around at the passengers. It seems that one's clothing here is far more important for conveying a person's status than apparel ever is in the West. They are their own moving car grill or logo of accomplishment. A good suit is a Cadillac man; synthetic fur hats convey the rank of old Chevrolet.

While hanging onto the overhead rail, I feel like apologizing to my own dead relatives. I'd address the first ones that left Ireland when the crops failed. Maybe, they danced a jig by the Statue of Liberty, but they came to try and make something better for their own unborn generations. I just can't let Matthew go back to a land where potatoes are no bigger than a child's fist, without a full heart-pounding discussion. Then, there is free choice.

Once in the city center, I head towards the museum buildings by the Kremlin. A father wants to photograph his young son at an angle, by the wall, where the red star will be visible in the frame. The child is full of movement and a big grin until the camera is raised. Instantly, he is solemn—even the time to smile can be a cultural dictation.

In the old armory are explanatory paragraphs, typed on cards, and mounted on the viewing glass. There's a sign in English to the right of the Cyrillic description.

The hall is almost empty. One man, with the slightest silver shading at his temples, moves to the front and side of me. As I glance over, his eyes are focused on the English print. I like his nose; it's long and narrow. It reminds me of a British novel that describes the "distinct aquiline proboscis" of a noble family. It's just a fast, free fall thought as he goes one way and I another.

It's almost noon when I see him again. Both of us arrive at the vestibule of an ancient church. His blue eyes are as distinct as his royal ski-jump nose.

"You are British?"

I can't help but smile. "I am from the *Have a Good Day* nation. If our generation designed the national flag it would be that yellow circle with two black-dot eyes and a grin."

He laughs, but the sound is real and not the noise that some people make when they are unsure of what to do.

He does have an accent. It sounds like the words have to traverse a nasal passage before utterance: "Ivan the Terrible is buried in here with his sons. Let's go see if we can find the graves."

I am his instant history disciple. He keeps talking. He makes Russia alive to me at the time of the czars.

It isn't until we get outside that he tells me his name and occupation.

"I'm Philip," he says. "I'm a history professor at a university near Adelaid."

I think how it's because of Australia that I moved back to Oregon from California. I received an invitation to give six weeks of lectures, starting in

Sydney. I had to transfer my children to Silverton schools, where they lived at Christian Renewal Center, our favorite retreat camp. When I returned, they all had reasons for wanting to stay. So I rented out my Topanga, California house and slowly transferred our goods north.

Philip never really asked me to join him. It's just understood; I love to learn, and he could win the golden blackboard award.

Through him, I can envision the icon of Christ being pulled down from the main gate in the Kremlin wall. Right after the revolution, the old believers were weeping and praying in the shadows. Working backwards in time, he makes me hear the cry of the architect of St. Basil's Cathedral; the czar put out his eyes to keep him from ever designing anything again that could compete with that building's beauty.

All my anxiety that has been mounting since we've missed our flight is blanketed by company. I have needed some diversion. Some women love the company of handsome men, while others feel a magnetic pull towards those in power. I couldn't care less and even purposely confuse CEO with UFO.

My second marriage showed me that charm can be deceitful, and there are more actors at large than the stage can hold. My divorce was like a bomb of such magnitude that I haven't encouraged any male relationship to grow; the air of romance has felt unsafe to breathe.

Once away from Red Square, Philip can turn the depleted grocery shops into lecture exhibits of contemporary times. I ask him how long will he be in Moscow. We are standing by an unlit display counter that has, hanging from chains above our heads, a simple painting of a blue sausage. There is no available meat but two kinds of fat—one white and lard like, while the other looks like bacon slices without any streaking of meat.

"I only have one more day in Moscow, and then I'm taking the train to Poland and on to West Europe."

He names capital cities ending the list with Rome. He has five more months of itinerary, returning to Adelaid in December.

I don't want to unravel all my travel problems. I only reply with the sure thing of train reservations back to Kiev in four days.

Outside, it's beginning to feel as if it can snow. The sky has become cold and gray. Moscow sidewalks demand attention from the pedestrians, and I can only take wing-shot looks at Philip and the rather dingy window displays. There are a number of cracks and holes along the walkway. Some are over a foot deep with visible angles of internal pipes.

While listening to Philip quote Nevil Schute, and highlight some Australian history, I can better understand the wake of energy between Matthew and Svieta. Attraction is such a high-powered motorboat ride.

We are at a street corner that is an access point to the metro. All pedestrians are required to cross under the road. It is dimly lit, and this one has puddles from a recent rain. All at once, there is a wave of people filling the tunnel, walking straight toward us. They are the discharged passengers who have just come up the escalator from the station below. They are marching at us like some soldier hoard.

I reach for Philip's arm in order to strengthen our width in a locked unit against the press and flow of people. When my hand makes contact, just below his shoulder, I can feel him shudder at my touch. It's not my imagination. In a microsecond, he turns from bones to steel and back to bones again. It is completely involuntary and slight, but I drop my hand, which has a seismograph sensitivity to the smallest tremor of rejection. Philip doesn't want me to touch him. The crowd, with its bags and briefcases, separates us until we climb the stairs up to the level of the street.

Philip is hungry. He has mentioned it before. Unlike Kiev, which has lots of small cafes, we have not been able to find one.

There is a line stretching more than two blocks to a shop window selling slices of pizza. I suggest that it might be the only thing he can find, and so he drops back to flank the end. I wish him a pleasant trip and stroll away. All of my great diversion is gone; I just want to go home. It is such an overwhelming desire to press some cosmic button and be back in my own Oregon house. My row of pastel roses should be in full bloom next to my front porch. I want to beat my own pillow, with my fist, on my own bed, and cry.

I walk as fast as possible through the end of the day crowd. It has a surreal feeling, reminiscent of a category of bad dreams. I am lost, not in the direction of the streets, but in Russia itself. Maybe, we will not get out for months unless we pay over $3,000 to Aeroflot. Maybe Matthew will not get out at all.

My image flows at the side of me in the window glass, bent and distorted. All the displays have an empty and dusty look. With nothing privately owned, there's no reason to create the art that beckons pedestrians inside.

Seeing a restaurant with white tablecloths, I stop to stare. There are no seated patrons, but a flurry of waiters setting glasses and utensils. I have to walk in, but my Russian doesn't soar beyond the primary dimension of nursery school talk. I can say both "Dog" and "Puppy," in addition to "Thank You" and "Please." A waiter motions me to a large couch over by the service door. The bustle and extravagant place settings seem to promise the best of Russian cuisine. I think of Philip in his miserable pizza line with a pang. I should try and get him. It's warm inside too.

I jump up trying to make gestures that, hopefully, communicate that I'll be back. The closest waiter's face registers that he perfectly understands my motions—I am a crazy windmill.

Rushing back over the blocks, I hope I'm in time to get Philip; they will have borsch and a rye bread with a sour tang. The salads are always finely diced. Sometimes there is both a fish and a meat, with a fried potato.

I see the pizza window. Those purchasing the slice get it right in their hands without a paper wrapper, which in the West is another kind of American flag of sanitation. Working my way back, I can see Philip in his navy blue jacket, and knapsack with the real leather underpanel. I go up to him being careful not to grab his arm. I declare the proximity and fact of the restaurant. I explain the lack of patrons by the fact they probably start service at eight.

He doesn't hesitate on leaving, even after paying his twenty minutes worth of dues, staring at dark wool backs. We don't talk, but set for each other an accelerated pace.

Once inside, I lead him over to the couch with its irregular plush cushions. I suggest this might be a restaurant that only takes hard currency. Philip nods that this is fine. His hotel is about $150 dollars a night, with a black and white television, and no ice. The in-house restaurant has been closed for remodeling. It would take more than a year of residence at my dormitory rate to approach his one-night sum.

"Philip, I really haven't told you very much about myself."

Now, I pause before the end of the high diving board. His eyes look back at me with blue intensity.

"I'm a Christian."

This kind of declaration has fallen far from being an honorable endorsement—if I had used *born again* as my prefacing adjective, most would subtract considerable points from my estimated intelligence quotient. In general, we have never invested in public relations.

I'm ready for the sneer, even if it's just the slightest tightening of jaw line muscles. Instead, this aristocratic face, just three feet from my own, begins to smile. It's such a beatific look that I wish we had met as students, and if I had married him, I would now know the history of the world.

"Laurel." Philip is looking up at the vaulted ceiling above the dining tables. "I'm a priest. Yes, I do teach, but it's a Catholic university; and I'm also the Father Superior or *president* of the school, as you Americans would say."

Instantly, I remember that he is on the way to Rome. I'm in shock. I'll choke if I'm now expected to address him as *Father*. He's probably Australia's greatest hope for the office of the Pope. Will he have to wear a big ring and have people in Latin America approach him on their knees?

"One of the reasons I've come to Moscow is to bring a gift of a gold chain to a family that once befriended a member of my order. They never knew he was a priest, and we feel their kindness deserves a reward. I'm to meet them tomorrow evening outside of my hotel."

The restaurant is ready, but no one comes in. It's like an act in the Theater of the Absurd. The napkins are folded, like a kind of cloth origami into wings of snowy birds.

"Another reason I'm here is to hunt for the Icon of the Black Madonna. Do you want to join me in the morning for my search?"

Matthew and Svieta's plans for tomorrow include locating the one McDonald's restaurant and probably looking for boats in Gorky Park where they can ride through the tunnel of love. They certainly don't want me with them.

Gladly, I agree to 9:00am and the lobby of his Intourist hotel. As he lists some of the art galleries where we'll start, I'm slightly disappointed. I had imagined looking through old village trunks or digging up a small container buried since the revolution in the back of a graveyard.

I can hardly believe how fast it has become late. I excuse myself because I have a distance to walk. With current desperate times, there are gangs and a new lawlessness. Philip offers to accompany me, but I decline. There is still a late raft of people for me to float with to my dormitory.

"Where have you been?" asks Matthew. His voice has the slight tone of a parent. Woe to his teenagers. The one overhanging light bulb adds an interrogation glow to his question.

I condensed my reply to the fact I met someone, and we were talking. It's amazing how much living can be squeezed into single sentences, and someday our whole life will be condensed into a two-paragraph obituary.

Svieta is sitting at the table sorting through a small pile of newly purchased cards. I walk by Matthew to see what she had found in a local shop.

It has been her own peculiar hobby to collect and organize greeting cards that exclusively use roses on the cover. I remember my first night in the Kiev dorm when Matthew sent her into my room. It was his idea that we should get further acquainted all by ourselves. To my amazement, she brought to me an enormous box and began to hand me a stack of cards bound with a rubber band. They were all in categories—like solid yellow, mixed colors, buds only, paintings of bouquets, etc. One by one, I looked with her at each picture. It took a couple hours, and she used some of them to tell me about herself. They were all straight biographical associations like: "I got this card the one time we had to move," or "My grandmother brought me this one from Siberia."

I can't help but like Svieta. There is an innocence about her that is missing in most western girls her age. Even her dresses look like they are part of a stage wardrobe from a 1950s play. She wears no makeup, and her hair is thick with an electric current of dark curls.

For the past school year, Matthew has written her almost every day and once a month would call. He even told me where he had the very first kiss of his life, on a public bench in a cluster of Soviet apartment buildings. He was twenty, and it was time to fall in love.

My objection is really not the fact that he would move to this far away place, even though I mutter about it. He did that in high school by transferring into Watts, an inner city Los Angeles school where he was the only student there that wasn't an African-American or Hispanic. We both like to practice radical Christianity.

Through his explanations, Svieta too, said "Yes" to God and then spent her winter months knitting Matthew a sweater that worked the entire Lord's Prayer into the back stitches. I was impressed and came to town ready to embrace my young and future daughter-in-law. I did think that maybe, this is where the wind has always been blowing Matthew.

But here a little, and there a little, has been evidence of a separate destiny. In our delay, I've gathered my lines and precepts. I can only hope that after all he has heard his entire life, that he will shake hands with wisdom. That is the best way for a boy to become a man.

The Disciple Doesn't Choose His Circumstances, Knowing They Are The Honing Instruments By Which He Is Conformed To The Likeness Of Christ.

Laurel's Journeys Around The World

Australia welcomes Laurel—1992

Laurel at a classroom in a Philippine refugee camp in 1993

In Aryan Land, Australia outback

Learning to make baskets in Zululand, Southern Africa

People's Republic of China 1993

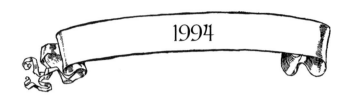

1994

January 2
Portland, Oregon

Anna did the decorating. It wasn't her usual twisting of crepe paper colors taped with balloons to the overhead light; she arranged dinosaurs on the tabletop. Fashion touches everything—even birthday party themes. Mary Elisabeth is eighteen.

While taking a serving platter back to the kitchen, I hear it for the first time. It's my children's new topic of conversation; the three of them are beginning to reminisce on their childhood. They laugh and speak of it as if their young adult status has earned them the "remember when" refrains.

I remain silent. I won't cover myself with any defense. It's true we all stayed in a Central American hotel that only had hooks in the wall, and the guests had to provide their own hammocks. I remember the heat and how I took Mary Elisabeth downstairs to buy us soft drinks. Then in the dining room, I turned from my wallet to remove soiled dishes from our table, and in that rotation, every cent of our money, plus purchased train tickets, disappeared. We were broke and stranded in a town that had more kerosene lights than electricity. I remember my feelings of despair while ushering my eight-year-old back upstairs. That was exactly one decade ago.

It's an amazing thing how time can translate one terrible incident into a humorous story. At that time, while I wallowed in despair, the children went right into prayer. Their requests had passion, and while they were still speaking, someone knocked at our door. It was all returned, by a waitress, without a word.

Anna, in a louder voice than necessary, tells that when I took her to Africa we went to an area of Swaziland that turned out to be infested with spitting cobras.

"Mom and I were afraid to leave the trailer."

It's Matthew's turn. He has the newest story: Three summers ago, we went to the Soviet Union. The school finally found our lost passports, and a teacher helped us get train tickets from his friend's tour company. Instructed not to talk, we joined our group boarding for Warsaw. It had already been an unusual Sunday morning. The television station kept repeating a tape of *The Swan Lake* ballet.

"When Mother finds out that the train is going to Berlin, she pays a twenty-dollar bribe to the conductor. Moved to another car, we have to keep changing seats to accommodate new passengers with reservations for our spots. At the last stop before Poland, our original group was ordered off the train to be returned to Kiev. In Warsaw, we learned there had been a coup, which really ended the USSR. We barely made it out on the very last train that was allowed to cross the border."

I can clearly see the theme for all my children's future reunions. As their hair turns gray, they will reminisce, and I will take on proportions of great eccentricity.

As the phone rings, I feel resentment at its intrusion. Tonight it's especially keen as I'm so aware that I am at the end of my full house mothering. Sometimes, I'm pursued by the melancholy of a soon empty nest. I don't want our evening to be dissolved. The girls have friends that need to know everything, and Matthew, being in love, could spend the next two hours telling Tina the shape of the clouds. Jumping up, I insist I'll get it, intending to make a quick dismissal.

The surprise is that it's for me. I hear the long ago voice of Mike Thaler. The last time we saw him was when we lived in Topanga, and he had come south to visit his mother. He explains that he is trapped in a house surrounded by another New York blizzard.

I assume that I'm his random choice from probably thumbing through a phone book. Every few years he'll scan the "L" page and think to make a call. His content is usually the status of a current girl friend and his children's book publications. I am usually the listener. Tonight he is all cold wind, and blue.

He requests some catch up paragraphs of our recent history.

I tell how we lived for well over a year at Christian Renewal Center by Silver Creek Falls. My best contribution to the camp was finding an ideal sled run through the woods at the edge of the property. Matthew was away for his first year at college, and I lived with the girls in the upstairs of a staff house.

Like her brother, Anna also wanted to go to a local University. She qualified for a track scholarship, but still the tuition bulged over this credit.

"When I went to enroll her, I inquired if I could speak at one of the required weekly chapels. My motive was not noble, but really, I was thinking of how I needed the honorarium. The dean must have misunderstood my request because he gave me a job

Mike Thaler

application form. Once hired, my children have had the opportunity of free tuition from a whole coalition of schools.

"Now, every first day lecture I use you, Mike, as an example." I describe one of his visits when he stayed for dinner. During the meal, he grabbed a knife off his napkin and waved it in the air, while his other hand held up the saltshaker. I quote how he cried out, "What is this, what is this?"

Then Mike declared, in a voice loud enough for the neighbors, that it was ASSAULT WITH A DEADLY WEAPON!

"My real point is that you next took out a little leather notebook and wrote it all down." I tell him how I'm impressed that he uses it exactly like a butterfly net to catch any bright, wing-span thought before it flies away.

Mike is quiet. "Something else, Laurel," he says in the lowest voice I think I have ever heard him use. "I believe now in God. I've had to have someone to talk to in all this long winter isolation. I am really different inside."

He used to laugh whenever I made reference to the narrow path.

"Laurel," he says, "I'll soon be in San Francisco to sign books at the American Library Association. When it's over, why don't I come up for just the weekend before flying back to New York?"

He makes it more of a fact than a question. I'm thinking how I'll have to clean the house and which of my children's rooms he can use. Even though the oldest two are in college, they commute from home.

Once back to the birthday party, they have moved from the hard chairs over to the living room's softer surfaces. I tell them who called and that he'll be coming for two days to visit us.

"I wonder if he still wears those funny clothes," says Anna, who works part time at a local garment store and sees herself as an expert on denim and right style. She now substitutes the word "spruce" for green and "golden-rod" instead of yellow, thanks to the Gap training manual.

"Remember when he lost the toothpick insert from his Swiss army knife in that fancy elevator in New York?"

I nod my head "yes." I learned that I could still feel embarrassed. When Mike realized it was gone, he dropped to his knees in his search and tried to enlist the help of the other passengers. Maybe children would have come to his aid or urban adults if he were looking for a contact lens. Instead, they had to pretend, in a very small space, that some interplanetary visitor had not landed in their midst.

"Look," I said ready to block another anecdote. "He's got well over a hundred published children's books."

Scholarship won't hush Anna. She has one last tale and turns her head to her siblings sprawled at each corner of the couch: "I had to walk with Mike and Mother through this long Manhattan lobby. When he said that he couldn't stand how it was decorated, he closed his eyes and made us lead him."

January 9

The ringing phone activates both daughters. It's their permanent challenge to get to the receiver before the second bell.

"Mom, it's for you. It's Mike Thaler who wrote a poem and wants you to hear it." Her voice sounds gracious, but I know the Bedlam judgment in her tone.

When sheep
Can't Sleep
Do they make a big fuss,
Or do they just go ahead
And begin
To count
Us?

He has lots of colored yarn, and unrolls skein after skein. He also wants to hear about the minutiae of my day.

I take the time for this peculiar verbal dance. Our words bow and sway. He says he'll call me again soon, another day.

March 11

Mike flies in tonight. I really don't want to care what I look like. Thoughts of my mirror's reflection are dominating me; I want to be free. My hair is long and exactly like I've always worn it, except its gray. "Lithe" has turned a bit more to "chunk" too. I've never cared about my appearance before in all our random criss-cross visits of the last eighteen years. We were just lower case, small-print friends.

Against everything practical and rational, I dress with a critical eye to how I look. Our telephone calls have become as regular as once a week. They have been effervescent, but that's dial-a-mind. Tonight is face to face. I understand why the general public hasn't demanded telephone camera chips and face screens, which are all technologically possible.

I finally decide on a black turtleneck with corduroy pants and leave behind a chair piled with my discards. I see numbers of cotton-clothing arms stretching down towards the floor in a kind of configuration of goodbye.

At the airport gate, I stand back a discreet distance while the passengers stream into the terminal. Family members stand the closest, loud in their greeting.

Mike Thaler is absolutely the last one. He's carrying a five-foot yellow pencil and explains it was a gift to him from the conference. It's odd we are so silent. One Saturday we talked for almost five hours, and now we are reduced to the smallest exchange of information. We even speak of the chances for more rain. It's night, and the street lights make the wet pavement look shiny. Mike isn't as rotund as in the past, and his beard is trimmed and tight, unlike the exotic bush that I remember.

We talk contract and book business. This was our old dialog from the past. He asks me what I'm writing. I can't move my hands from the steering wheel, but I feel like inverting my pant's pockets to show they are empty. I only have the lint of a spare, couple-paragraphs-a-day diary.

I explain that teaching three writing classes each semester means lots of student papers. It's an avalanche of white sheets. I can hardly dig myself out from circling bent phrases or underlining paragraphs that are overstuffed with words.

"Now, I love it too," I counter. The students are the same age as my own. Mine have become too grown up to hardly give me eye contact, so it's fulfilling to have all those classes record, and even memorize, what I say.

Mike laughs, but I know him well enough that he's not in agreement with anything that would separate a writer from his task.

I gave the house a five-star cleaning. It's easy to see the tracks that Mike makes. I come downstairs, as the day's last act, to turn down the heat. It's my equivalent of lowering the American flag, and there was baby powder, like a milky way galaxy, all over my bathroom hooked rag. He must have helped himself to more bread too, as there were crumbs on the table with a path washed through them by a sponge.

March 12

Last night Mike had argued against leaving the house at 7:00am. He said he would take a taxi and join me later at the university. I told him that idea would cost him probably a million dollars, and I've never even seen a cab in my commute to and from Newberg, Oregon. He first hinted and then asked for me to come back and get him at the time aristocrat's rise, but my morning's classes are locked together.

I like the ride; the sky goes from black to a palette of gray. I point out the Christmas tree farms, and fields that fill with pumpkins every autumn. There are the raw wood frames of a new housing tract. To me they are like wagon trains still coming in to domesticate the wilderness.

Most of my students feel it's the ultimate suffering to start a class twenty minutes before 8:00. They cross the campus under tree branches where the squirrels are still sleeping. Loose roosters, at large, might be an aid to early waking. Mike, in the front row corner, has the same rounded angle of slouch as the rest of the class. He even has on a baseball cap over finger-combed hair.

No one takes a class; they only take a professor. I feel a challenge to cut through that sleep deprivation glaze and their mechanical duty to come at dawn. It's my salute to their parents and the double-digit tuition.

Within ten minutes, Mike rouses himself, stands up and wants the chalk. He's an animated lecturer, illustrating his points with an economy of backdrop, cartoon lines. He sketches a baby with a mallet and a huge block of stone. The child keeps chiseling the giant rock that shrinks as he grows old. Finally, he's an aged and bent man who dies, and his life's work was the now completed grave stone.

I don't know all the different gates women walk through when they first identify the feeling that they are falling in love. These long sleeping endorphins are beginning to stretch. I am really afraid their years of hibernation could end; I want to stay safe. Heart wounds have a potential to produce the greatest decibels of anguish.

Mike walks with me to the school cafeteria for lunch. He looks around, amazed at the islands of food. There must be twelve kinds of cereal. The salad bar is another grazing field. We do an Indian arm wrestle with words, of who will pay. I open my purse to finger dash for my wallet, and it's gone. There's that shock that begins to inventory my lost wad of small bills. I'm hoping it is in the car where I may have jumbled it while reaching for my briefcase.

Excusing myself, I suggest that Mike begins, and I'll be right back. My voice has no quivers. I know how to put a mask over worry. Life always has some mosquitoes that buzz in an ear. Students from the morning lecture volunteer to be Mr. Thaler's guide.

"No," says Mike. "Your problem is my problem too."

To me it is the equivalent of an eighteenth-century gentleman throwing his cape over a puddle so the lady can pass.

The brown wallet is wedged between my car seats. I know it's sheer romantic nonsense, but I feel it's only there because he came with me.

I declare it too. Let him see more of my crazy swirls of thought.

"Yes sir," he replies. "I'm a living rabbit's foot. I'm the horseshoe nailed above the garage. Look, you're in the clover, and I have all four leaves."

April 5

I try and explain it to my friends, Judy and Sylvia. We are sitting in the booth of an Italian restaurant chain that will give you all the bread, salad and soup you can eat for five dollars. They are absolutely quiet now that I've told them that when Mike flew back to New York our pattern of phone calls changed. Never again do we talk once a week—now it is every day.

These women have known me a long time. I met both of them when I was a school bus driver's wife. One talks caution, like a yellow light, and the other speaks only brakes and stop sign.

They are right. They have the experience of fingers that have always worn the same wedding ring. Mike and I are like the Sharks and the Jets; we belong to different West Side Story gangs.

I can hardly look up from my minestrone soup. I just keep stirring it and listening. My spoon chases a grated carrot slice with unusual intensity. I know that Mike is a city boy. He has often said that he likes sidewalks, restaurants and antique stores.

I love to go to villages that are so remote they have cow dung floors. I have also spent 26 years going to church, and give me any first line, I know hundreds of hymns by heart. He doesn't share any of that paradigm.

By the time the chocolate cake comes with three clean forks they give their final assessment: "Laurel, you are just used to a full house. Your children are almost gone. It's a big mistake to jump into a marriage because the issue here is really one thing—I think you might be afraid of living alone."

I acknowledge to myself that some of what they say is true. I have considered how living alone can be a selfish life. Once I quit teaching, my days will move without shape, like some amoeba. I could eat standing in front of an open refrigerator.

I tell my friends what I really want is to join the circus, but they won't put it in my contract that I don't do tumbling.

I'm using a joke as a swinging stick because their words are getting close. They can't see my lap. I've started shredding my napkin into tiny little bits. I completely agree with their logic. They have real facts, and feelings can be transitory and deceptive. But, how can I tell them that we never fail at being able to talk good poem/bad poem. I've never done that with anyone. Every evening our speech seems high, and higher.

They leave me in the parking lot. On all four sides is a strip mall that's in duplication all across America. Off hand, I can't pick out my car from the rest. A million of us bought the same white Honda. Feeling depressed, I make myself look straight up. One lone airplane can't cover the sky.

April 9

Matthew is cutting the grass. He chooses diagonal strokes across the lawn. Tina must be somewhere nearby. Being formally engaged, complete now with a summer wedding date, they have a couple's gravitational pull of nearness.

I turn off the ignition of my car and just sit watching the even lines mown into the green. There are some flowers blooming by the low stone wall. On impulse, I detour from going through the front door and sit on a rock. I begin to pluck the bed's intruding dandelions. Their seed caps range from tightly drawn white skirts to fluff ready to twirl into the air. Each spring they win more dancing sites. I wonder when my whole yard will be a yellow ballroom.

Matthew shuts off the lawn mower, and peace replaces the drone. As he turns towards me, I notice that he's wearing his old summer khaki shorts. It's wonderful when the weather allows a reduction of yardage below knees and shoulders.

"Tina and I have talked a lot about this. We are really in agreement that you shouldn't let yourself get serious with Thaler."

He's like a parent full of advice. Every sentence seems to start with "no" or "don't." I thank him but drop my eyes back to the roots that resisted being extracted.

April 11

I'm convinced. There is wisdom in a multitude of counselors.

Yet I can't stroll by all of Mike's honesty. He's a Jewish boy that loves to pray and in his scholarship has a magnet's draw to the prophet Isaiah. If I pull that ancient gift wrap, could he see his own Messiah? Would he find the stepping stone? I can lose my breath in the risk.

April 25

I have written down all the information. The directions are scribbled in an open notebook next to me on the passenger's side of the front seat.

Mike is doing an unexpected Visiting Author program in a Washington school. He is on a tour, but it will give us a few hours. I have a tank full of gas, and I'm slightly exceeding the speed limit.

I'm preparing myself to let all the doubts and fears speak forth. Since this is the *Dead End* sign, it should be a face to face contact. I've got to let him know that my London bridges are falling down, and we are never going to cross them into a marriage. My world is all cockney dialect compared to his.

It's strange that he never formally proposed. It was just an assumption that he made somewhere along our hundreds of talking hours. Just because something feels right doesn't mean it is right.

I love the vista of Mt. Hood that's a white triangle to the east. I'm crossing the Columbia River, which is the border of two states. Out of all my car windows, I scan this wide wonder of water. There's even an island that has no access except by boat. This bridge that covers the journey trail of salmon should have a majestic name, not *Interstate 205*. Engineers could build it, but they never should have been allowed to name it.

My fingers are tight on the steering wheel, and I'm not turning on the classical music station. There's nothing in me that wants to float and swoop with sound. It's not easy to be a firing squad to hope.

I have some trouble finding the grammar school. The residential streets circle themselves like a peculiar maze, and I'm losing some of that precious time that we were to have together. Finally, I pull into the visitor's parking where a sign states that I have to report first to the office.

The main hall is like a whimsical gallery of bright art. Hand prints have been turned into an aviary of stylized painted birds. There are egg carton caterpillars tacked around another school room door.

I find the auditorium by a banner welcoming OUR FAVORITE AUTHOR, all in bold print. Mike, who has his back to the door, is adjusting an easel. He greets me with exuberance and introduces me to the principal, in stiletto high heels, and to a giant bear of a man named Don from a book fair service.

The administrator is talking program times with Mike and leaves to organize the younger classes for the first assembly. Don, the book fair bear, is apologizing that even though they brought the costume, there is no one available to wear it. It's explained to me that it is the uniform for one of Mike's favorite characters, a teacher named "Mrs. Green."

"What do you need," I ask.

"It's simple," says Mike. "You could do it. Just when I read the book, come out and waltz around."

Agreeing, they slide over a heavy-duty cardboard box that looks like it once contained a refrigerator. Don offers to carry it to a side-stage bathroom where I'm instructed to wait there until he comes for me, when Mike starts his opening story.

Once alone, I look inside and pull out an acrylic green head of a stylized crocodile. It has a hair bow and wire-rimmed glasses. A round hoop waist is supported by shoulder straps and covered with a bright sky blue dress. The biggest part is the tail, like a giant anaconda, that trails on the floor behind me.

I practice walking, and there is a slight odor of old perspiration from the previous masqueraders. It could feel like I am trapped in a tiny closet. Thinking to venture out, I slowly lumber down the hall to the stage behind the drawn curtains.

As I reach out my green gloved hand to search for the opening in the curtain, I can hear Mike talking with his friend from the book club. When he uses my name, I stop to listen. He has no idea that I'm just three feet above him.

"I really don't know if Laurel will ever be able to make the leap of faith and marry me. This would be the final tragedy of both of our lives. She seems assured, but she's been injured, and I sometimes doubt she can trust a man for the demanding intimacy of a marriage relationship.

"And for me, I've never been so sure of anything in my life; I know its God's very plan."

This is my moment, eavesdropping in a lady crocodile outfit, with a size 75 waist, that I really say "yes" to Michael Charles Thaler.

I go back to the bathroom, with my wet eyes concealed by three inch, black-net pupils.

Don finally knocks and leads me down the stairs. I keep checking if my tail is well connected. I can hear Mike's voice, and as I get close, his tone turns into words:

"This is called *The Teacher From the Black Lagoon*. It's the first day of school, and I wonder who my teacher will be."

As I'm swooping among the children making them shriek and laugh, I think how I will be marrying a long-time bachelor. We will learn all the places where selfishness will need a stake in its heart. I'm just holding onto the words, "God's Plan," or I will bolt and run to Mongolia now that it's open to foreign English teachers.

May 3

It is the second time tonight that Mike has called. He wants to explain again how he has lived 25 years in the same upstate New York home. He has started calling it "his little palace." He is definitely Mr. Roots. I have to be the one that will be airborne. He wants me to move east at some point after we're married.

Our conversations have definitely moved from sonnets to kitchen sinks. There is lots of negotiation. He acknowledges my points of being accessible to my children, and the fact I have to finish my teaching contract.

I've moaned my subjective reservations to him too. His house, even at three stories high, has no view.

Turning with the phone, I look out my back windows. It's dusk, and the fading light gives the pine trees a hue reminiscent of classical oil paintings. They slope down to the Willamette River. In the winter, when all the leaves are gone, I can see an island. Sometimes deer roam like visitors from a past tense world.

The Thaler property is flat, and the window over his kitchen sink has in its cross hairs a mongrel on a chain in his neighbor's yard. It barks in its random doggie code.

I have a recurring image. I tell it to Mike too; I'm not keeping secrets in any false relationship pose. I feel I'm on a very high dive, and far below is a swimming pool. Everything refreshing is in that water. But, what if I hit the concrete?

"We'll wait," says Mike, "until the board is floating in the water. Then, we'll do a safe cannon ball jump together into marriage."

Words, like his reply, help a lot—but then I later see again that tiny aqua colored dot so far down below where any wind or miscalculation means we strike cement. I have old divorce scars that ache when courtship has turned serious.

Deciding to snack on crusty bread, I head for the kitchen. For me, this kind of anxiety provokes appetite.

Besides my swimming pool phantoms, I think again about Mike's house. I saw it only once, years ago, when Anna was sixteen, and the two of us made a trip to New York in early December. I was stunned by his quirky tastes. I couldn't believe that my first art critic once painted some flat rocks yellow, making a trail to his back door. It had mostly peeled away, scrubbed by shoes and weather. We passed a picnic table that looked unsafe at any speed.

I remember Mike's back porch that had been adapted to be a close-at-hand garage. There were boxes of things that looked like leftovers from a mechanical flea market. It ranged from about-to-rust to being orange in its state of full metal decay. Besides a "NO SMOKING" sign, there was another printed message that instructed all who were about to enter to "REMOVE YOUR SHOES." I don't remember anyone ever doing it.

That evening we were in a hurry as he was to drop us, at a certain time, by the home of our one time California neighbors. We waited as Mike dashed upstairs for his street map of Rhinebeck.

The kitchen walls were painted a shade of yellow like fresh egg yolks. There were five doors in that single room making it the hub to the basement, front hall, dining room, pantry and outside. In a burst of bad-taste-whimsy, Mike must have laid large yellow and black linoleum squares. A bulletin board was covered with decades-old concert announcements.

Anna pointed out to me his windowsill art above the kitchen sink. I just glanced at the collection of small ceramic Easter rabbit sculptures. There was no dishwasher, and above the sink was that distant grim view of a chained animal.

Tearing off the other heel of the loaf, I thought how this coming June I will be going again to New York, and I'll see for myself all of Mike's house. In just a couple days, I will be taking a group of university students to study for a month in Kiev. I've been doing it for a number of years; it is a schedule set in cement. I will live without the props of calls or letters.

Rinsing out my bowl for the dishwasher, I look out my kitchen window into a true forest of Oregon firs. From a very distant street, I can barely hear the sound of a single dog barking.

May 6 to June 5
Ukraine

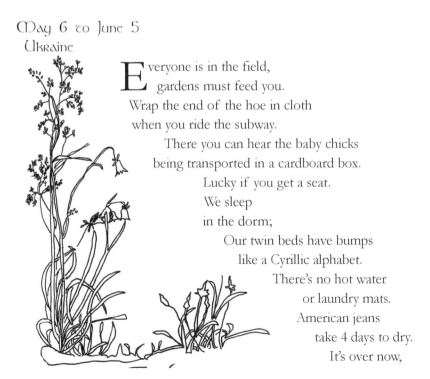

E veryone is in the field,
   gardens must feed you.
Wrap the end of the hoe in cloth
when you ride the subway.
    There you can hear the baby chicks
    being transported in a cardboard box.
      Lucky if you get a seat.
      We sleep
      in the dorm;
        Our twin beds have bumps
        like a Cyrillic alphabet.
          There's no hot water
          or laundry mats.
          American jeans
            take 4 days to dry.
            It's over now,

or in a new form of Mafia.
Please show me,
in secret,
in your two-room apartment,
your old communist membership card.
We laugh.
Toast each other
on state made champagne.
[It's a dues book—
listing dates and amounts
of rubles that vanished
into a Swiss bank.]

I'm glad
you learned English
so well.
You had to go to school
on Saturday,
while my classmates
watched cartoons,
and put our hands
in open cereal boxes.
There are still lines
for bread.
Those round brown loaves
are shoved across the counter
by big women wearing white starched hats
like crowns (bakery queens).
Every month the price goes up.

Packing is such a revelation in how I've tripled in goods. I wrap the painted Easter eggs in dirty clothes. I can't wait to see the familiar—to see Mike.

July 9
New York

It's the same kind of heat as a sauna. We don't have such humidity in Oregon. Mike is waiting for me with a bottle of peach flavored tea.

In the drive to his house, we have all the windows down. He has no air conditioning. I'm doing most of the talking. It seems impossible to really push the whole of Ukraine over to him in paragraphs, but I still try:

"I'm on the upper bunk in an old Soviet train, and I can't help but watch this older man sitting below at the tiny table. He unwraps two hard-boiled eggs from a newspaper page and pulls out a bottle of vodka from his vinyl bag. It's stuffy in the car, and he takes off his shirt revealing a huge tattoo of Lenin."

I'm noticing that I somehow work the fact of the temperature into most of my stories. Mike is wearing a yellow tank top, where I have on denim sleeves. After living so long in Oregon, I've become used to days of mist and overcast. No one watching national weather should feel sorry about the dark green shading that indicates precipitation in the Northwest. A lot of us have learned to like rain.

I'm keen to see his house, but I'm afraid again of the emotional gymnastics it will require for me to go two hours from the Pacific ocean to two hours east of New York City.

The closer we get to Stone Ridge, the more excited Mike becomes. Like a teeter-totter, he is rising to the top with animated explanations. I'm swinging down to short sentences and finally single words.

It is pretty out the window. There are meadows that shimmer with sunlight, vistas of rolling hills, and some remarkable houses built of stone.

"That one has the wide King George boards on the floor. That was a forbidden timber that the colonists were supposed to send back to England."

My one small glimpse of mail box 223 and the driveway to the back door was on an early winter evening. Now it's a tunnel of giant bushes and overhanging limbs. I like the house. Built in 1929, it has a look of solid straight-line character.

"I don't use the front door."

"Let's talk about that later," I laugh as we pass by a covered porch where the first carpenter took time to ice it with delicate scallops of decorative wood.

It has a huge lawn—at least one half acre, but there's no sense of gardening. The flower beds have been left to multiply and tangle. Birds plant the seeds.

I follow him through the trail to the back porch. It's as I remember it. Once inside I go around the ring of downstairs rooms. The bones of the house thrill me with the natural woodwork and antique glass doors. I declare that the glassed-in sun porch, off the living room, is where I'll stay during my visit. Mike puts my bag next to the twin spindle bed.

The way he has fixed the rooms makes my senses reel like the victim of a hit and run circus train. The walls are tipsy with every kind of oil painting. Some canvases look like stylized neon highway lines or enlarged science slides of everything that bubbles. Between, and on top of these contemporary expressions, are some delicate seascapes and portraits.

There's an element of cartoon in his choice of furnishings. One giant velvet cactus is next to a director's chair with bright toucans on the canvas.

Mike is smiling. The world in here is one ring of Thaler, an absolute individual whose style overlaps with no one.

"On the next floor up," he says, "are my two offices and a museum room. Then, the whole top floor of the house is my bedroom. I had the attic converted with a bathroom and a deck."

As I follow him through the remaining rooms, I have a single question: *Will you really let me change this?* If I have my way, not one thing, except your office, will remain as I now see it—I don't want to move in and face a continual series of negotiations and compromises. I am the one that is rigid. I doubt my ability to ever sleep as Mike's wife next to a toy racecar collection that covers almost the entire floor with at least eighteen small teddy bears dressed in racing goggles.

If I could construct my own visual chaos, I could probably retire between stacks and stacks of hardback books. They would shift from those "not read" over to the piles that were. That would be an opium reader's dream; we each have our own compulsion.

July 11

Except for the fact we sleep on different floors, it's like playing house— and a peek into what life would be like with him. I learned not to just believe the telephone for content. Mike writes, makes jokes, likes to eat potato salad, and is ready to listen, like a friend.

My fingers wrinkle from the bowls of soapy water, and I put bags of garbage out by the garage. I found two drawers stuffed so full of rubber bands that they resisted being pulled open. I doubt if Mike has ever thrown away any aluminum foil. There are giant yard sacks full of it in the corner of the pantry. Mike has made towers of empty Kleenex boxes and yogurt containers in the basement. Every empty vial used once for pills now chokes the upstairs linen closet.

I think about the elements that helped shape these peculiar swirls in Michael Charles Thaler's personal fingerprint. Maybe his nurture became his nature. His father, Benjamin, immigrated to America at age sixteen and eventually made a successful business selling zippers and buttons to clothing manufacturers. At night, Mike said, he would draw pictures while listening to classical music. He would tell his son, "Keep your head in the clouds, but your feet on the ground." Maybe there was also a steady whisper not to waste.

One of Mike's genuine concerns is to get a good idea and not have the tools to write it down. I found one closet full of cases of tiny notebooks, and there are unopened boxes full of golfer's pencils. Always ready to record, it's carried in his hip pocket with the pencil pushed into the spiral.

"They have to be short," Laurel, "or they will protrude and stab my leg."

There was an all around curiosity for Mike's friends to meet me, and I was equally interested. I was living with the possibility that my whole world could tip to the east.

As we drive to Woodstock, I know that Marvin and Joan have a gallery, and both of them are artists. Mike has a collection of Marvin's pottery. Their distinctive feature was a glaze that resembles iridescent rainbows, like a swirling oil slick on water.

While waiting for them to be free of the day's end customers, I wander through their gallery looking at the expensive things. I still have Ukraine in my eyes where every shop was exclusively for basic needs like hammers and shoes. When we go to a local restaurant, I keep translating the menu prices to be equal to about three weeks of Kiev salaries.

Joan asks family questions.

"I have three children," I reply.

"We have a teenage daughter, and a much younger son. In between them," she said, while lifting her scotch and water, "I had an abortion."

It's all pronounced in the same tone as "pass the mustard."

It is just another culture jolt, and she would think I'm absolutely crazy if I put my arm around her and cry. It is more than the loss of that tiny baby artist, but my increasing voltage of loneliness. Everything is foreign.

I try to talk to Mike about it on the way home. Summer evening air is blowing in from both of our open windows. Mike looks bright behind the steering wheel in his golden pineapple shirt and yellow baseball cap. His silver gray hair curls up in the back.

Taking his eyes off the road, Mike shoots over to me an eye to eye look.

"Think of all your friends Laurel, like a chorus, blending their voices. There's my own glee club here, singing in harmony. Mine can't believe I would be engaged to a woman, and I've never slept with her. And yours is just as surprised that you would violate the sake of appearances by just staying alone with me in my house.

We are back, and I just feel like using the front door. I forget that not only is it locked, but Mike once fastened a rack across it that is covered with his collection of hats. Hurrying back around, I come in and see he has already punched in the burglary alarm code on the box by the stairs.

I remember how surprised he was, to learn during his visit, that I never even lock my house while he has wires and security company decals on most every window.

Sunday

It is raining. Leaning over Mike at his desk, I see he has printed a new poem in block letters:

> A HILL GIVES ME A PLACE TO SIT,
> THE EARTH A PLACE TO STAND.
> THE SKY GIVES ME A PLACE TO JUMP,
> THE GRASS A PLACE TO LAND.
> THE POND GIVES ME A PLACE TO SWIM,
> THE SUN A PLACE TO DRY,
> AND IF, BY CHANCE, I FALL ASLEEP,
> MY BLANKET IS THE SKY.

He's so intense—rolling sounds, in whispers, over his tongue that he doesn't know I'm there. I want to go to church, but I can't borrow his car because I've never learned to drive a stick shift. I know he doesn't like to be interrupted when he's working, but my need makes me tap his shoulder.

I explain how I could just stay home and read some scriptures, lapping them like a bowl of cream, but I want to see the neighborhood congregation. I think denominations resemble Sherwin William's chips of colored paint. There are thousands of hues.

Mike promises to come down and get me.

Since it's early, I decide to attack all the layers of hats that bar the front door. I get a bag for transporting them to some cleared shelf, and a screwdriver to remove the rack. All doors should open.

I'm so engrossed that I hardly hear Mike on the stairs behind me. Some of the treads squeak.

It's time for you to go," he says. "I phoned our village congregation." I wish he would come, but he's wearing sweat pants and an old tee shirt with so many small holes that it looks like the cotton is imitating Swiss cheese.

Church should be a kind of first aid station for people like me that feel grazed by arrows. There can be balm in song, but this particular congregation murmurs the first and last verse from a hymnal that was distributed before World War II. I'm used to singing something over and over again as I move from my own small, rolling-dice thoughts to adoration.

The congregation is mostly older women, and the bulletin invites one to come to the basement midweek to continue making crafts to sell at the Christmas bazaar.

I came for bread, and in the whole of the service, I hardly found a crumb. No one talked to me when it was over; it is strange to feel completely invisible. *If they can say "hello," to only those they know, what more are they doing than others.*

Once home, I knew we had to talk.

"I'm afraid," I said.

We had climbed to his third floor room and gone out through the sliding glass doors to his deck. The rain had stopped, and taking a towel, we wiped off the chairs and pulled them over to face each other.

I explain as best I can the keen loneliness and distance I feel here from everything familiar.

"I'm like a Lego that can't snap in; I just don't fit."

"What about two homes?" Mike suggests, without a pause. "I like Oregon. We can make that our primary residence, and then come here too."

I'm moved by his willingness to suggest such a change.

"And, there's something else, Mike. It's important to me that we go to church together."

I went on to list the differences between what I know at home and what I experienced this morning. The sermon was a dead letter in the mailbox.

Mike puts up a hand to ease what will be a string of metaphors. "That I can promise, but I'll always insist, Laurel, on the front row." I know for years he went to classical concerts, and is fully convinced that these are the best seats.

"Look, Laurel, This is my greatest concern—I don't want to sink my whole being, two becoming one, and have you die with cancer."

We both wrestle with the phantom fears of what could come.

Will you always be so nice?

Will you always be so well?

We end our truth-with-terror talk and go back to our separate occupations. One floor down, Mike turns back towards his office. From my hall view it's so choked with papers that one can imagine a forest was sacrificed for its pulp.

I go back to excavating caps while thinking that I can't reassure Mike Thaler like he can me. Just four years ago, I had to go climb into the cancer ring again for a third bout. It wasn't Hodgkin's disease, but a malignant mole that required a second surgery to remove a lump of surrounding flesh.

The doctor had first phoned with the news of cancer just as Matthew was about to knock out our kitchen ceiling. We had been involved in a remodeling project that was transforming the kitchen to be almost two stories high. Who needs an attic when you can alter the lines of a shoebox into something expansive?

Talking with the physician, I had completely forgotten that I was about to tape a plastic sheet over the door. As I hung up, down crashed all this swirling debris. It was a small bomb's worth of dust. It was a perfect symbol of how I felt. I just walked straight out to the backyard asking, through layers of sky, for another increment of time.

The surgery determined that there were no malignant cells around the mole. I could rip away any leash that was connecting me to the hospital.

After bagging the last of the hats, I finally get the door open. The whole hall fills with the smell of rain washed air.

My twelve-day visit on the East Coast is almost over. Almost as soon as I get back, Matthew will be marrying Tina.

I realize that they have been talking, through their whole courtship, about wanting a big family. I could actually become a Nana. Like the grand-mother of my past, Ada Belle Watson, I could dye my hair a very pale blue, but I would forgo her obligatory gloves, hat and costume jewelry.

July 20 to August 5
Portland

Matthew objected to my one mother-of-the-groom dress because he said it was too low cut, so I took it back.

Tina asked me to really think about the professional wedding photo-graphs as my summer purple suit wouldn't work with the shades of the bridesmaid's dresses.

Two days before the ceremony, I purchased a green dress that later I learn gave Tina's mother some concern because it was the same color as her newly purchased suit.

My concern was not the day's linen and silk skin, but my own emotions. I am like an ocean of sentimentality; I could be drowned in memories.

Matthew, when a toddler, preferred to drink water out of flower vases and refused to eat anything but spaghetti.

He used to clench his fist and make a pretend razor to shave his little boy's cheeks.

He would cry at railroad crossings if there wasn't a train he could see.

It's baby, going, going, gone.

His plan for dating girls was to take them to a five-dollar-a-plate spaghetti chain restaurant and give them a battery of values questions.

In questioning Tina, he learns she taught school: check "yes." He had wanted a wife that had the same holiday spread as his own. There was no insanity in her family, and she had spent her summer doing literacy work in Hong Kong. She was active in church and loves children—maybe have four, five, or six.

After they promise the great vows tonight, they will leave from the reception to fulfill a two-year teaching contract in Guam, some little spot of land that protrudes from the Pacific somewhere by the Philippines. Matthew was thrilled they could time this journey with their honeymoon.

They are in that same strong magnetic field of the future, like I once was. All generations compare to being like successive waves of the sea. Tears are salty, and I go into the bathroom to get wads of Kleenex for my purse. I'll be in the front row, and I don't want a wet face.

August 25

"Mike it's funny how, as a parent, one counts forward with their births, and now I count backwards," I tell him on the telephone. A family of four has become a family of three.

I'm talking to him while wrapping the cord around my arm, and off again. It's a strange mannerism, and I've stretched out some of the tight loops.

"Now, last night Mary Elisabeth came to tell me that she wants to attend the University of Guam, fifteen airplane hours away. She says it has the best marine biology program."

My words to Mike are just family equations. He sympathizes, but can't really understand the feelings, as he has never had a child.

Telling me about his trip to Hershey Pennsylvania and buying antique cars at a toy show, I think how he doesn't know a parent's denial either. Mike Thaler goes and gets whatever he wants, almost like a boy with a gigantic allowance. I know the contents of his house; he doesn't need another racecar.

I've always had to think first of milk and children's shoes. And now it's college tuition for Mary Elisabeth and semester textbook bills. I straightened Mary's teeth and got both Matthew and Anna their first computer.

As for myself, my personal expenditures don't exceed small purchases—like buying an on-sale turtleneck in a gorgeous shade of purple.

Once off the phone, I'm still aghast that Thaler spent three thousand dollars because, as he tried to explain it to me, there were molded, human-looking figures in it, and it came with the original box.

We are certainly going to be—him, as Jack Spratt, who could eat all the fat, and me, the wife, with the lean ...

January 4, 1995
Portland

It is one of my litanies; Mike Thaler is 57 years old and has been a bachelor for a very long time. Those who know human nature have coined certain enduring phrases. At one end of the life cycle are the *terrible twos*, and then time arcs to the truth of *set in his ways*.

Mike has one of the worst senses of color and clothing than anyone I have ever known. The trouble is he is stubborn and resists any suggestions that would make him look like someone a bank could trust for a loan. He simply likes anything gaudy and bright.

Garment manufacturers need Mike because he will buy their moment of bad judgment in stocking red or yellow pants. Often his purchases come from a clearance rack. He feels clever and will crow how much he has saved.

I know the truth; no one in their right mind would purchase it. The odds in a store finding a buyer are not as good as winning a New York lottery.

It was mostly okay with me. I had gone to Berkeley in the sixties where, to a new degree, we had collectively celebrated individualism. I love people who are truly unique. In our dating encounters, I was amused, and got used to the public's second glance and long sidewalk stares. Mike truly never noticed.

I called him to talk about wedding clothes for our March ceremony. It is going to be small, private and in my living room. There will only be a hand-ful of friends. Yet, this time it really matters what he will wear.

"Well, Laurel ..."

I could tell by his tone that he had never even thought about it.

"I want to look special."

"You don't own a suit. You don't own a tie," I reply.

"I will wear silk. You know my mustard colored sports jacket and that bright purple shirt? I have aqua pants, and you know my yellow belt that I bought in Rome?"

I *know* Mike; this isn't going to be negotiable.

Still thinking about adages, I remembered another one later that has also endured. I thought of it as being as high as a skyscraper. It was impossible to look over it and see the other side:

You don't marry a man with the idea of changing him.

I couldn't see around it or underneath it either. No one can.

I'm being reckless with hope, but now I believe, with obedience also.

February 12

Once Mike Thaler arrives in Portland, we both agree that our invitations should be hand made. There isn't time for any other option; our date is fixed to the cusp of spring break.

We go to separate desks to fish for our announcement's cover art. I know Mike employs a loose line and will be quick to land a choice drawing. Always in contrast, I grip the pen for a slow tight cast. I'm pulling exact five pointed stars onto the page. After adding a balloon, I erase it; there were just too many years of doing birthday invitations. Mike bounds up the stairs bearing his trophy work:

It is us, in cartoon sketch facing each other in the pose of a dancing jig. If he had not made such broad smiles under both pug noses, it would be the classic profile of prize fighters, dukes up.

Mike suggests that I add some stars and do all the printing on the inside.

1995

March 3

On my wedding morning, I see the sky is a pearl-gray velvet. My excitement can't be put to work—everything is done. Even the living room chairs have already been arranged to face the stone fireplace, the spot of the pending ceremony.

I have pushed back my closet clothes so my dress can hang alone. I have matched it to Mike's colors so we can look like tropical fish swimming down the stairs, and to and through, our vows.

Needing some occupation, I am feeling giddy. Where is calm? The part of my brain that can act like a radio is monotonously repeating a tune from the 1950s Hit Parade:

"Love and marriage ...
Go together
Like a horse and carriage.
Let me tell you, brother
You can't have one without the other ..."

I throw on my most real me clothes—baggy corduroy pants and a turtleneck. I have already heard Mike's voice in the room beneath mine droning on the telephone. I know he had planned to jump into business for his morning hours so we can take our tiny, honeymoon vacation, like a parenthesis in our unrelenting schedules.

Stepping outside, I see spots of light now turning the sky into swatches of overcast tweed. I remember my small sack of flower bulbs on a bench by the side of the house. They are much more patient than the nursery's containers of plants. Those yell for water and earth.

Spooning out holes in the front bed, I am thinking how a young bride could plant a sapling, and half a century later sit under its branches. In August my gladiolas will bloom—we have to live condensed lives.

Everything that is usually daily and common is being imbued with significance. It's a wedding day, and not some legal interaction.

250

A friend who knows I never go to beauty shops gave me a certificate for hair and finger attention. The last time I sat under a hair dryer was probably for my junior prom in 1962. Some smells provide an instant sense trail back to the original sniff. The styling chemicals haven't changed in 33 years.

I want my hair a common way I always wear it, but the French braid is like a perfect back head zipper.

Once home there are people who have come to help. It's like the river has developed a new current. Eventually we are banished upstairs with a couple of friends to dress in separate bedrooms. Then, we wait together, occasionally glancing at the mirror's reflection. We're silent, waiting for the summons to come down once everyone is seated.

Time is in rapids. We can feel the waterfall.

The bottom stairs are banked at the end with Joanne Small's gift of flowers. Somehow, I begin to think how I'll put poinsettias there for the month of December.

Then, I see the people. There's so many more than we expected. They are even standing behind the rose patterned couch and leaning against the bookcase.

I see some new, silver friends, and those old and gold, representing all my decades. If there were a secret ballot, maybe even the majority here might rule that I'm making the mistake of illusion. But, I'm infused with the rightness of us. It is a mysterious green light; this is God's plan.

Anna is my only child that can be here, as Guam is so far away. She is as thin as a spring stem standing up at the left side, across from Jared, Mike's illustrator. I'm afraid if I lock eyes with hers, we'll just start to laugh; a nervous joy can turn funny corners.

She didn't like Mike in the beginning, but once she knew him, she changed her mind. My daughter gave consent.

As the pastor talks psalm and scripture, it feels very serious. We each say "yes" in the ancient covenant of promise.

I can only see Mike's eyes, and for the first time I realize they are the same

color as mine.

His family came from East Europe to New York, and mine from the British Isles through the deep south of America to this cross hair of time. Israel Thaler's grandson marries Jackson Moore's granddaughter.

The instruction to "kiss the bride" makes everyone laugh, and later I learn that Anna, at this point, began to make funny faces. Everyone owns some cells of a comedian.

The food comes out. I have a best friend, Marilyn, who graduated top of her class in a Paris cooking school.

We had decided to stay in the house the first night. So many people came from airplane distances, and we want to be with them. This is a consideration when the bride and groom have hair the color of snow.

Later, and finally alone, we climb the stairs to bed. It's so comfortable. Mike keeps telling me to be careful, I'm in stocking feet, as if I'll slip, be paralyzed, or die before we reach the top.

We both stand in the doorway and stare into the largest bedroom. Someone has taken the time to surround the bed with all the upstairs house plants. I recognize my botanical garden from the bathroom's bay window. I suspect

it's the pair of university students that came to help with serving. Interspersed among the foliage are lit candle pillars, fat with wax, to burn for hours.

"It looks like some pagan altar prepared for the rites of spring," I murmur.

"Yes," says Mike. "It's to sacrifice the virgin."

I'm sure this really is the beginning of living, "happily ever laughter."

March 4

"We'll always travel," says Mike. "It's not like the factory lets us out for one week a year.

The irony is we're still in the house and it's almost noon. We have set plans to drive through Washington to Vancouver and return through Canada's Victoria Island. The suitcases are in the car, and I've been ready for hours. Mike is stuck in event replay. He is now looking at wedding cards and eating, with a tablespoon, from a large pan of left-over potatoes.

Standing near the door, I start picking at Rain Forest Crunch, one of the confections from a large gift basket of specialty foods. I've even put the flowers in the car to give away while they are still in one-hundred-watt bloom; it's hard for me to waste anything.

"Look," says Mike. "This isn't hard time. We don't have an airplane to catch. Do you think we should go and rest a little more upstairs?"

"No, I've driven to Spokane before, and it takes a full day. I would rather spend the time at the Bed and Breakfast where we've been given two free nights."

We've had time wars before. Mike doesn't own a watch. I'm exact, and I could salute the 12 at every minute's rotation when I'm anxious to go.

I take his potato pan into the kitchen and see he has eaten off the entire top crust; Mike takes my can of Rain Forest candied nuts to the car, and complains that I've picked out all the almonds. I love how we sound like matching shoes in a long-time marriage.

By the time it turns dark, there's snow on the highway and slow-moving traffic. We creep into the Victorian inn very late. Our room has no closet but an antique wardrobe Two interior hooks are decorated with a top hat and a white bride's veil. I choose the side of the bed where those wedding clothes are the last thing I see, as Mike turns off the light.

Much later that same night, we have our first heat skirmish. I prefer a room to be cool for sleep, and I wake covered with sweat. I had long thrown off the blankets, but the air is reminiscent of a July afternoon. I don't know where the wall thermostat is that Mike adjusted. Creeping to the window, I slide it open thinking I am saving our lives.

Welcome to all suicidal snow flakes; I want the North Wind to whistle away our discomfort.

"What are you doing, Laurel?"

A grizzly bear sized lump shifts on the bed.

To my cry of "heat stroke" and "fire drill," Mike rises to adjust the wall thermostat to some realm of compromise.

"This is more evidence that we are from different sides of the moon," I murmur.

"Yes," says Mike reaching out to cover my hand with his own.

He whispers,

> *"Does a polar bear wear underwear,*
> *When the temperatures are zero?*
> *Or is he naked under there,*
> *A hardy, happy hero."*

I carry my work with me for our week. It is a full bag of fifty freshmen research papers to grade, and I keep it closer to me than my own purse. Everything bears the mark of my red pen, but a percent carry peculiar moments from our journey. Canadian breakfast butter spots mark "The Vanishing Timber Wolf" and jelly on an analysis of "New Age Cults." The water spray from a ferry stained five folders. I rolled on a remnant in my bed permanently creasing the computer-typed lines. Mike tugged one out of my hands in a Vancouver antique store tearing away a thumb-sized corner. He was just excited to show me a *netsuke*, a small 19th century Japanese carving.

I will have to offer an apology that I don't really feel. I am nostalgic about my first week as a wife, and all those blemishes produce in me a pleasant recall.

May 1

Mike gets the mail from a neighbor; I check my flower beds for new green curls. Once inside, the chairs are still straggling in all directions. We each carry our own bag up to the bedroom. After pulling out two shirts and fishing for hangers, Mike asks for half of the closet.

I have been a wife of perfect courtesy, until this request. I flatly refuse that he should get a full fifty percent.

"I'll clear out some space; I have so much more stuff than you."

"No," says Mike. "I want half."

"Wait a minute! Let's just think of this like theoretical communism; you should only take what you need."

Before Mike came, I had spent hours ordering my clothes between winter and summer, peasant to fine.

"No," repeats Mike with only half a smile. He has turned up the volume on his voice. It is obviously not negotiable. It's funny too, because we thought we had talked about the issues that make up the stuff of argument. We know we sit on opposite ends of many a teeter-totter. On politics, we have always been elephant versus donkey. On money, he thrives on splurge as I do for thrift. Our genealogy includes Rabbis and Baptist pastors. We never once considered temperature wars or the friction of redrawing closet boundaries.

One concern I had about moving to New York was fearing his ability to be flexible. He was so grown through that house, like tendrils of Thaler, that there wouldn't be much room for any of my designs. Realizing I'm the one doing this, I begin to remove all my "not so often" and "maybe once a year" garb.

"Okay," I say pulling out my orange and black flannel shirt that only is used at Halloween. I also have a whole section of "once I lose some weight" apparel that can be transferred downstairs.

Mike turns his attention to the large bedside table. I can't help but call out as he begins to move an arrangement of full-blooming African violets.

"Think about the French impressionists!" I cry. "Keep that purple fire right there!"

Unmoved by my pleas, he carries all but one plant into the bathroom. He begins to place on the table his Kleenex, blood pressure medicine, spiral notebooks, a flashlight, and chapped lip balm.

What's selfish in me, wanting things exactly my way, is large and alive. It's actress, deep breaths, and biting the back of my hand.

"Mike, you've made that table look like something out of the "I Am Completely Broke Trailer Park." It just needs a couple cans of generic dog food.

"Well, Laurel, how can we compromise?"

His tone isn't at all sarcastic like mine, but his voice is still louder than usual. I think marriages win or die in how they handle conflict. Lucky for me, I've married some of the spirit of William Penn. I go get for him a roomy antique basket, with a lid. He especially likes the amber-colored bead on top.

While watering my downstairs houseplants before retiring, I can see there are more spots of husband with his liberal distribution of Kleenex boxes. I remember how his house in New York had tissues in almost every room. I just don't believe that everyone who sneezes has to have some visible soft paper aid within a five-foot radius.

Once upstairs, I explain to Mike the in-drawer, in-cupboard places where I've stored them all.

He's facing the bed with his back towards me.

"Laurel, I understand now the real difference between the genders.

Women love to put fifty pillows on a bed where you really only need two."

I retort that he has crowned "Practical" as king, where I have little allegiance to that throne.

"Beauty and aesthetics are far more important."

Only then does he turn and launch two pillows at my chest from across the room. He's provoked by my slightly haughty tone. Both shots are a bull's eye. He may have had more practice than me with all that East Coast snowball weather, but I've had three children and clocked a lot of pillow fights ...

It's a truce.

Winter still tugs at the weather. It's the heavyweight in Portland's central ring, yet spring delivers some warm and scented blows. The students have to know that we are like them and also can't wait for school to be over. We would love to be airborne.

"You see," says Mike, "I really was a *hobbit*, you know. I love naps, I drink tea, I have cozy slippers. I had my favorite chair in New York and would sit almost every night and watch old movies. You know, you did come into my life like Gandolf, to finally convince me that Jesus is my Messiah, and you showed me that maps can actually talk and beckon."

This is Planet Earth. There is gravity, there is dust, there are problems. Yet, they were not between us; I had married the court jester of children's literature.

The Problem came in a plain envelope towards the end of summer. The return address was IRS, and it was not a refund check, but a summons to an audit. It included an order to call them and make a September appointment. I was to bring all my records for 1991 and 1992. My bones turned to stone.

With three children coming and going to college, boxes had been pushed around, or an empty carton was created by dumping my papers somewhere else. I could find journals, letters and certain scraps that were nostalgic, but nothing numerical.

The little dog laughed to see such a sport, but my checks had run away with the spoon.

I had faxed my summons to my accountant. His assessment was based on the fact it had been years since I had book royalty income. "They want to show your occupation as a university teacher and writing as a side hobby, which puts your deductions in question."

When he whistled while telling me how many thousands of dollars it could cost, I thought that accountants might be one of the worst professions for having any comprehension of a bedside manner.

To me the IRS is a wolf that can scratch through the door.

September 4

School started. The semester is like a giant elevator that picks up faculty and students on a long, golden day then descends to the cold, pinched light of mid-December. It felt like it was going to be a long stretch before Professor Ed Higgins could wrap one of his hats with battery-lit noel lights.

September 12

Mike was Mr. "Don't Worry," but of course, I did. He permanently camps on the side where all will be well. In contrast, I was thinking how the IRS has the power to force a house sale, and we'll have to look to Jimmy Carter to build us a habitat.

September 24

In the extended forecast, there will probably be record-breaking heat tomorrow. This seems ominous for my appointment day, but so would rain or overcast skies.

September 25

I have learned a lot of things from students. Many of them were experts in the art of appearing as if they had fulfilled an assignment, where really they had barely typed their name near the top line. This was especially true in Autobiography, where they were required to keep a detailed semester journal.

I had a scheduled conference in my office where I was to review, in front of them, their account of their lives. Some would come with volumes of papers and press into my hand anything with the semester's dates, and explain it's like a collage, an expressive array of themselves. I was forced to look through letters to hometown friends and essays on dead music composers.

Now, I am doing the same thing. It took my largest backpack and a three-foot long, giant willow basket to carry all the vaguely relevant information. I wore my nicest shorts and a white blouse that had a dry cleaner's starch, like a hair spray for cotton; I cannot wrinkle.

After parking in a city garage, I'm glad it's a downhill walk to the federal building because of the weight of my bundles. The lobby guard looks suspicious; the Oklahoma City bombing happened this past spring. The elevator passengers seem to regard me with pity once "IRS" lights on the panel as my choice. I am self-conscious with all my stuff, and no one has on shorts.

There is no waiting room, but just chairs to the side of the check-in desk. Everyone else has real cowhide briefcases. Nothing is vinyl but our seat cushions.

Different auditors come out and call a name. I can actually detect their relief when anybody else, but me, stands up. I'm in a visually determined category, like a street musician with dread locks. I do all my accounting with walnut shells.

Finally, a middle-aged man calls, "Laurel Lee." His laminated badge states "IRS" in such bold letters above his photograph that it can be read at distances by the vision impaired. It strikes me as odd that he is wearing the same shirt today as the one in his badge picture. I wish for a magnifying glass so I can trace that laminated plaid into visual infinity.

I follow him back to a simple cubicle made with portable sound-padded boards. It's so small; it is a testimony that no tax dollars are lavished here. I recognize my forms on Mr. Barry's desk. Wanting to be real and human, I hand him three school shots of my children while announcing that these have been my life's major deduction. Without pause, I hand him next a picture of our house. I've practiced my speech too.

"Writing," I explain, "is not a hobby like collecting Avon bottles or this new craze for Beanie Babies. It's a job, but writers do collect words ..."

At this point Mr. Barry takes charge and begins to fire questions.

"You bought a car in 1991. Show me only the proof of payment for this Honda Civic." I am so glad that somewhere I have the actual price tag that was hanging down from the rear view mirror. I stored it as a kind of souvenir of progressing to a middle-class income.

He asks about my California house sale, quickly adding that he doesn't want any pictures—just the legal papers from the Realtor. After some shuffle, I actually find the folder to hand to him.

"You bought a computer. What kind of computer games do you like, Laurel?"

I know it's a trick question because it's so out of character, but I tell him my highest scores on Columns and Tetris.

"Okay, you use it for entertainment, and I'm only going to allow half the deduction. Now, I want to know about your office."

I explain how I created it in the basement because it's away from the traffic of the house, and it also stays cool through the summer.

"Oh, come on," he replies in a rather nasty tone. "Why would a sensitive, artistic person like you make a place to write in a dark basement?"

His sarcasm is like its root word, "serrated." I feel cut and want to cry. I have to keep thinking, I am an adult. Mr. Barry can behave like a playground bully, but there is no teacher on duty or parent to take up my cause.

I only hand him photographs when he queries for hotel and restaurant receipts. One was taken on the highway out of Calcutta. I had stayed at one of the frequent truck driver stops where there were no walls, but ropes that separated the simple cots. I point out to him where I'm sitting on the left with my back to the camera.

For a brief moment, he is wistful, and even mentions that he had once thought of doing something like that with a motorcycle, but it was a long time ago.

I had heard of the Stockholm Syndrome, when the victims begin to attach themselves and identify with their captor. It happened in a Scandinavian bank robbery where the perpetrator took hostages. It tries to explain one of the odd ripples that acute stress can produce. I truly understood it as I found myself actually beginning to like my examiner. I even offered him any of my pictures. He especially liked the refreshment hut that was almost buried in coconut shellswhere I ate in Pakistan.

The interview lasts the maximum allowed time. Completely exhausted, my brain aches as if it had been forced to chew stiff and stale gum. I stuff everything back into my pack and basket. Mr. Barry says the results will be calibrated and sent in the mail.

The lobby's doors continually flap in the massive five o'clock exit. I ask the afternoon guard if I can momentarily leave my things while I get my car. He nods, as the temperatures are peaking and it's all uphill. It's a traffic sludge to any residential neighborhood. Finally, I reach our driveway and turn to get my bundles from the back. Nothing is there; I left it all in the federal building. My intelligence quotient feels as if it has been reduced to a padded-helmet status.

Mike meets me at the door. He leads me to the living room couch and wants to cheer me with his poem of the day. He believes that nonsense is one of the best antidotes for all that is sober.

He says he's dedicating it to the IRS:

> *A shark is never*
> *really still,*
> *He is a fish*
> *In motion.*

From snack
To snack
He swims along
His dining room's
The ocean.

To retrieve my documents, my husband first phones the IRS office, which has already closed. Next, he tries the police, and then as directed, puts a call into the FBI. He thinks it's all very funny, and I can hardly muster a smile as we get in the car to retrieve my baskets.

OctobeR 1

I decided not to tell anyone at school that I am leaving for Alaska. My Tuesday and Thursday teaching schedule will not be interrupted, and why let the right hand know what the left hand is doing. It is Mike that will be addressing the state's English teachers; I'm just the pal in his side car.

On the plane, I'm feeling Celebration at being on the other side of the IRS mountain. In contrast, Mike seems more grim than usual. His lips are pressed into a tight line. We are sitting next to each other like a living pair of happy and tragic drama masks.

While pulling out the pretzel snack from the seat pocket, I ask him what is wrong.

"Look at it down there, Laurel. It's just wilderness."

"So. When I was 21, it was the goal of my life to be in a little house in those big woods."

He reaches over me, tapping the window with is hand. "That indicates an extreme shortage of sidewalks, which means no book stores, antique shops or restaurants. I prefer civilization."

If we were a couple in an earlier century, I would be arguing for the Oregon trail, where he would be gripping Boston so tight, his knuckles would be white.

The Fairbanks airport is decorated by taxidermists who stuff select creatures that roam the giant state.

"You know the polar bear, Mike, will stalk humans."

He's very easy to tease.

We are in the second largest Alaskan city, but it would be a small town in most other parts of the States. Some one-room log cabins have been absorbed by the urban-growth boundary.

We are brought to a hotel, and our upstairs room has a balcony. Once unpacked, I look in vain for the Northern Lights.

October 2
Fairbanks

Mike is scheduled to give assemblies for the primary grades before his conference begins in the evening. He is dressed completely in yellow. Even his shoe laces look like they have been dyed as a match for melted butter. I walk through the school doors feeling that I'm in the company of a rather husky buttercup.

The gymnasium has been transferred into an auditorium. It's interesting that when Mike hints at needing a volunteer the students almost levitate out of the seats in sheer enthusiasm to be picked. Yet, I know that the adult audience tonight, hearing the same request, will avert their eyes and compress to cement. There's a gain with age, but also a loss.

Once the assembly has been dismissed, Mike begins to draw posters for the school. As he colors in Mrs. Green's tail, I begin to explore. In one unlocked closet is an abundance of indoor sports equipment, including racks of roller skates. A bright pink pair, embossed with an "8," will fit me like Cinderella's dancing slippers. I recall gliding on Illinois sidewalks and how the texture changed while crossing the street.

Letting my right foot lead, I begin to roll rapidly towards my husband. It is a surprise that years can subtract so many digits from balance. I have Mike's attention, but it isn't any performance that I intended. My goal is to just stay upright and reach the single, central Samsonite chair. I'm barely vertical, and then there's the pain of falling and rattling bones.

I cannot get up. Mike goes to see if there's a school nurse. Her assessment is to get a wheelchair, load me into the school station wagon, and go to the city hospital.

Hospital

The initial X-ray confirms that I have shattered my pelvis. The specialist tells us it's like a donut, and it just can't break in one part.

"This, of course, means a hospitalization, Mrs. Thaler."

"What?" asks Mike in surprise. He is 58 years old and has never spent one night in any medical institution.

Finally, I get an injection for pain. It feels exactly like I'm being filled with clouds, but there's a tip of the mountain, above the fog, that still hurts. When the nurse brings the enrollment papers, she asks how I'm now feeling.

"Just like a calendar picture I once saw of Mt. Fuji."

I realize I've been too obtuse when she asks an associate about my initial narcotic dosage.

After recording our insurance and address, she also asks questions that reflect how close we are to the wilderness:

Do you carry all of your water into the house?

Do you bring all of your wood into the house?

Do you use a generator, or do you have electricity?

Mike comes with me as I'm transferred to a bed. I groan at my shrinking world. I'm between one bedside curtain and a window view of plain red brick.

A nurse comes with more forms. She asks how the accident happened. I want to bargain my story for a better bed, but I'm abruptly told that everything is full. Emergencies from around the entire state are either air-lifted here or to Anchorage.

I wonder if she's telling the truth, or just trying to avoid extra labor. She will not look at me in the eyes.

"I was roller skating and should not have tried to jump over the chair." I will not look at her in the eyes either. Mike turns his laugh into a cough.

Later, my new attending physician comes in holding my chart. "I see you are up here from Oregon as a professional skater."

The other enrollment notes include that I'm 49 years old and overweight.

October 3

I am being kept on complete bed rest, and I'm drowsy from the medicine. Sometimes my narcotic dreams turn the hospital into a care center that includes injured wildlife. From a great distance, I can hear the bellowing of crippled caribou. Walruses and sea lions moan in two distinct tones.

Mike visits me as often as he can. Sometimes he's wearing tee shirts that are embossed with characters from his books, over turtlenecks. It's cold outside. The first winter snow can come at anytime.

"I've learned, Laurel, that you must be hospitalized for at least one week. They are going to wait until you are stable enough to travel in a wheelchair. Also, there's a chance that you will not be able to teach this semester. I'll call the Writing/Literature department for you."

"I'm always checking too," he added. "And there are no available rooms with a view." He has pulled a chair up to my side. Somehow, he's holding several sheets of hospital stationary. He explains that he's making drawings for the children of the nursing staff. I must have fallen asleep because he's gone, and I can see a stack of pictures piled up on my bedside table. On the top there's a racecar being driven by a lion.

October 4

I am transported by a gurney to ultrasound so they can further evaluate the extent of the fracture. It's a room in tones of twilight, operated by a woman who has a whole console in front of her like the controls for the spaceship, Enterprise.

Once parked back in my featureless dock, I can hear my neighbor making muffled crying noises. She is on the telephone, and I can hear her stammer, "they think it's cancer." For the first time, even her television is off.

Once she hangs up, I have to talk to her. After an apology for intruding, I share how I had cancer over twenty years ago, and contrary to everything the doctors knew or said, it all went away. I underline that nothing is impossible with God.

What happens next is better than thunder in the sky. Within the half-hour her doctor returns. I'm listening to every word. He says he has just come from a conference where several physicians have examined her test results, and although it looks like cancer, it is not. She can go home.

She asks if she can be allowed alcohol with all her new prescriptions.

My physician comes in the afternoon. I'm surprised because he is only a morning caller during the duties of grand rounds.

"Mrs. Thaler, I've examined the films taken today in ultrasound. We can clearly see three tumors. One is considerably larger than the other two. To be evaluated, they will have to be removed. This is going to require abdominal surgery after you return to Portland.

"We will get in touch with the necessary physicians in your local Kaiser hospital."

I feel like an Account Due bill has been delivered, requesting a staggering amount, and a possible eviction notice.

There's an irony that I delivered such a fair and golden speech to my neighbor, who has now been discharged. This fresh dread has been activated by the word, "tumor." It's already assaulting the nightingale that can sing such high notes about trust.

Fear can pick through its own bone pile.

I've always been bothered by the case of Charlotte Bronte. I detest how she died during her first year of her marriage. I've read the biography. Taking a walk with her husband, Patrick, she was caught in a rain storm. Contracting pneumonia, she fell on the side of time before antibiotics.

Our seven months of marriage have been like colored balloons up in the sky knotted together—we seem to float above the earth.

Mike has spent a portion of his adult life in the role of a boyfriend. He's internalized the acts of a suitor. I get notes, like five in one day, and the hour I'm to open them. I get flowers. The last bunch was carnations. I get compliments. I get free will-hugs. After all the relationship rejection, I need a husband whose mode is in *romance overdrive*.

There's a lot of women who helped in his training that I should thank.

In the evening, Mike comes on his way to a reception being hosted in the local artifact museum. I can't believe he is wearing his favorite Hawaiian shirt over a bright orange turtleneck. Tonight, if I were well, we could have had a clothing discussion. I would have been tempted to point out that the event is not a costume party.

Instead, we have a real problem, which reveals the superficiality of any other concern. Clothes are not life or death. Looking for the right words, trying to find a synonym for "tumor," I tell him myself. I can't have Mike get the news in *doctor-gram*. This was his courtship fear of what could happen.

While the stun gun of facts is still taking effect, I let him know that I got to compare the anxiety of a tax audit versus a suspicious X-ray. It's field research.

"There's no question that the IRS is worse."

While holding both of my hands, Mike makes up a joke just for me. He says, "What's the most beautiful letter and number in our language?"

After a silence long enough for me to shake my head, he says, "B, NINE."

"Do you get it, Laurel? That is what we are going to believe together for this tumor, BENIGN."

We are holding each other. We are both going to have to make a real effort to stay on the sunny side of the street.

October 5

The morning nurse has news while recording my vital signs. A room with a better window is now open.

Two women, who usually clean, move my bed. Finally moored to my new dock, I can overview a parking lot, helicopter landing pad, and beyond the street, a woods.

Sometimes, I almost catch the ghost of myself walking down that very highway on my way to hitchhike to Anchorage. I was bone thin, hungry, and really only had my diary to talk to.

October 6

Mike tells me that the Alaska doctors have communicated with our Oregon HMO. The first day we can be back, I have a priority appointment. He kisses me and is gone to an appointment at a school. He is my anchor newsman.

I have to learn the transporting art of crutches. A physical therapist is to teach me the full range of possible movement while suspended by sticks. Like in all things, there is to be progression. I will learn how to mount and remain upright at a gallop. At the end of the hall is a stairwell. These will be my fences to jump, while astride, one floor to the next.

October 7

It happened after the hospital staff had peddled their sleeping pills and passed out the canned fruit snack with crackers. It was right before the night duty staff came for their eight-hour shifts. Settled with grape juice, I looked the million billionth time out my window. There they were. The Northern Lights moved through the sky like a great waltz in fire.

I found myself reaching deep into vocabulary, as if it were a drawer of cash, and finding myself bankrupt for words. Language lacks the gold for expressing first time wonders, like seeing the sea.

Mike called, also mute to explain such beauty. His hotel balcony is just at the right angle to see the performance.

Once we've disconnected, and the night is again void of those dancing skirts, I am painfully sad. I remember a movie scrap from the 1950s. Every soul was evaluated to mark for each a time to die. The decision included a check list of experiences:

1. Ever licked dew, or tasted fresh snow?

2. Ever picked fruit and ate it from a tree? And somewhere in that giant list was, "ever known real love?"

Now, it can be added, "Laurel Lee has finally seen the Northern Lights."

I'm that much closer to having finished my course.

October 8

Mobile with my wheelchair, I now have rounds that I want to do. It is my last night. I will wheel down to the pediatric wing, and then I want to go and visit the pastor who fell off the roof and injured his spine. I'll bring him my cache of accumulated fruit juice cans and an assortment of small breakfast cereal boxes. He has a lot of company.

October 9

Mike loves to get on a plane during early boarding. He has explained to me that there is no problem then in storing overhead luggage. He likes a full magazine selection too. I've watched him take off his baseball cap because he thinks he looks older and actually shuffle by the door where the tickets are monitored. He shamelessly enters the plane with women and infants.

Now for our Alaska Airlines flight, with its medically altered tickets, we will be the first of the first. I see them coming with the abbreviated wheelchair that's as wide as the aisle. I will be pulled like a beverage cart, and due to my ingested pills, will slump and sleep to Oregon.

October 21

My wheelchair and surgery date, in just eleven days, rains on the traditional gags for my fiftieth birthday party. I'm waiting for my friends to come. Mike has organized a potluck dinner. The standard jokes are to bring such things as canes outfitted with a horn and rear view mirror, yellow pages listing retirement homes and adult diapers. I've watched people unwrap bogus deeds to cemetery plots. It's all to laugh at future shadows and eat cake with nuts while you still have teeth.

October 31

I feel a million years away from Halloween. Downstairs, I can hear Mike exclaim over the costumes at the door. I bet he is secretly hoping that someone would pick one of his book's characters for their night's theme. He's told me he has seen two *Cat in the Hats*.

I am sitting in the bathroom. Tomorrow's 8:00am surgery prohibits any kind of food or beverage, except for this prescription liquid plumber. This has probably ruined lime flavor for me for the rest of my life.

November 1
Hospital

We drive through the dark and quiet streets. I feel a diffused envy for normal people, sleeping in all these homes, with health.

Neither of us is talking. Mike has assured me so many times that everything is going to be all right, that I'm rather worried about him. He's called every friend with continuing updates on my medical status. In contrast, my style is to be quiet, very private, and if possible, make everyone laugh.

The waiting room for surgery is right by the hospital's front doors.

They fastened around my wrist a plastic information band, which includes 1945, the year I was born. I am thinking they can never type in a patient's weight because some women might saw it off with the hospital dinner knife. There are enough humiliations in any day.

As patients, we used to be able to see our rooms first, put away our things and then have the gurney come. Now it is more like a conveyer belt as we all sit together for these last moments, with our private concerns. None of us knows where we will wake up.

The most serious operations are scheduled first, and I see a couple much older than us, looking at photo albums together. I rage, wanting them to have this intimacy of reminiscing without all the pedestrian observers. Few people at 5:00am are reading magazines.

Wheeling my chair down the hall, I have to get away from the sights that keep invoking my heated editorials. I decide for the practical; I braid my hair to prevent a maximum of pillow-rub tangles.

Mike is anxious and outside the door. They have called for me twice. We enter a bustling long ward of curtained cubicles where I am stripped of all civilian clothing and begin to be attached to machines. I even have mechanical boa constrictors wrapped to each ankle that huff and puff to prevent blood clots.

Mike asks, "Am I holding your hand, or are you holding mine?"

The same pastor who married us is escorted to our stall. I am impressed because he had to get up even earlier than us to get here, and he plans to sit with Mike through the morning.

Greg asks to read Psalm 91. I like to hear his voice alter to purple robes and pulpit tones:

Because he has set his love upon Me,
Therefore I will deliver him;
I will set him on high,
Because he has known My name.
He shall call upon Me, and I will answer him;
I will be with him in trouble;
I will deliver him and honor him.
With long life I will satisfy him ...

Three times we are interrupted. Two different nurses have offered me a shot for anxiety, like a little dim-it-all cocktail in a syringe. Shaking my head, *no*, I don't even want the slightest erasure.

The hospital's official chaplain is making rounds too. He bobs in and out, like an elderly lifeguard making sure that no one is drowning. I bet he's got pockets of lifesaver literature.

I can hear them beginning to roll out the beds for the designated surgery rooms.

Mike kisses me again goodbye. Our passion must be surprising to the miscellaneous staff. How can they know? We are just two days short of eight married months. As they roll me around the corner, I want to call back to him that the sun is just coming up. There are streaks of first light behind the hillside trees.

The last turn is into a wide hall without windows. It's like a strange habitat under the sea. Everyone is in aqua, with masks.

Most of the surgical team is waiting for me. I'm transferred to a cold and hard table. No mattress salesman has ever been here. I only know Dr. Zenhoffer and the specialist, an abdominal oncologist. The HMO has even put out extra money for his morning service.

I want them all to know I'm wide awake.

The anesthesiologist is talking to me like I'm an idiot child about the primary range of numbers from one to ten. The last things I see are the brown eyes of Dr. Zenhoffer. They are the warm blanket, bedtime story, and last prayer. I don't get a glass of water.

With first consciousness, I check my face to see if I have a tube down my throat. I was warned that if they found some extra problems and had to increase the scope of their probe, I would find such a device. Relieved there is none, I fall back to sleep.

As soon as I'm wheeled out of the recovery room, Mike is there. He's standing with some of our friends. I moan for water like a character out of a late-night desert movie. My float doesn't stop in the hall, but I keep moving through the mists of waking and sleeping, and wishing for something to drink.

I think, sometime in the middle of the night, I get ice chips.

November 2

Dr. Zenhoffer is at my bedside. Because of his surgical mask yesterday, I couldn't see that he's in his first week of growing a beard. It does make him resemble some friendly derelict that has wandered in from a park.

He explains that everything looked good, although the complete lab report will be comprehensive. Besides extracting three tumors, he says that my uterus was also removed.

"How is that going to affect our chances on having a child?"

He just stares back at me, unable to think of a thing to say. The preposterous can be so funny, except it hurts to laugh.

November 3

I barely noticed that I have a roommate. Yesterday, there was just some motion and light across from me. My awareness has now expanded beyond that single cell vision. She and her visiting family have turned on the TV and have filled the room. They have even brought in an ice chest, on wheels, to add to their party atmosphere. Everybody seems to be a sister, aunt, or a cousin.

Mike has given them the two chairs from our side and is carefully perched on my bed. He holds my hand, and we just kind of listen to the sound of them. Our pronunciation is so flat, like straight-line speech, where they have rounded and honed every tone. I love African Americans. My first congregation, back in the sixties, was in inner-city Portland. They welcomed the Jesus freaks and gave us our first real bottles of milk.

Some of them are chortling, then all of them are laughing. One of the younger women, with the toddler, calls out to us the joke.

"Mary Lou's doctor said he's not going to let her go home until she starts to fart! We're going to hide both her sisters under the bed to get that discharge!"

To me it's funny too. Mike isn't laughing like I am. He has been worried because we haven't heard the lab results. We both clearly understand that humor can be a campfire. We are safe when we laugh. There are too many things right now that bite and tear at us when we wander too far from light.

November 4

A young woman doctor is making the morning rounds. She is all stern looks and tough speech.

"To get well, you must be ambulatory. If you don't walk, you increase your danger of blood clots and the complications of a stroke. You don't want that for yourself!"

She adds that the surgery had been delayed until I had healed from the pelvic fracture. She concluded that she wanted me up and walking today. She has got the right manner of insistence. No doubt, her children will always do their homework.

It takes me an hour to sit up. It's torture to slide my feet to the side of the bed. The nurse gives me a shot in the stomach for pain. I have my crutches just in case. I can stand, but I am bent and feeling like a pretzel knot that can ambulate. I will crumble easily.

I am out in the corridor when Mike comes in the afternoon. His enthusiasm can be seen and heard. He doesn't see any of the reproachful looks from the nurse's desk. Most of the time he lives in proportions that are a little bit larger than life.

"And," he shouts, while whipping out an envelope from his jacket pocket. I can read the INTERNAL REVENUE SERVICE return address above his thumb. "There's no change in status," he quotes. "That means we don't have to pay anything!"

I always love the part where Goliath falls.

November 5

My friend, Judy, brings me a plant; Sylvia, who sat with Mike through surgery, has promised us a chicken stew as soon as I'm discharged. More friends will be coming this evening, and everyone wants to know the surgery results.

November 6

I have a room to myself. No one moans, but me, and only when I want to. There's no television; I prefer solitude. The curtains have been swept back as far as possible. I want every side inch of light.

Dr. Zenhoffer comes in. Every day he has a darker chin.

"I have the pathology report," he says, while pulling up a chair.

A now sitting physician doesn't seem like a good sign. He has always stood in his morning rounds; he has lots of patients to see. Doctors see time like a ticking parking meter. This is *bedside manner* behavior; he must have to talk to me.

"It really did look good during the surgery. We couldn't see anything abnormal. The report confirms that all three of those tumors were benign.

"What I'm concerned about is this nurse's note that you were vomiting last night."

Relief at this news breathes out of every pore.

I confess that Mike brought in some Thai food, and I drank a little too much soup made with coconut milk.

"That is going to cost you one more day here," says Dr. Zenhoffer as he stands.

Mike is early. I had called as soon as our doctor left, but he was already on his way. It is better as eye to eye news anyway.

"Well, what are we going to do next?" he asks after wiping his eyes with the back of his hands and then getting tissues for both of us from the drawer.

"Ukraine," I answer. "I know a language university in Kiev, where we can lecture. Also, we have an invitation to teach writing for one month at a university in central China. It's a faculty exchange with a local university. By contract, we'll get a room, an allowance, and the use of two bicycles."

Mike and Laurel in China

"I'm ready," says Mike. "You know Scholastic books will send me to the Arab Reading Conference in Baharain. There's international school invitations to Buenos Aires and the Department of Defense schools in Europe for their *young author festivals*. Why don't you get yourself one of those little suitcases with wheels?"

He is making these suggestions while pacing between my bed and his turn around spot by the pleated curtains.

The future feels like it's in Technicolor.

Hearing this, I get up, and limp over to the windows where I rest against the plate of glass. It is completely overcast weather, but I know the sun is up there. In the distance is a vector of some late migrating geese. November winds always get the last of the leaves air borne. I watch two of them swirl by me in an updraft and out of sight. I've been given another season.

1997-1998

April 26, 1997   First Grandchild
Hospital

I can't get over the facilities of the Adventist family birthing center. Tina explains to me that she will stay the whole time, like the other patients, in just one room. The bed is built like a transformer, labor to delivery, all in its moving parts.

I had been with my daughter-in-law and son in a grocery store when Tina began bending over the green peppers in a spasm of hard labor. We got to the hospital in time and made the phone calls summoning family.

Anna is sitting in the chair with a video camera, in the most modest angle, up by Tina's head. She's already panned the sky and taped some of the morning's random radio to make a record of this day's weather and music.

The baby's heartbeat fills the room due to some monitor, and the sound is exactly like pounding hoofs, as if she is galloping towards us from some golden place in space.

Matthew stands at the doctor's side. He wants to cut the cord. He looks like he is about to cry.

Mary Elisabeth is next to me. She is actually rocking in anticipation. We want to see the baby crown, and I think I'm forgetting to breathe.

In contrast to all of us is Tina's mother, Linda Palaske, who is perfectly serene; she has a nursing degree.

Rebekah Faith Lee is born. I have a granddaughter with wide open blue eyes.

We were so afraid we would miss her as we leave in seven days for Kiev. Now, I can bring pictures.

September 21, 1998   Second Grandchild
Hospital

I have Madame Cao Feng Ting with me. She is the Communist party secretary from her university in Wuhan, China. We were in her house last May, and this is her first day in Oregon. I was going to show her the sights of the city, but instead we are here at the hospital. She is shocked to find Tina sipping from ice chips.

"No pregnant woman is allowed to have anything cold during their whole last month of pregnancy," she explains.

There is a lot to contrast.

Anna has the video camera by the chair. Mary Elisabeth is standing by me. We are all here, just like before, except for Tina's mother. She has been watching sixteen-month-old Rebekah, but will come as soon as the new baby is born.

Things go from normal to tense as the baby's heart beat drops. The doctor orders oxygen for Tina and says they might have to do a Cesarean. Madame Cao comes out from the corner and takes my hand. I had forgotten about her. In China, no husband, family, or friends are ever allowed into a delivery.

Mike is pacing outside. Never having had any children, some of those earlier blanks are being filled in. He missed Rebekah's birth by having to be at a book signing.

"It's stable," says Dr. Sargent, "but keep pushing."

"You have a girl," cries the nurse.

Of course, we all knew the gender before hand; ultrasound is much more advanced than two decades ago.

Matthew is much calmer at the birth of his second daughter. Anna reminds him how last time he declared that his wife's uterus had come out. She loves it when he makes mistakes because he was a biology major.

Elizabeth Grace is now under that first warm light, where she will be weighed and measured. She has her mother's full lips.

Rebekah comes in to meet her sister. This is Day One of siblings. Looking down from my arms at that round, brown, down of hair, above the folds of flannel, she pronounces it's a "Basketball" and asks to go "Color."

The Lee family, with its infant daughters will soon return to their isolated village in Alaska where Matthew teaches an entire middle school of twelve students. I'm going to keep looking with Mike for a farm house we can buy that will just have more room, and maybe a porch for a sunset.

Matthew Jonathan joined his sisters on July 19, 2000

2003

October 20

As I slept, Anna was shot through the forehead with the serious findings of my inoperable, advanced pancreatic cancer. Kaiser would enroll me immediately in a hospice program. While I dreamed of donuts, she drove me home from the hospital test and called Matthew.

It was odd to wake in my daughter's home and find both my children in her guest bedroom. Matthew explained to me the facts that his sister just called him in tears. My first comfort was to have the news come from the mouths of those I love and not some Dr. Grey-Face.

I want to wait and call Mike in Vermont. He's on a short tour visiting elementary schools. He is such a mighty tree, and how I wish to protect him from that axe's bite.

I woke later that night asking, "Is it true?" Snapping on Anna's television, a gospel quartet sang, *"When we all get to Heaven what a day of rejoicing that will be. When we see Jesus, we will sing and shout the victory!"*

October 21
58th Birthday

We, in plural, went to the doctor. Anna, with Matthew, waited two hours in the examination room for the doctor who five weeks earlier removed a benign tumor with two-thirds of my liver. The room was so small and grim that they had to laugh at times, or the circumstances could eat them.

"You have only three to eight months." Dr. Purloff then related a story of caring for an aunt with a purposeful overdose of morphine.

"Don't worry," said Matthew. "We'll let God choose the hour of your death."

For the afternoon, I drove and collected things to finish my second room in the barn. A house fire several months earlier had made it necessary to convert a one-time cow barn into a temporary home. Mike's homecoming in a week is my goal. (I almost wrote deadline, and find I can still laugh.) He is going to need an office with a view of fields and woods.

Suzanne, a friend from when Anna was in baby days, encouraged me to sort images and write.

Maybe it is my time. The two-edged sword is often quoted with plenty of back-up scriptures that, *"By His stripes we are healed."* But, my portion might be the other sharp edge, *"Precious in the sight of the Lord is the death of His saints ..."*

I have peace. The standard reply to any deep tragedy is an affirmation that God can do anything. Although this is true, God is not a waiter. We don't order from the menu of life, and just by saying, "In Jesus' name," pull the napkin across our laps. "One big heaping of ten more years, please."

I don't want to diminish the time I do have by constantly interceding for more. My altitude comes in trusting in Him with all my heart and not leaning on my own understanding.

I've gathered pretty things for the new room. They're the trophies from fishing in many a thrift store and trolling through the minnows of garage sales.

Mary Elisabeth has announced on her birthday phone call to me from San Francisco that she is getting married. Ah, it's all style and the individuality of fingerprint. She wants to go from maiden to wife with wild animals in Kreuger Game Park, South Africa. Several months from now and a twenty-two hour plane ride is a long way away.

Mike will be back next Wednesday. He cries into the phone and declares his assurance of me being healed. I have my interior steering wheel directed at acceptance with whatever happens.

I have thought of a grave site back in the wooded acreage of our farm. Its been the place of such summer laughter and picnics. Its been the brier versus the blackberry. There my bones will be dust. Mike wants to be next to me and laughs that with our grandchildren it would become a pet cemetery with departed hampsters, cats and dogs. He elects for us someday to instead be placed near the small prayer chapel at Christian Renewal Center where he committed his life to Christ.

October 25

Anna took me to church in magnificent golden sunshine and unheard of warm temperatures for the end of October. We sat in the back, and after announcements I came to the front to thank the people and explain how I think the wind is blowing.

All the worship choruses held meaning.

We drove to the farm before the sermon. People came to help in the afternoon. While I slept, it was an ever-changing equation. I remember the sound of water washing the windows. Suzanne came as I later rested in a chair. Still exhausted, and feeling the embers of deep back pain, I greeted her with the statement, "I'm dead ... tired." How odd the permeating word. There's deadlines, and dead ends. It accompanies our mortality, waiting for the last dance.

October 29

Mike came home—the airport reunited kiss was joys of poetry during the horrors of war. Mike was very quiet—from the flowers at the barn door to transformed rooms. He had left our summer *camping* house of pumpkins and come back to a glass coach.

The oriental rugs had come out from the tomb of storage to cover his new office floor. Add to this hundreds of extras with new beds and folk-art walls. Sylvia brought flowers, chicken soup and a foam bed pad. Matthew was installing lights, and I could leave for Heaven from these pleasant, simple rooms. Our big

farm house behind us is still under construction from the fire that licked away much of Mike's art collection and my unpublished diaries. It seems I replaced my clothes in thrift stores within five minutes. No one was hurt, and I had been glad that I could now change the color of the roof.

Mike's hope and insistence that God promised us more years than the nine we have been together does effect me.

All the edges of how to run a house are severely blunted, and I ache like bullet holes.

Once alone with Matthew, he gave us the new TV introductory lecture. It was a gift from Suzanne and Tom. With Mike, our lives have spanned its black and white arrival in the 1950s to now hundreds of channels plus techno complications.

September 11, 2002 fire that destroyed the top two floors of Mike and Laurel's home that they shared with Matthew, Tina and the children. Photo courtesy of Canby Herald

Mike has the exhaustion of the East Coast meeting the Western watch. He is needing bed by 8:00. He is kind with my ups and downs for medicine. By 2:30am I retire from diary and pills to sleep in the outer room. Hospice provided a bed where a button switch moves the back up and down.

October 30

Mike is combing out the tangles in his office. Matthew sits at the kitchen table working on the lights and electrical parts. I'm balancing medicines and my day's schedule for morphine and Dilaudid. It's the continual worship music on tape that adds oxygen to the air.

October 31
Friday

My only sight of Halloween was seeing my granddaughters in curlers in the back of their van waiting to be turned into princesses. All of their faces, including Jonathan and Hannah the baby, are one of my hardest good-byes. We had a couple years of all living in the community of an extended family. They had their own floor and kitchen, while we had ours. The shared porch was for the performance of sunsets. "See, the clouds are God's puzzle pieces," said Rebekah. Sometimes Matthew brought his guitar— there were age-graded, summer scoops of ice cream.

November 1

My nurse, Robert, came from Hospice. I had hoped for an older woman with big bosoms. Robert in his cowboy boots does seem absolutely efficient. He immediately changed my meds from an every-three-hour dependency to a twice-every-24-hour, time-released morphine. It was explained to me again that to be referred to the hospice program by my physician meant a life expectancy of only a few months.

Sunday

I drove with Matthew and family to Christian Renewal Center to chase the hope of snow in the new cold of coming winter. We found small transparent spots of white and a rainy mist. There was one snowman on Tim and Julie Hansen's yard.

While wandering, I met a staff worker in the kitchen. She gave me a Xerox of all scriptures that mention Heaven. "No more sorrow, crying or pain for the former things are passed away." Four more verses down in Revelations, it lists those that can't get in. We all need mercy, and the hymn: "Who can wash away my sins? Nothing but the blood of Jesus ..."

Anna and her new husband, Peter, came with a beautiful dinner that I couldn't eat. My daughter packs my medicines for the week like arranging chess pieces. As they left, I took a tiny sip of nap, and Matthew came with his oldest daughter. She was gentle love, and reading one story wears me out. My discomfortures mount, and energy flees, but her tender love climbs in bed with me to snuggle.

I sleep like a yo-yo, up and down, and write until I sleep in my chair.

Just this past July, I had three hospitalizations for unchecked nausea. They found a tumor like the size of Mississippi burning in my liver. The transport ride to surgery was a first view of torture. I have too much imagination for the narcotic weight of five days in intensive care. Dreams are too thick, elaborate, and I'm under their waters with ripples of dark hallucinations. Anna's touch is tender. I hear her say she loves me, and Mike commands me to breathe. He knows anxiety.

I began to get well, comforted by the benign report. Mike could leave for his trip in peace. But my body had a hidden bullet. When there was no relief to pain, the medical school emergency room found the spot on my pancreas.

Anna stood alone, wearing for me my wedding ring during the procedure, and was the first to hear I'm dying.

November 3

It's an early visit with Matthew and Mike to the oncologist. My choice becomes whether to try palliative (not curative) chemotherapy. Will it help shrink the tumor and stabilize my condition to some degree, or am I taking a discomfort axe and cutting up what they purport as my few remaining days of life? Matthew's feelings are to go for it, where Mike is more cautious.

Matthew wanted information; Mike wanted to support me, and I felt apprehension at the range of weapons medical personnel can fire at the patient with their tongues.

Since this is incurable, the doctor's approach was the warm and fuzzy of do what you want. Matthew was outraged because there have been good results for a very few patients, using one particular chemotherapy agent. One in over a million tumors can shrink.

I was appalled when the doctor told me they would have never done the liver resection. Presurgery, I would vomit on every car ride and be regularly poisoned by nausea. They would have left boulders in my already rocky path.

The doctor gives me a paper for legalizing marijuana due to nausea. The 1960s has bumped into me.

I speak for chemo and get scheduled in the morning.

My nights are long. It's journal scribbling and naps.

I sing inside—*God knows the way through the wilderness, and all we got to do is follow* ...

November 4
Tuesday

Mike holds me in the night and says he will stand with me if I quit the chemo. Again as we dress, he offers to turn around. My memory from 1977 chemotherapy has a pitchfork horror quality.

I'm a bit of a shaking leaf on the hospital floor that's first a long row of Lazy Boy chairs and beds, all separated by curtains. It looks like a peculiar Flanders Field where the poppies grow. I'm put in a private room for the three-hour process due to the need for an extra IV of liquids.

With the nausea drip and sedative, I sleep and then begin. I have no ill response. Even 48 hours later there are no ill effects but the most prevailing exhaustion.

November 5

For the first time since before the surgery, I slept all night. Slyvia came and helped me bathe and oiled my dry crocodile skin. At 5:00 we went to see another doctor that a friend recommended from her Sunday School. He suggested an oncology hospital in Houston, Texas. I'm afraid it would be a long trip and a lot of money to hear the same thing.

God is my crosswalk guard.

Riding home with Matthew, I mentioned that all waking hours is a weight of knowing and feeling so ill. "It's like the pressure of a laundry iron." Then came the picture of a bride getting her wedding garment ready. There will be no spots or wrinkles.

November 6

Decent sleep—woke on my back. At 7:30am, after no food or drink is a preliminary pain bloc.

The morning air was like penguins crossing blue ice. I was glad for hot blankets and a covering of a soft sedative. After positioning a key nerve out of

280

the pancreas, they dulled it and asked if I feel better. I had also just had my morning morphine and said, "Yes," hoping my affirmation is genuine. The real pain bloc will be in a week.

Robert, my nurse, came to the barn around 4:00pm. He has a gentle calming manner. He has eyes that buckle me in for my peculiar thrill ride descent. It's the same eyes of the surgeon just as they begin the anesthesia drip before surgery.

Will I be wrenched out of my flesh? How tight will I be tied to mortality? May it be the most gentle hand reaching into mine. "WELL DONE" are beautiful words, and to have some works that will praise me in the gate.

November 7

At 6:00 we meet with Dr. Way. Again, it's sober news—the entwining position of the tumor is around the aorta artery. We have booked a house for two nights at Thanksgiving, and with Matthew's help, a visit to South Texas in a week. We are going to make such a journey to support Mike. He's considering canceling a raft of visits to schools that have organized so long for him to come. We don't like to be separated.

November 8
Saturday

Anna comes in the late afternoon at the same time as a high school youth group. They play paint ball, running in the woods. I hobble between rooms. The babies throw crayons or eat crumbs from off the floor. Rebekah and Elizabeth create with couch pillows a set for "Create Your Own Adventure." After a tour of the house that is under construction, I can barely negotiate the stairs. Later Anna takes me to the grocery store.

Our moment of foreshadowing would be Matthew passing by with Rebekah on the motorcycle. She shrieks, "I love to go fast."

Anna got the call by the shopping carts. She heard how Rebekah had reached over and adjusted the throttle once she assessed this would accelerate the motorcycle's speed. Rebekah has one broken leg, and we'll get a wheelchair. As Mike goes to bring everyone pizza, I go with Anna and her new twin-sheet bedding. We stop in Sellwood to meet Peter and have dinner. I sleep at the table before the meal is served. They take me back to their house and the room where I first learned the news. How much further down the laundry shoot am I? How much further is the real hot water?

November 9

A friend comes with lilacs. They are the traditional flower of the bride. The company blurs. They are dear people. Some with soup, all sweet faces and well meaning prayers. I want to wear the petitions for health. I long to wake up girded in strength and appetite. Sometimes I think about my last breath and the transformation of my first on the other side.

November 11
Tuesday

Chemotherapy; vomited lunch—later vomited morphine in the evening. No pain relief. No relief with anti-nausea suppositories. Mike had to call the hospice hotline and Matthew for help.

November 12

Mike left for Texas. I'm again physically stable but Hospice came— pancreatic cancer is like being captive to the inescapable company of death.

November 13

At 7:30am Matthew took me to Kaiser pain control to destroy some of the pain-effected nerves coming out from my pancreas. *How many IVs must this dove have before she can sleep on the sand?* The woman physician warns me of the possibility of paralysis. I sign the agreement form. The procedure is to be done under the CAT scan machine for exactitude.

Some mechanical voice says, "Take a deep breath; hold it." Then after an interminable time, one is released to "Breathe." Will I be able to wiggle my toes again?

I'm drugged, and a friend comes to help me pack. It's crazy hard through the fog of sedatives. It's hard to imagine hot Texas in Oregon chill. Like others, Suzanne is a solid gold friend. All the raft of my age—fifty something pals—are alive. It's their parents who have failed or are failing. I have strong and dedicated buddies that drive and have their teeth.

I went to Matthew's house for the night. The baby is sick. She is a darling that likes to growl to make people laugh. I move upstairs to find less living, swimming cold germs.

Next day is Yiddish for *crazy*. Meshuguna was a gift to me from Mike's childhood vocabulary. In all, the plane cancelled due to mechanical failure. Matthew and my oldest two grandchildren sleep in a complimentary hotel two miles from the airport. Tina comes with Hannah and Jonathan who finds the traveling snacks of food while the baby growls and sneezes. God, keep us all!

November 15

Matthew cuts back my morphine dosage. The pain bloc seems successful. My night is colorful sleep. My dreams extend all plots and illustrations. Elizabeth joins me near dawn.

Our wake-up call is 6:00am, and walking out the door, I see Matthew's shaving kit in the bathroom. In the elevator, I realize we forgot my wheelchair, which my son quickly gathers. At 7:00am Rebekah and I are being closely checked, shoes off, with the security wand. I can hear the six-year-old telling how she broke her leg, with the resulting purple cast above her knee, by riding a motorcycle too fast.

As Matthew looks for pain meds, he leaves the five-year-old to roll her six-year-old sister down the corridor. It's a down hill ramp. I'm at the drinking fountain with three 30 mg. morphine tabs when I alert him to his daughter's play or folly.

We board without incident in a little quad of four seats. Landing in Dallas, Elizabeth suggests we go to one of the many houses she sees with a swimming pool and ask for a plunge before our next flight to South Texas.

In McAllan, Texas is Mike. We are home with each other in the most beautiful love a couple can experience. We even dance to a slow song on the radio.

Matthew and Rebekah find a big armadillo in a flashlight hunt on our host's lawn.

November 16
Sunday

We went into Mexico in two vans. There are throngs of folks, streets of goods. I napped in the front seat while our party had its main course dinner. Exhausted by 6:30 pm. Matthew continues to look for armadillos. Elizabeth swims with Rebekah, calling teaching instructions to her from the side of the swimming pool.

November 17

One day I can wave a flag for relative comfort, and the next morning bury it for nausea. We had Mexico adventures, ate well, the girls each had disposable cameras to take pictures of the sky or the bush beside the intended star pig in the yard.

November 18
Tuesday

A contrast to Monday—bed ridden, nausea, more than a body can hold.

Wednesday

Went to Mike's school to see a performance and back to Mexico to Matthew's favorite parakeet-wall restaurant. I'm pushing myself to move.

Thursday

1:30—dry heaves, sick like I'm tied on the mast going into the great barrier reef. Near dawn I asked Matthew to get us home one day early.

Friday

Crept to Dallas on a full flight and on to Portland. Anna took me home. Illness receded. Tom and Suzanne brought Mike home from his later flight.

Saturday

I couldn't get out of bed or eat. Sylvia gave me a bed bath. A kind sister is a well-watered garden. Matthew set up praise music and urged the impossible to dine. By evening I could move, and friends came for prayer. "The Lord will do what you want—health or home," one said ...

Oh, axe of a question—when I feel good, I want to be up for Kingdom work, so purged am I now from the world's goods and vanities. But sick and tortured, I look for the dear Hand to pull me to the celestial family.

Sunday

Slept all night with no sleeping pills. Dawn comes through thirteen barn windows.

November 25
Tuesday

Thanksgiving is coming, and Anna wants all the family to be the first to sit at her wedding china. With Mary and her fiance' coming from San Francisco, I count twelve ever moving, oxygen-breathing guests.

To me, it's so precious to be together that I want more than a tightly packed hour. I ask Mike to rent a house on the Oregon coast. It takes six bedrooms, and its location is advertised as having windows onto raw beach. In the right century we could watch the explorers land.

November 26
Wednesday, the day before Thanksgiving
The Oregon Coast

For someone who put on seven-league boots and strolled the earth, I'm tied now to the most feeble frame. I'm whittled to a nub by the twisting mountain road and the penetrating cold climbing to the front door. One couch is mine by the gas-heated fireplace. I turn the room into Miami's weather.

Evening

The family comes, all with cartons of food; Tina is first, with the children. I want to hold each one and talk like a Hallmark card that entwines my affection with its prose.

Once alone with Anna and Peter, they tell me I probably won't live to see their children. "We don't know if we'll have a rugby team," is their preface. "We have decided if there is a daughter, she'll be named Laurel."
"I think Laurel Cairney sounds nice," says my daughter in a soft voice.

I am moved and can now only hear the waves. The sound of the waters feels once again to me like the generations. I'm beating my own parents to the shore. And so we come. The little children grow to be parents stretching back into the waters. The unformed generations still wait in the deep.

November 2003—Laurel and her parents
Pat Moore, 90, and Jim Moore, 85,
with 18-month-old Hannah Joy who arrived April 8, 2002.

November 27
Thanksgiving Day 2003

While mothers everywhere stuff turkeys in Manzanita, Oregon, the rest of the coast population strolls the beach. Everyone owns a dog. My window view is like animated calendar art. I can almost see the wind.

The labor is not mine. I watch how adulthood has filled all but the grandchildren. There's no shrinking or complaint. Everyone rolls up sleeves. They make an enchanted table from the dinner lamb to magazine-cover turkey.

I give the Thanksgiving grace. My gratefulness doesn't stand alone like a little bouquet of well-said words. It arches back to my earliest cry to live from Stage IV Hodgkin's and raise three tiny children to adulthood. The needs and wants of my decades, with all those loose short ends, have been tied with gracious provision. I have a husband that exceeds any telling.

I can go home to New Jerusalem. There's family there too. My father once told me that the Moores have a history of itinerant preachers and church builders. There are many to love on both sides of the sky.

EYE HAS NOT SEEN
EAR HAS NOT HEARD
IT HAS NOT EVEN ENTERED INTO THE HEART OF MAN
WHAT GOD HAS PREPARED FOR THOSE THAT LOVE HIM

Epilogue

Matthew Lee graduated with a biology degree and his teaching credentials from Warner Pacific University. With his wife, Tina, a George Fox University graduate, they taught Chamorro Indians in Guam. Later Matthew taught Upik Eskimos on the Norton Sound in Alaska. Currently Matthew helps run the family farm and works for a marine automation company. Sometime in the near future, he and Tina, with their four children, intend to move to Southern China where Matthew will teach full time at a university.

Anna Lee earned a Master's degree in teaching, both English and Speech. She taught at a Portland area high school for several years before becoming the sales director for an on-line educational company. Today Anna is working for Tiffany and Company. Anna also continues to be involved in all aspects of the equestrian community. In 2003, Anna married Peter Cairney, a M.B.A. graduate from the University of Notre Dame. Anna and Peter currently live in Portland, Oregon.

Once Mary Elisabeth Lee graduated with a degree in writing and literature from George Fox University, she joined the Peace Corps. She taught high school in rural Zimbabwe, Southern Africa. Moving to San Francisco she has become active in the fashion industry. This has included modeling, coordinating fashion shows, and working as a stylist. Mary has designed her own line of clothes and assembled outfits out of used clothes that are carried in shops with one of her own labels—"Found by Mary Lee."

Anna, Matthew and Mary

Laurel and Her Grandchildren

Rebekah Faith Lee, age six, says, "I want to be a teacher when I grow up. Maybe, I want to be a fire fighter. I'm good at climbing trees and making pictures."

Elizabeth Grace Lee, age five, says, "I want to be an artist when I grow up because I draw so good. I like to draw hearts."

Richard C. Owen Publishing

Laurel, Matthew, Elizabeth, and Rebekah

Matthew Jonathan, like his father at age three, loves trains. He also likes to "be cozy and sing."

Hannah Joy, at one and a half, is a climber. There's no table too high for her emerging skills. While her sisters prefer stuffed animals, Hannah loves to carry her toy baby doll.

Laurel with Hannah

For additional copies of Tapestry:
call 866/876-3910 Order Line
or go to www.lighthousetrails.com
For updates on Laurel
go to www.lighthousetrails.com/tapestry.htm